MW00993928

SAILING *by* STARLIGHT

SAILING *by* STARLIGHT

The Remarkable Voyage of *Globe Star*

ROD SCHER

Essex, Connecticut

An imprint of Globe Pequot, the trade division of
The Rowman & Littlefield Publishing Group, Inc.
4501 Forbes Blvd., Ste. 200
Lanham, MD 20706
www.rowman.com

Distributed by NATIONAL BOOK NETWORK

Copyright © 2022 by Rod Scher

All rights reserved. No part of this book may be reproduced in any form or by any electronic or mechanical means, including information storage and retrieval systems, without written permission from the publisher, except by a reviewer who may quote passages in a review.

British Library Cataloguing in Publication Information available

Library of Congress Cataloging-in-Publication Data available
ISBN 978-1-4930-6569-1 (hardcover: alk. paper)
ISBN 978-1-4930-7076-3 (electronic)

∞™ The paper used in this publication meets the minimum requirements of American National Standard for Information Sciences—Permanence of Paper for Printed Library Materials, ANSI/NISO Z39.48-1992.

This one is for my daughter, Rachel.

You were always so proud of your dad, even when there was little reason to be. And you left us so soon and so unexpectedly that we didn't get to say goodbye or to tell you that we loved you, but I suppose you knew that; we'd certainly told you often enough. And now we all have Rachel-sized holes in our hearts that will never truly heal. Not a day goes by that I don't think of you.

Why do you go away? So that you can come back. So that you can see the place you came from with new eyes and extra colors. And the people there see you differently, too. Coming back to where you started is not the same as never leaving.

—TERRY PRATCHETT

CONTENTS

CONTENTS

ACKNOWLEDGMENTS

So many people contributed to the writing of this book that it's difficult to credit them all and be sure I haven't forgotten any, but I'll try anyway.

First, to the Creamer family: Thank you for entrusting me with your father's story. I've told it as best I can, "warts and all," as I said I would. Thank you also for sharing with me your memories and for providing access to hundreds of primary research items that any writer would love to have when writing something like this: letters, notes, snippets of conversations, poems, bills, receipts, Marv's own manuscript and journals, and much more. I hope I did him justice.

To Katie Dolan, a wonderful writer and editor in her own right, for thinking of me when Marv's daughter, Lynn, was telling you her dad's incredible story. You're the one who put this whole thing into motion. I'm proud to have been your colleague and gratified to be your friend.

To Jen Jackson, my research assistant, for hours spent tracking down and documenting image permissions and the occasional pesky fact. As I told some folks who were slow in getting back to us with photo permissions, you're a bulldog, but a delightful one. No one could have done a better job.

To Rick Brown, who helped clarify Marv's approach to celestial navigation, and to Fred Schneider, who helped with Rick's illustrations of Marv's method. I trust that readers will benefit from Rick's explanations of my explanations of Marv's explanations.

To the dozens of people who corresponded with the author, many of whom also participated in video and telephone interviews: the Creamer family, Lynn, Andra, and Kurt (and not forgetting Marv's ninety-five-year-old "little sister," Evelyn Creamer Daniels); Ben Trimble and Richard Scott, Marv's friends and colleagues at what is now Rowan University; Rob Cheshire, Marv's friend toward the end of his life; Lin Pardey and Patricia Wood, stellar writers who also happen to be experienced sailors;

ACKNOWLEDGMENTS

Herb Benavent, a professional rigger who took time out of his own sailing to speak with me; consulting oceanographer Michael Tomlinson; Captain David Jackson, USN (Ret.), and CDR John Harrington, USCG (Ret.), for sharing their nautical expertise; Dr. Steven W. Ross, ichthyologist at the University of North Carolina at Wilmington, and Dr. Richard Searles, Professor Emeritus of Botany, Duke University, for their opinions on Marv's use of oceanic fauna as one of his position-finding tools; Kathleen Saville, author of *Rowing for My Life*, a spellbinding book recounting her (and her late husband's) singular triumph—rowing across both the Atlantic and the Pacific Oceans; Dr. Rüdiger Trimpop, of the Friedrich-Schiller University of Jena, for his insights surrounding risk-taking behavior; Ted Brewer, esteemed designer of many blue-water boats, including the one Marv and his crew sailed around the world; Ted's wife, Betty, for help in rounding up specs, sail plans, and design documents; Dr. Daniel Schneider, for insights into the whys and wherefores of shoulder separations; Ralph Harvey, a good friend of Marv's and the man who, almost single-handedly, kept the *Globe Star* voyage flame burning for all these years; William Nixon, an exceptional journalist who prefers to be referred to simply as "the Irish sailing writer," so that's how we'll refer to him; and Dr. Richard Dienstbier, for insights into the psychology of self-confidence.

The crew of *Globe Star*, many of whom are no longer available to speak with, deserve special mention. Thanks especially to Bob Rout, Nick Gill, Bob Watson, and Jeff Herdelin, who endured dozens of emails, video chats, and more in an effort to fill in gaps, explain what it was like on board *Globe Star*, and whose testimony provided important perspectives that would otherwise be lacking.

And last but far from least, thanks to my wife, Lesley. I love you. It was a rough year or so, and I know I was holed up and distracted for much of it. Thanks for sticking it out with me. Yet again.

PROLOGUE

All that is gold does not glitter,
Not all those who wander are lost.

—J. R. R. TOLKIEN

THE THREE MEN SAILING THROUGH THE INDIAN OCEAN TOWARD Hobart never saw the wave that knocked down their boat. The vessel, a 35-foot steel sloop named *Globe Star*, weighed some ten tons—20,000 or so pounds, including the 6,200 pounds of lead ballast she carried. Nevertheless, in the stormy, swirling waters, the boat was tossed about like an insignificant scrap of paper swirling 'round a gutter.

We can't say exactly where a given wave forms, but we do know *why*. When wind blows over a segment of an ocean, it causes ripples, and if the wind continues, the ripples eventually become waves. If the wind blows hard enough, and consistently enough, and over a great enough distance (oceanographers and mariners call that distance the *fetch*) in the same direction, waves can grow to be enormous, partly because of the energy equalization at play when seas become fully developed. Oceanographer Mike Tomlinson, a consultant formerly with the University of Hawaii at Mānoa, notes, "What sailors call a *fully developed sea* is a situation where the wind has blown steadily over a sufficient fetch (e.g., the open ocean) long enough that the energy put into the sea to generate waves equals the energy lost by the waves due to breaking. For example, if a 40-knot wind were to blow over a 710-nautical mile fetch for 42 hours, the significant wave height (i.e., the mean of the highest one third of the waves) would be 44 feet, and the highest 10% of the waves would be 57 feet." Tomlinson also points out that such waves can exert a tremendous amount of pressure. "A 39-foot wave has the force of about 6 metric tons per square meter, or 1,230 pounds/ft²."[1]

In fact, the wave that struck *Globe Star* need not have been huge, so long as it was large enough to spin the vessel such that her bow was no

Windturbine   Generator

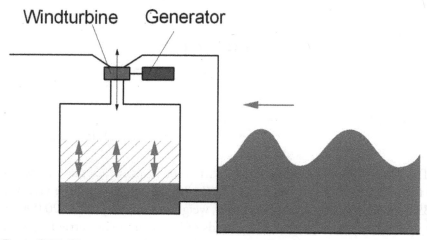

Figure P.01. Waves generate a great deal of power, most of which is eventually "wasted" as the waves dissipate. Recently, however, attempts have been made to capture that energy via a variety of mechanisms. In this simplified diagram, a pneumatic chamber uses wave surge to power a generator.
(IMAGE USED UNDER THE TERMS OF THE GNU FREE DOCUMENTATION LICENSE.)

longer headed into the oncoming wave. She was then in a position to broach, or turn broadside to wind or wave. Waves are plenty powerful enough to do that if the direction of the wave is unexpected or if the wind shifts suddenly, especially if the helmsman does not react quickly enough. Says Tomlinson, "Remember that the pressure applied is force per unit area; therefore, the total force on [the] boat would have been the wave force times the cross-sectional area of the affected hull and superstructure. The forces involved would have been tremendous."[2]

So picture a wall of water looming above your boat. Looking up at it (not that *Globe Star*'s crew could see it very well in the dark), you know that a (literal) ton of water is about to crash down on you. If it's not under perfect control, a thirty-five-foot boat (or a 350-foot ship, for that matter) can be hurled about, and the surging sea can flip the vessel broadside in an instant, and untethered crew (or supplies and equipment) can be washed overboard.

A broach of this sort makes a boat ripe for a knockdown, which is exactly what happened next.

One of the crew, Jeff Herdelin, a young man but an experienced sailor, had just gone forward to add a staysail. In rough weather, such as the waters in which *Globe Star* was sailing, a staysail is often used alone or in combination with another small sail to maintain control of a boat without sending her scudding along too quickly, pushed relentlessly by strong winds and possibly burying her bow in an oncoming wave and pitchpoling or losing steerageway and then broaching. It was a prudent move, but it had—as many prudent moves do—unanticipated consequences.

According to the skipper, retired geography professor Marvin Charles Creamer, "Jeff had just positioned himself on the foredeck when a towering wave crashed into *Globe Star*, rolled her on her port beam, and sent her scudding to lee."[3]

Creamer was in the cabin at the time, so he yelled for the other crewman, Rick Kuzyk, to check on Jeff. For a few tense moments, there was no sign of Herdelin, and the other two men were frantic, thinking that the young man might have been washed overboard by the force of the wave and the lurching of the boat.

Creamer feared the worst. The best he could hope for, he felt, was that they might find Jeff overboard, dangling by the tether of his safety harness.

A few moments later, though, Jeff appeared, raising his head above the top of the cabin. At the moment of impact, he had flattened himself between the two dorade vents on the deck and hung on for dear life. It was a wise move; if he had stood up, even if he had grasped a stay or the mast itself, the force of the wave and the sideways motion of the boat would almost certainly have thrown him off the deck and into the dark, churning waters.

The sailors were okay, but their boat was a mess.

"In the knockdown," says Creamer, "a winch handle had flown across the cabin and broken one of the galley stove grates. Water poured in through the sliding hatch and charts, records, tape recorder, gun, and many other items were drenched."[4]

In addition, glass jars containing spare parts were shattered and strewn over the two vee berths in the bow of the boat.

Their troubles were not over. Moments after Creamer started the engine, *Globe Star* was knocked down again. In the tumult, a flying item (perhaps an air horn used to sound fog signals) struck and turned off the engine's Master switch while it was running. For the moment, they had no engine.

But the men were dealing with something even more worrisome than a debris-strewn boat and a dead engine: They had begun to wonder whether the heavy, steep seas that they had encountered were in fact a sign that they were nearing land. Waves and swells tend to build heavily and quickly as they approach land, and it was possible that these steep, breaking seas signaled that land—unseen in the stormy dark—was perilously close.

Oddly enough, the men had no precise idea where they were, nor how close they might be to land, and it was their possible proximity to land that concerned them. Sailors far out at sea are normally safe; at sea, they're not worried, for the same reason that pilots at altitude are not worried: If anything goes wrong, the sailors—and the pilot—have time and "sea room" to sort out whatever the problem might be. On the other hand, sailors close to land—and pilots at low attitude—worry a great deal when problems occur because they may find that they have little or no time to address the problem before they make an unexpected, and sometimes deadly, landfall.

Which, of course, brings up a question: Why were the three men sailing through a wild, storm-tossed ocean with no real idea of their location? Therein hangs a tale. It's the story of a dedicated, some might say obsessed—in any case, a singularly *driven* man—and what some said was an imprudent decision to battle nature while eschewing most of the safeguards that sailors commonly use when crossing the sea.

CHAPTER I

GROUNDWORK

Only those who risk going too far can possibly find out how far one can go.

—T. S. Eliot

THE VOYAGE OF THE *GLOBE STAR* SHOULD HAVE BEEN THE FIASCO THAT many had predicted. The skipper, Marvin Creamer, was a seemingly mild-mannered professor of geography at a small college in New Jersey. Slender and sandy-haired (and with the receding hairline typical of many middle-aged men), he was sixty-six years old at the start of the voyage, an age when many college professors are content to retire to decorous, book-lined studies, relax, mentor former students, and give the occasional (usually sparsely attended) lecture concerning their areas of specialization. Marv's area of specialization was political geography, a subject that generally fails to excite much ardor in the hearts of even the most dedicated students, dealing as it does not simply with geographical boundaries but also with the political machinations that created those boundaries. Not really very exciting stuff. Creamer, however, was not really the retiring type. Instead of staying home, working in the garden, and enjoying the quiet pursuits of most men his age, he had opted to go to sea—again. He had crossed oceans before, but now he had an even more lofty goal: nearing seventy years of age, Creamer intended to sail around the world.

The boat Creamer intended to sail around the world was a gem: a 35-foot steel, soft-chined beauty, a cutter-rigged sloop designed by Ted Brewer, one of the deans of small yacht design. *Globe Star* was beautiful, and while she may not have looked as sexy or as speedy as a transoceanic

I

Figure 01.01. Marv Creamer aboard *Globe Star*.
(IMAGE COURTESY OF ROWAN UNIVERSITY ARCHIVES.)

racer, her lines were nonetheless pleasing to the eye and she was stable, sturdy, beamy, and well found.[1]

"I tried to design the size and type of vessel that I would want for long range cruising," says Ted, the author of *Understanding Boat Design*. In fact, "a sister to the steel-hulled boat that Creamer used was [selected], a couple of years later, by a solo sailor to do a complete circumnavigation."[2] *Globe Star* was a solid, sturdy boat, one of Brewer's best designs; her rounded-bilge, metal-hull construction was the forerunner of many more radius bilge designs, but *Globe Star* was one of the very first. (For more information on *Globe Star*'s specifications, see appendix D.)

She was as solid an ocean-going vessel as one could ask, but when the boat was delivered, just twenty days prior to the day of departure, she was also missing many of the items that make a sailboat usable. Trucked overland from the Huromic Metal Industries factory in Goderich, a small town in Ontario, Canada, the boat lacked sails, rigging, a mast, provisions, a galley stove, and countless other items, both large and small. At this point, *Globe Star* was an empty shell, a new, untried vessel in which Marv Creamer and his crew were about to risk their lives by sailing into the windswept Atlantic with only the vaguest idea of where they were headed.

That their heading was vague was no accident. The men proposed to use—and this was crucial to the whole point of the voyage—no instrumentation at all: Creamer and his crew intended to set off on an around-the-world voyage utilizing no compass, no sextant, no astrolabe (a precursor to the more modern sextant), no depth-finder, no radar, no LORAN (which had mostly become inactive in North America by the 1980s, anyway), and no GPS or chart plotters (civilian versions of which did not in any case exist in 1982, when Creamer's voyage began). The boat didn't even have a clock on board, and neither Creamer nor his crew brought with them a watch or chronometer of any kind. (There was, however, a custom hourglass, which the sailors intended to use to divide periods of the watch.) Creamer's objective was to show that ancient peoples could have traveled the globe using no instruments other than their brains and their five basic senses, so he set sail on a frigid New Jersey morning in December 1982, carrying with him none of the modern devices that

Figure 01.02. This is the custom hourglass carried aboard *Globe Star* and used to denote the hours of the watch. No other timekeeping devices were on board. (IMAGE COURTESY OF ROWAN UNIVERSITY ARCHIVES.)

contemporary sailors use to find their way and ensure their safety.[3] It was, to say the least, a risky venture. As Creamer himself noted, "Doomsayers had had a field day. They reckoned we would be lucky to survive for as long as two days." One TV interviewer asked the boat's Canadian builder, Bob Patterson, "Is this guy normal? Does he have all his bolts?" Patterson's answer went unrecorded.[4]

They were adventurous, but they were not stupid. It may have been a daring—some said foolhardy—undertaking, but the man behind the adventure was anything but stupid, and he was most definitely nobody's fool.

Marvin Charles Creamer was born in 1916 in Pittsgrove Township, New Jersey. The small town (the population at the time was about 2,100, and even today there are scarcely 9,000 people there) is miles from any sea or ocean.[5] The sea was not in Marv's blood, at least not yet.

During Marv's younger years, his father, Sereno Todd Creamer, was a small-scale farmer and then a metalworker, carpenter, and machinist for the Civilian Conservation Corps. He was by all accounts a self-reliant, resourceful man—as Marv would turn out to be. In fact, the elder Creamer was resourceful enough that when he received word that the new Ford automobile that he had ordered would not be ready because it had not yet been assembled, he didn't let that stop him: Sereno Creamer and a friend simply harnessed a horse and wagon and rode the eight miles to the Ford agency in Elmer, New Jersey, assembled the car themselves, and drove it home in time for a Memorial Day weekend outing.

Thus began for Marv a lifelong and fundamental passion: the idea that things could be fixed, that obstacles were there to be overcome, and that they *could* be overcome by dint of hard work and by the application of reflective intelligence. In truth, it couldn't even be said to be a mere fixation; it was part of him. Integral to his very being was the notion that there was a solution for every problem and that the appropriate answer could be arrived at by thoughtful consideration of the facts.

Creamer's family was well aware of his outlook, and also of his penchant for studying and solving problems rather than allowing them to defeat him. Asked what was the best advice her father ever gave her, Dr. Andra James, Marv's eldest daughter, noted:

> *I think that it was more than advice. It was role modeling the idea that problems are solvable. It's possible to get yourself out of a fix. You can come out ahead, you can live your dreams and you can integrate them within you.*[6]

Of course, the notion that problems could be studied, analyzed, and solved is not at all uncommon, especially for farmers, carpenters, sailors, machinists, and others who work with their hands, building, fixing, planting. Farmers, for example, have to be resourceful and self-reliant; in effect, many become machinists of one sort or another even while still working the farm. When machinery breaks, it must be fixed, and fixed *now*. A broken tractor may eventually need a trip to a machine shop, dealership, or mechanic, but first it must be able to finish the job for which it was being used at the time. A plow, even back in 1916, was a fairly complex piece of machinery; a farmer had to know how it worked, why it might quit working, and how to get it working again. Ditto a pull-behind harvester or a crop seeder. These were not sophisticated pieces of equipment, as we think of such equipment today (that is, electronic, computer-controlled, often guided by GPS), but they were complex, multipart systems, and they were often balky and temperamental, as were the draft animals that, in the early days, pulled them. The farmer's livelihood and family's subsistence depended on the ability to diagnose and repair issues, to analyze and solve problems. Farmers were—and are—problem solvers. (All of this is, of course, in addition to being able to grow, sustain, and protect crops. Farming might sound peaceful, bucolic, and simple, but it's a lot of hard work, and the work never lets up, no matter the season.)

Creamer took those lessons to heart. He grew up to be a machinist himself, a tinkerer, a builder, a fixer. Overcoming obstacles was simply part of his nature, whether working around the house or sailing around the Horn. Marvin Creamer grew to be a consummate problem solver.

Marv graduated high school at sixteen, having attended a one-room school that housed eight grades, and having advanced rapidly through all eight of them. Then, in 1932, he went to work. This being the heart of the Great Depression, jobs were scarce, but not as scarce as in the big cities; there was work to be had, if you were willing to work hard and do menial jobs. Marv and his older brother Richard did construction work and carpentry, built and hauled burial vaults, and picked up whatever part-time jobs they could.

But when the opportunity presented itself, the two brothers also fished, hunted, and boated, often on eighty-acre Parvin Lake, located in a New Jersey state park a short distance from where Creamer's father had moved the family when Creamer was a boy. (It is no coincidence that Marv's mother's maiden name was Parvin. The land that became the state park had previously belonged to her family.) That lake was where Creamer got his first taste of sailing, in a sixteen-foot converted rowboat that was none too stable and none too fast. Then again, as Creamer noted, "There were no regattas on Parvin Lake."

"The same boat that more often than not would wet the seat of our pants," said Creamer, "would always whet our desire for a bigger and better boat and a bigger puddle to sail it in."[7]

Several years after graduating high school, Creamer would attend Glassboro State College (now Rowan University), where he acquired a degree in education and became a teacher and a school principal. The army interrupted his career and, as a school principal with clerical and administrative skills, he spent most of his time in the service working in the payroll department at Mitchel Field in Long Island.

Not long out of the Army, his alma mater called: Glassboro State College had need of a geography teacher to work in the school's Social Studies Department. Creamer went to work at Glassboro, and attended the University of Pennsylvania, earning a master's degree in education and then a master's degree in geography from the University of Wisconsin. He did PhD coursework at UW, but he never finished his thesis, ending up (like about 50 percent of all doctoral students) ABD: All But Dissertation.[8] Creamer never would finish his PhD (though he would eventually receive an honorary doctorate from the school at which he taught), but in 1964 he became the chair of the Social Studies Department at Glassboro. In between, he married Blanche Layton, a New Jersey teacher

Figure 01.03. Faculty at Glassboro State College (now Rowan University) in 1956. Marv Creamer is in the back row, second from right. (IMAGE COURTESY OF THE CREAMER FAMILY.)

and a graduate of the college at which Marv now taught. The Creamers had three children. Andra, the eldest, is now a specialist in maternal-fetal medicine who practices and teaches at Duke University. Lynn, the second-eldest, is an RN and an administrator at Nebraska Medicine in Omaha, Nebraska. The Creamers' youngest child, Kurt, is a research engineer connectivity manager at a biotech company in North Carolina.

Creamer retired in 1977, although he maintained his ties with the faculty, the administration, and with many former students. On a more profound level, Marv never really "retired" from teaching; being an educator was part of his DNA, and he continued mentoring students, and especially young student-sailors, many of whom would sail with him on various voyages.

Shortly before his retirement, Creamer discovered serious sailing. He'd played around before, taking his eighteen-foot outboard motorboat far out into the open ocean in the 1960s, but in 1970, he acquired *Scotia*, a thirty-foot Allied Seawind.[9] After viewing the boat, Creamer said, "I called the owner, a Presbyterian minister in Larchmont, New York, and told him that I would buy his secondhand Seawind for thirteen and a half thousand dollars. I hung up the telephone in a fit of nervous shaking. No one that I knew personally had ever spent that much money on such a foolish idea."[10] It's worth noting that, allowing for inflation, $13,500 in 1970 is equivalent to about $90,000 today. For the sake of comparison, the salary of a high school teacher in New Jersey in 1970 was $9,130 per year.[11] In 1970, $13,500 was a lot of money to spend on a sailboat.

The "foolish idea," though Creamer may not yet have admitted it even to himself, let alone to his family, was this: at fifty-four years of age, Professor Creamer was planning a transatlantic crossing. This would eventually lead to an even *more* "foolish" idea: crossing the Atlantic without instruments.

Creamer would make several voyages in *Scotia*, including trips to the Azores and Bermuda, sometimes taking his children or his brother along as crew.

Ironically, it was on his 1974 return from the Azores that Creamer started thinking seriously about an instrument-less crossing, and it was

Figure 01.04. Ben Trimble and Marv at the latter's one hundredth birthday party. Trimble taught with Marv at what is now Rowan University. He remembers Creamer as an excellent teacher, and in fact he audited the celestial navigation course that Creamer taught in his later years at the school. He recalls that Creamer was generally a friendly man but could also be a harsh taskmaster. *(Photo courtesy of Ben Trimble.)*

mechanical failure that gave him the final nudge: "Almost nightly compass light failure began to overload us," said Creamer. "One night it would be the bulb, and then the socket, splices in the wires, and connectors. All were in good repair when we left our home port but the constant exposure to splashing salt water was taking its toll. And the almost daily repair was encroaching on our sack time."

The repeated failure of the compass light prompted Creamer and his crew to forsake its nighttime use and rely almost entirely on the stars for guidance. This worked surprisingly well; after a night of sailing by the stars, Creamer took a sextant reading and discovered that he was almost exactly where he thought he was. Steering by those stars invited a pair of seemingly unorthodox thoughts: *If it's possible to steer fairly accurately at night without a compass, would it be possible to steer with reasonable accuracy in the daytime? And could one use those stars to determine his location, or at least his latitude?*

Those questions would become something of an obsession. It was a problem, and Creamer was, after all, a problem solver. Surely there was a way to use the sun, even without a sextant, to determine one's position. It would be fairly straightforward, he thought, to use the sun's rising and setting positions to calculate latitude, but what about from midmorning to midafternoon? What about on an overcast day?

Creamer was not like most of us, drifting sedately through life, not paying too much attention to the world around them. He really *looked* at his surroundings, and he sought to understand what he was seeing. As a geographer—and as a problem solver—he truly lived *in* the world. And what he saw when he looked out from the cockpit of *Scotia* was . . . waves. Large, heaving swells; smaller waves that coursed and bounded along the surface; little wavelets; small ripples; and his boat bobbing happily among all of them. Why not use the surface of the sea itself as a guide in determining direction?

"Long distance swells are directionally constant for a relatively long period of time; perhaps they could be used," thought Creamer. "And if no swells were discernible why not key in on the direction of the waves generated by the currently prevailing wind? And what if there were neither waves nor swells to use for direction? There would be no problem because

Figure 01.05. Blanche, son Kurt, and Marv Creamer, circa 1978.
(PHOTO COURTESY OF THE CREAMER FAMILY.)

that would mean there was no wind and without wind there would be no *need* for direction."[12]

After twenty-nine days at sea, Creamer and his crewmate, Ed Twardowski, arrived back at Cape May, from where they had started. By that time, Creamer had convinced himself that finding direction by day without a compass was entirely feasible.

Now he began looking for a way to determine latitude without a sextant. He pondered the problem for many months, continuing to sail all the while. In 1976, he sailed to England; on that voyage, rough seas and knockdowns literally knocked two compasses out of the cockpit binnacle in which they rested. If anything, this made him even more determined to find a way to sail without such instruments because they were proving themselves finicky and prone to failure. It was in England, in response to a reporter's question, that Creamer first spoke publicly about a possible ocean crossing without instruments.

Creamer knew that for centuries sailors had been "sailing down the latitudes." That is, they would sail northward or southward to the latitude on which their ultimate destination lie, and then sail east or west knowing that, if only they sailed long enough, they would (sometimes quite literally) run into their destination. The key, then, was finding latitude without a sextant.

The professor, about to retire, kept pondering, knowing that there was a solution somewhere. He played with the idea in his mind and on paper, sketching angles and horizons and azimuths and declinations. There *had* to be a way. Soon, said Creamer, he "had eased from soft fantasy into the hard reality of planning an ocean crossing without instruments. I felt compelled to dream up a way of finding latitude."[13]

And, as he often did, he found a way.

The trick, he realized, was in judging whether a particular star was at or near zenith. One would have to point to an imaginary spot in the sky and identify it as being directly overhead. This is difficult on land, but on the deck of a pitching, rolling boat, it *really* took some doing. So Creamer practiced in his front yard, identifying stars that would pass near the zenith, trying to guess when they were on the local meridian, and then estimating the angular distance in degrees between the zenith and the chosen star.

Marv's son, Kurt, recalls many nights watching his father trying out his methodology, wandering out to the front yard to look at stars, jotting down notes.

"I have a very vivid memory of him in a particular window in our house. He would put a little pan of water on the window sill and then use a sextant to measure the angle of the celestial body. When you don't have the ocean available to you, you can use an artificial horizon created by the pan of water."[14]

It turned out to be possible, but the results were frustratingly inconsistent. Creamer was stymied until he realized that some simple geometry could be used to work out a star's meridian transit.

"For practical purposes the northern pole star, Polaris," says Creamer, "is at the center of the apparent rotation of the nighttime sky, thus it is on the meridian in the northern hemisphere. If a line drawn from Polaris to a star, e.g., Vega, divides the sky into two equal parts, an eastern part equal to a western part, then the star, Vega, is on the meridian. To find latitude from Vega you would (1) choose a time of year when it would stand at or near your zenith some time during the dark hours, (2) draw an imaginary line between Vega and Polaris, (3) watch the imaginary line, as it is pivoting on Polaris, rotate counterclockwise as Vega rises in the east, (4) determine the instant when the line divides the sky into two equal parts, and (5) determine whether Vega is at the zenith or, if not, whether it is north or south of the zenith and by how much, making the judgment in degrees of arc."

Just five "simple" steps, but those steps assume that (A) you know some basic geometry, (B) you can identify a fairly large number of stars, (C) you can determine when and where an extrapolated line will appear, (D) you can observe closely enough that you can tell exactly when a line divides the sky into two equal parts, and then (E) determine just how far off—in degrees—north or south of the zenith a point might be. And you have to do this on the slippery, rocking deck of a boat, often in freezing temperatures.

Kurt sailed with his father on a later (1978) transatlantic voyage from Ireland to Cape May, New Jersey. Already possessing a decent knowledge of celestial navigation, Kurt was awed by his father's ability to judge how far north or south of the zenith the selected star might be.

"What's truly remarkable about Dad is that, on a pitching boat in the middle of the ocean, he was able to look up at the celestial body—lining up, first of all, with the North star so that he knows that he's on the same longitude as the star—and then decide, is that star directly overhead? Or is it one degree this way or one degree that way? The most remarkable thing about the method is that he could decide accurately whether it was

Some of the concepts used by Professor Creamer to determine latitude may be better understood if presented visually. Rick Brown, of the Prairie Astronomy Club of Lincoln, Nebraska, has provided further explanations, and he and graphic artist Fred Schneider have provided images that may clarify Creamer's process:

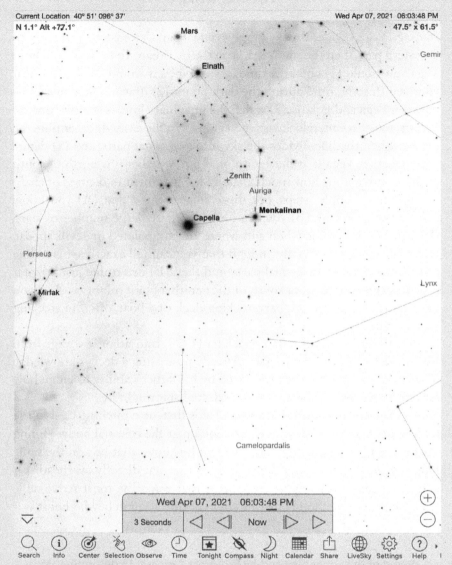

Mars

Elnath

Gemir

Zenith

Auriga

Menkalinan

Capella

Perseus

Mirfak

Lynx

Camelopardalis

Wed Apr 07, 2021 06:03:48 PM

3 Seconds ◁ ◁ Now ▷ ▷

Search Info Center Selection Observe Time Tonight Compass Night Calendar Share LiveSky Settings Help

Figure 01.06. This image shows the star Menkalinan near zenith. But the right time to measure its distance from zenith is when the star is highest in the sky, which also is the moment it crosses the local meridian. If it's east of the local meridian, it still has some climbing to do, and if it's west of the meridian, it's already past its high point. *Reaching its high point* is also called the star's *culmination*. That's when you take the measurement. (IMAGE COURTESY OF RICK BROWN AND FRED SCHNEIDER.)

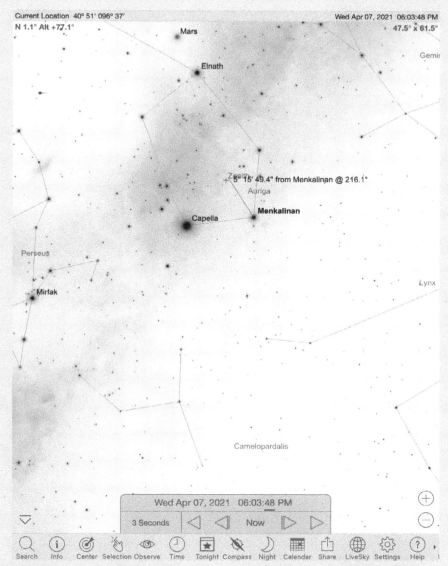

Figure 01.07. This image is the same as the first, except that it shows that the angular distance between Menkalinan and zenith is about 5 degrees, 15 minutes. It turns out that if you hold your hand out at arm's length, the width of 4 fingers is just about 5 degrees. But this measurement is worthless unless we know whether the star is at culmination or not. Creamer's problem was that it was just too hard to discern the moment of culmination by looking at the star alone. (IMAGE COURTESY OF RICK BROWN AND FRED SCHNEIDER.)

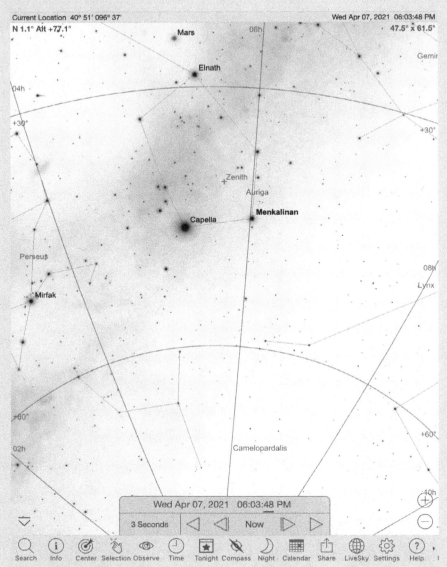

Figure 01.08. This third image illustrates Creamer's solution, which was to draw an imaginary line passing through the star, down and through Polaris, the North Star (not shown), which is basically the location of the Celestial North Pole, around which all the stars appear to revolve. All of the radiating lines you see in this picture also pass through Polaris, though Creamer only used the one line that passed through the chosen star. This line rotates counterclockwise around Polaris like the spoke of a wheel, carrying Menkalinan with it. This made it easier for Creamer to visualize whether the star was east of, west of, or directly on the local meridian at any given moment. (IMAGE COURTESY OF RICK BROWN AND FRED SCHNEIDER.)

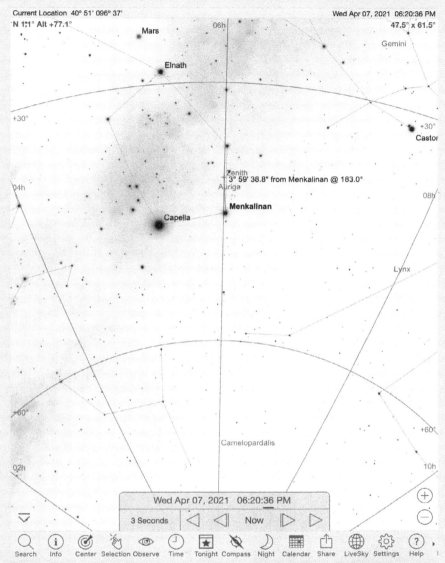

Figure 01.09. If we wait a few minutes for the sky to rotate, Menkalinan (and its radiating spoke) are now directly on the local meridian—which is the same as saying that Menkalinan's "spoke" now divides the sky into two equal halves, east and west. Now is the time to measure the star's angle from zenith, which in this illustration is now just under 4 degrees. And finally, we combine that information with Menkalinan's known declination (from memory or star charts) to calculate our latitude. (IMAGE COURTESY OF RICK BROWN AND FRED SCHNEIDER.)

Figure 01.10. Kurt Creamer, pictured in 2008. (IMAGE COURTESY OF KURT CREAMER.)

directly overhead or a few degrees off. Because if you're just one degree off, if it's 89 degrees overhead and not 90 degrees, you're going to be 60 miles off. Now, if you're trying to hit the coast of North America, which we did on the first trip where he tried this, that's one thing. But if you're trying to hit an island and you're 60 miles off, that's a catastrophe."[15]

Kurt's European voyage was his last on *Scotia*. In 1980, Creamer sold *Scotia* and purchased and outfitted *Navstar*, a thirty-nine-foot Southern Cross built by the C. E. Ryder Corp. *Navstar* (hull #2 from the company) was large enough to offer room for more crew members, as well as more storage for food, water, tools, and spare parts. The larger crew and additional provisions were essential if he was to accomplish his next goal: a round trip from Cape May, New Jersey, to Africa and back. The trip was to be made without instruments.

On April 11, 1980, Marv and a crew of three set off for Dakar, on the northwest coast of Africa. They would return via Bermuda on July 19, having battled thirty-five-foot seas near the Azores. In fact, Creamer had actually intended to *visit* the Azores on this voyage but had doubts about whether he was actually on track to intersect the series of islands comprising what is officially the Autonomous Region of the Azores. (Which awkward name goes a long way toward explaining why most simply refer to the islands as "the Azores.") Later, Creamer's wife, Blanche—having viewed data sent from a transmitter on board *Navstar*, a transmitter to which her husband did not have access—would reproach him, asking why, when he was headed straight for the Azores and only forty-four miles from them, he had turned away. (Note that in Creamer's notes, journals, and manuscript, he sometimes differentiates between nautical and statute miles, but when he does not differentiate, distances here are generally expressed in nautical miles.)

"The answer," says Creamer, "was that I did not believe I could judge latitude, with any degree of accuracy, from a platform that was being constantly buffeted by turbulent seas. I felt sick. The methods had worked but I had failed. I resolved never again to lose faith."[16]

Soon he would break that promise while transiting on *Globe Star*, disbelieving his own calculations and potentially imperiling himself, his boat, and his crew.

CHAPTER 2

DEPARTING CAPE MAY ON BOARD *GLOBE STAR*

> We shall not cease from exploration, and the end of all
> our exploring will be to arrive where we started and
> know the place for the first time.
>
> —T. S. ELIOT

IT WAS NOT AN AUSPICIOUS BEGINNING.

Globe Star, having been delivered only twenty days prior to departure, was a beehive of activity, with volunteers of all stripes busy loading food and gear, installing the gimballed stove, filling water and fuel tanks, and attaching lee cloths to the berths to act as safety nets to keep occupants from tumbling out of the berth when the boat heeled or rolled violently. The custom mast had been ordered earlier but still needed to be stepped and stays rigged.

There was a *lot* of gear to load, and a great deal of food. Marv liked to cook and he liked to eat, and he knew that hardworking crewmembers also liked to eat. In fact, he knew very well that there are times aboard a sailboat during a long passage when there's not much else to *do* but eat—or *think* about eating. Thus, with Blanche's help, he made sure *Globe Star* was well stocked with all manner of edibles: canned and dried fruits, vegetables, soups, soup mixes, canned juices, flour (Creamer loved to bake bread and pies while at sea), oatmeal, spaghetti, macaroni, cocoa, cheese, oranges, apples, potatoes, carrots, cabbage, onions, eggs (coated with Vaseline to retard spoilage), canned fish, and a supply of meats that had been canned by Blanche Creamer herself. Food would eventually become a matter of some contention with a couple of crewmates, but it wasn't because Creamer hadn't tried to anticipate the need for healthful and varied provisions.

Globe Star was docked at Greenwich, a small township (population approximately nine hundred in 2020), after the crew attended a media event held at Red Bank Battlefield Park, intending to sail her down the Delaware River, which runs between New Jersey and Pennsylvania, from Greenwich to Cape May, New Jersey, her true point of embarkation.[1] It being the end of December, the weather was not conducive to a pleasant launch. The temperature had dropped to 17 degrees Fahrenheit in nearby New York the night before, and was now in the mid-30s in New Jersey. Several inches of snow covering the boat and the dock had to be removed before the volunteers could begin loading *Globe Star* and finishing up last-minute details. It was cold and blustery and none too comfortable for the crew, the volunteers, and those who had gathered for the sendoff.

The last-minute details were eventually taken care of, though Marv was never quite sure just where all these people came from and why they all worked so diligently to see him off. *Globe Star* started her engine, a three-cylinder, thirty-six-horsepower MD17d diesel furnished by Volvo Penta of the United States that was to give them no end of trouble as the voyage progressed, and cast off. (The boat came stocked with a two-cylinder, twenty-four-horsepower diesel, but Creamer and the builder agreed that more horsepower would not be a bad thing, so a larger engine was installed.)

The boat, with Marv and crewmembers Jeff Herdelin and George Baldwin aboard, immediately began heading up the river—the wrong way.

Or so it appeared. In reality, Marv had purposely decided to head about a half-mile upriver in order to clear some shoals, and only *then* turn downriver toward the bay. A smart-aleck onlooker shouted, "Open the bag! Open the bag!" referring to the sealed package of instruments that the boat carried (at Blanche's insistence) and that Marv intended to open only in the event of real disaster. (In addition, consultant and Smithsonian project director Lee Houchins had arranged for a joint Smithsonian/

National Weather Service project to sponsor data collection and position transmission via an ARGOS transmitter on the boat, but Marv and his crew did not have access to that information. The transmitter, it turned out, did not always work correctly, in any case. The sealed bag of backup navigation instruments was to be made ready for inspection immediately upon *Globe Star*'s return to Cape May, New Jersey. Only in dire emergency, Marv resolved, would he open that bag while at sea.)

Creamer and crew *did* carry some charts on board, so one might argue that they had at least *some* "modern" advantages. However, the charts they carried were few and, in some cases, not terribly useful.

Bob Rout, a crewman on a later leg of the voyage, points out that charts are only truly helpful when they are of the appropriate scale. On a long-range transit, broad-scale charts are relatively handy; closer to shore, more detailed charts are necessary—or at least desirable.

"We had not-very-detailed charts of South America," says Bob. (Rout sailed with Creamer from New Zealand to the Falklands, skirting South America.) Instead they had a large book that showed currents and wind patterns for trading, "just a very large-scale world map of wind velocities and directions at times of year, and it included a very broad-scale chart of South America. We did have a detailed chart of the Falkland Islands and that, as it turned out, was very fortuitous for us. But we had no detailed charts of southern South America, which was kind of the tricky part of . . . the voyage."[2]

Of course, the charts Creamer had on board were actually not much different than the rough drawings and sketches carried thousands of years ago, when voyagers set off, and that were sometimes provided by natives when voyagers put in at various landfalls.

In addition, many ancient voyagers used mapping tools that predated modern charts but were used in a similar fashion. One example is the Polynesian "wayfinder," a 3D latticework of bent twigs and cordage, the shape of which is meant to indicate currents, wind and wave directions, and the presence of atolls and islands. Comparable tools were used by the Micronesians and others.

These and similar tools were used by South Sea Islanders and others as "charts," which they would consult as they sailed. Not at all coincidentally, ancient navigators also used wave, swell, and cloud formations to indicate both direction and the location of and proximity to islands and other landmasses. Creamer and his crew used similar "tools" on his voyage.

One Tahitian navigator, Tupaia (with the aid of some of Captain James Cook's officers), actually drew a fairly complex and quite accurate map of Tahiti and its surroundings for Cook in about 1769. Tupaia's map (and his advice) were used by Captain Cook aboard HMS *Endeavour* as the Tahitian traveled with Cook's expedition to New Zealand. Tupaia died aboard Cook's ship in 1770, having contracted either malaria or dysentery. Cook, on the other hand, was killed by Hawaiian natives in February 1779 when, not at all surprisingly, the natives reacted unfavorably to his plan to kidnap their chief in response to the natives stealing a small boat from Cook's modest fleet; the exchange resulted in Cook being clubbed, then stabbed to death. Because he was held in some esteem by the natives, they removed the flesh from his bones and eventually returned his skeleton to his crew. The respect with which the natives undertook these funerary rituals apparently did not mollify the angry crew.

Thus, ancient mariners were not without tools of their own when it came to navigating, including (sometimes rudimentary) maps, charts, and other representations of the surrounding seas. In large part, though, the main instruments those navigators (and Creamer) used were their brains, their senses, and their knowledge of the sea and of geography, some of it passed down from generation to generation. One can still encounter this mode of instrument-free ocean travel, though it is becoming exceedingly rare. Bob Rout notes that when he lived in Oman, he would see large wooden sailing dhows that Middle Easterners would "sail down to Africa, down to Zanzibar on the Northeast monsoon, and then they'd come back on the Southwest [monsoon]. And they didn't have navigation aids, they had the knowledge of the skipper who had done it all his life."[3]

Creamer *and* ancient seafaring people shared more than just the desire to traverse oceans and visit unseen lands; they shared an ability to use their knowledge of the world to make those voyages possible. (See chapter 7 for more information about ancient navigation techniques.)

The *Globe Star* expedition, meanwhile, was unfolding at a rapid pace. The two crewmembers who accompanied Creamer on that first leg were,

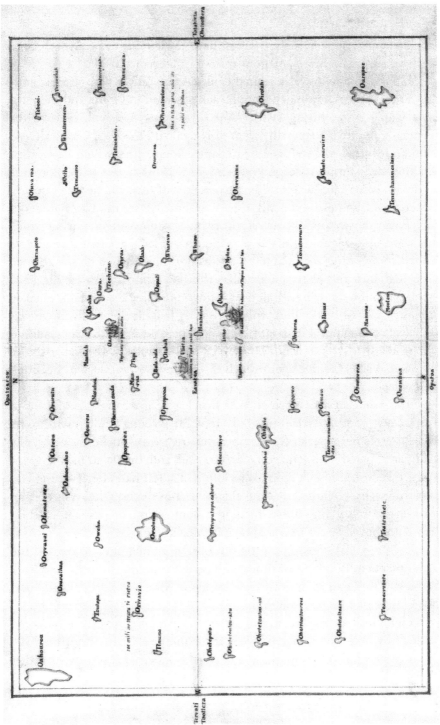

Figure 02.01. Tupaia's map of the area surrounding Tahiti. (IMAGE IN THE PUBLIC DOMAIN.)

in some ways, opposites. That might have turned out to be an issue, but, perhaps surprisingly, no antagonisms ever materialized.

George Baldwin was a retired career Army officer who, after spending a few years as a primary school teacher, served in China and the Panama Canal Zone during World War II, followed by some years in the Pentagon. Baldwin eventually went to Korea with the First Cavalry Division and retired in 1961 as a lieutenant colonel, after which he worked for Bell Labs until his second retirement. With that sort of background, and with some blue-water sailing experience of his own, he was a steady, experienced, and assured hand to have around. (After the *Globe Star* voyage, Baldwin was to make several other blue-water voyages, during which he acted as navigator.) His trip to South Africa on *Globe Star* almost ended shortly after the boat left Cape May, though, when he was thrown face-first into the chart table when the boat rolled, gashing his head open. With blood dripping all over Baldwin's yellow foul-weather jacket, Creamer closed the wound with a butterfly bandage—luckily, there was an excellent first aid kit aboard the boat. There wasn't much he could do about Baldwin's broken nose, however, and it quickly swelled to twice its normal size. George spent much of the next several days in his bunk belowdecks.

The other crewmember on that first leg (Cape May, New Jersey, to Cape Town, South Africa) was Jeff Herdelin, a young student with some coastal cruising experience but no familiarity with offshore sailing. He had participated in organized races, however, and, thanks to having spent some time working in a sailmaker's loft, had a deft hand both setting and repairing sails. He jumped at the chance to join the expedition but began with a few misgivings about making a noninstrument passage. Luckily, those doubts were put to rest almost immediately.

Says Jeff, "I [worried] a little bit, but Marv had already crossed the Atlantic before, a couple of times with no instruments, from Ireland back to New Jersey, and then from New Jersey to Africa, to Senegal and back. So, I knew that he had done this."

Herdelin had wanted to sail across the Atlantic ever since he was a young boy, and the passage had become something of an obsession. "The Atlantic was sort of always there, and you'd wonder what was on the other

Figure 02.02. Jeff Herdelin, many years after the *Globe Star* voyage.
(PHOTO COURTESY OF JEFF HERDELIN.)

side," says Jeff. "It had been something I had wanted to do and I was looking for a way to do it."[4]

Ultimately, Jeff became interested in learning how no-instrument navigation worked, and Creamer was an excellent teacher; after all, that was his profession. Not surprisingly, the two developed a teacher/student relationship, Creamer acting as mentor to young Jeff, with Herdelin keen to learn all that Marv could teach him about navigation and Marv, as always, happy to teach an eager student.

Still, when imagining his first (and, as it turns out, his only) transatlantic passage, Herdelin admits that traveling across an ocean without any instruments wasn't exactly how he'd pictured his initial crossing. He had imagined a more traditional passage, one that utilized compass, radar, sextant, and other such tools, but instead found himself signing up for an unconventional voyage that lacked such modern niceties. "Once I found that out, I guess that sort of explained why there wasn't a long line of people getting ready to jump on board," he says.

Jeff Herdelin and George Baldwin seemed unlikely partners, especially in an enterprise in which they held each other's lives in their hands. As a staunch churchgoer, a military man, and a lifelong member of both the American Legion and Masons, one might have expected that the presumably conservative and perhaps somewhat conventional Baldwin would have little in common with—and perhaps little to say to—the bearded, bushy-haired younger man. But that turned out not to be true: Although the two men's backgrounds and outlooks may have been different, they shared a love of the sea, an appreciation of each other's talents, and an understanding of the fact that teamwork is what makes a successful voyage.

According to Jeff, "George was not the gruff army officer stereotype you might think. He was certainly friendly to me, a kind man, and pretty easygoing most of the time."

One thing that George might have had some trouble with, according to Jeff, is that, "as a career officer used to manuals, policies, and procedures for everything, he might have struggled a bit with the unconventional nature of the expedition, especially the no-instrument navigation, since there was no manual on it; *Marv* was the manual."[5]

In the end, all three men—with Creamer as their acknowledged leader—found that they complemented each other and worked well together.

The three sailors set off (going the "wrong" way, as noted) on December 21 at about noon, intending a short jaunt from Greenwich to Cape May (their official debarkation point)—and immediately ran aground.

Says Creamer, "It took more than an hour of prodding, rocking, tugging, sweating, and tidal rise before she broke loose and got under way. I wondered when we might expect the next exciting adventure."[6]

He got his answer almost immediately. As *Globe Star* beat its way through Delaware Bay and toward the Cape May canal, Creamer started the engine and heard a strange sound, which then turned into what Creamer described as "a deafening clatter."

They dropped anchor, and Creamer checked out the engine, quickly determining that the rocker arms had worked loose; the result was that the pushrod clearances were excessive. He used feeler gauges, wrenches,

Figure 02.03. Marv and Jeff Herdelin on the day of departure.
(PHOTO COURTESY OF THE CREAMER FAMILY.)

and the engine's manual to rectify the problem. Half an hour later, they were underway once again.

The boat had not even begun its journey, and it had already suffered through two mishaps; a lesser man might have viewed this as a bad omen, portending still more—and more serious—trouble ahead. A lesser man would have been right.

But this overcoming of obstacles, this constant finding of solutions, reveals an emerging theme illustrated repeatedly on this journey: the need for self-reliance. One might be forgiven for thinking that Marv *liked* problems, for problems required rational thought and analysis and the calm consideration of options, and those led to solutions. Those solutions would lead in turn to feelings of accomplishment, a sense of satisfaction at having resolved what had started out as a baffling issue. Added to this was the fact that solutions to thorny problems *impressed* people, and Marv—as he would probably admit—liked impressing people.

Figure 02.04. Marv speaks to the press on the day of departure.
(PHOTO COURTESY OF THE CREAMER FAMILY.)

Figure 02.05. Jeff Herdelin in the cockpit as *Globe Star* heads into the Atlantic.
(PHOTO COURTESY OF THE CREAMER FAMILY.)

All of his life, Marv Creamer sought solutions to problems, some of them considered insoluble. This voyage would present more than its share of such issues, and every time Creamer and his crew encountered an obstacle—a balky engine, a broken rudder, a cranky stove—the voyagers would put their heads together to find a solution, even if that meant crafting parts from leftover pieces of scrap metal.

But as Jeff Herdelin points out, while everyone helped out, the majority of solutions came from one man.

"We had to figure out how to fix stuff. And when I say *we*, most of that knowledge was Marv," says Jeff. When it came time to find a way to fix a problem, "Marv just had an amazing ability to think that through."[7]

Like his father before him, Marvin Creamer was a resourceful, self-reliant man. That would stand him in good stead as the voyage progressed.

CHAPTER 3

THE OPEN OCEAN, GALLEY FIRES

*Man cannot discover new oceans unless he has the courage to lose sight
of the shore.*

—ANDRE GIDE

SAILORS AT SEA FEAR MANY THINGS; THE OCEAN, AFTER ALL, IS A POW-
erful and fearsome thing, and one does not trifle with it. It's not malevo-
lent, not really; it is simply cold, uncaring, and capricious. The ocean is
beautiful, and danger sometimes lies in beautiful things. On a boat, one
must guard against adverse weather, the threat of capsize, broken rigging,
torn sails, balky engines, damaged rudders and tillers, electrical systems
gone haywire—the list seems endless. (And we can add to that list an
impressive catalog of *human* frailties, both physical and psychological.)

Perhaps this is one reason that sailors are a superstitious lot; one cannot control *every* variable, and over the centuries, an impressive collection
of seafaring superstitions has gained currency. Thus, some days are just
generally considered unlucky, while others are thought to be ill-omened
for specific reasons. For instance, it has long been thought unlucky to
begin a voyage on a Friday. (No one is quite sure how that one came about,
although it may have some connection to the fact that Jesus was said to
have been crucified on a Friday.) Similarly, most of us recall the sailors'
maxim, "Red sky at morning, sailor take warning; red sky at night, sailor's
delight." (There is actually a meteorological basis for this one: A red sunrise
indicates that a high-pressure system may have passed, potentially giving
rise to a low-pressure system—with its attendant bad weather—moving in.
In addition, a red sunrise can indicate the presence of moisture in the air.)

It is for some reason considered unlucky to have bananas on board a ship. Boarding a boat left foot first is said to be bad luck, possibly because of the sinister associations with the left side of anything. Whistling while on board is likewise considered to be bad luck. Some *people* (called "Jonahs") are considered bad luck, and this includes pastors and priests. Women are also thought to be unlucky, especially redheaded women. (A redheaded woman who happens to be a priest or pastor must be presumed to be especially risky to have on board. And yet a glance through the annals of just the U.S. Navy corps of chaplains reveal that many are female and several of those are redheads.)[1]

Of course, there are also *positive* superstitions. Cormorants and cats are considered good luck on board ships. (The former because they are thought to embody the spirits of loved ones lost at sea who have come to visit, and the latter possibly because they kill rodents, which were likely to destroy ropes and stores of grain.) St. Elmo's fire, which neophyte sailors might view with some trepidation, is an electrical discharge that sometimes occurs at the mastheads of boats; in spite of its fearsome aspect, many (but not all) sailors view it as good luck.

Superstitions aside, there is one thing that sailors fear above all else, and that is *fire*. Fire on board a boat or ship is terrifying. (The difference between a boat and a ship continues to be debated, but for the sake of simplicity, let's assume for now that a boat is generally quite small compared to a ship and does not—as most ships do—carry aboard it any full-size boats. That is to say, a ship can carry a boat, but a boat cannot carry a ship. But then other questions arise: Could a *ship* carry a ship? *Any* ship? The debate about these terms has gone on for centuries; it will not be settled here.) The reason that an onboard fire strikes terror into the heart of any sailor is simple: When fire strikes your home or apartment, you have options. At least most of the time, residents can escape through a door or window; after their escape, they generally gather in front of the residence or huddle with neighbors while they wait for the fire department. In the worst-case scenario, the occupants of the burning home might have left the home with only the clothes on their backs, and they might end up having to stay with friends, or perhaps the Red Cross or other such service group will arrange temporary housing. As bad as it might be to see your home and your belongings go up in flames, most fire victims do escape and can contemplate rebuilding their homes and their lives.

Fire on board a boat is different simply because once the fire begins to spread, *there is nowhere to go*. If a skiff or life raft is available, the sailors may find themselves adrift at sea with few supplies and perhaps no means of propulsion. If no skiff, tender, or life raft is available (or if it was destroyed in the fire), the sailors must jump into the sea, where their odds of survival may—often depending on the temperature of the water—be dismal indeed. A burning boat will simply burn down to the waterline, leaving nothing but a burned-out husk of what may have been, only minutes before, a well-equipped yacht. (And if the hull's integrity is compromised, even that husk may not stay afloat for long. As for *Globe Star*, her hull was made of steel and would therefore not have burned in any case, though the rest of the boat might have gone up in flames.)

BoatUS (Boat Owners Association of the United States) has been insuring boats for over fifty years, and the organization has kept track of fire (and other) statistics. The group notes that fire ranks number five among causes of boat loss. About 32 percent of those fires are electrical in nature, while another large percentage (26 percent) are started by "off-boat sources," that is, something else that is on fire (another boat, a dock, etc.) comes into contact with a boat, starting a fire on that boat. Other causes of onboard fire include engine issues (7 percent) and fuel problems (5 percent).[2] The bottom line is that a fair number of boats burn every year, and people occasionally die.

Note that fires from cooking stoves are not explicitly mentioned in BoatUS's statistics, partly because they're not terribly common, especially with today's modern stoves, which is why Marv was so shocked in early January when he stepped into the galley to check on some bread he was baking, only to find the galley on fire.

"Four columns of flames and black smoke shot upward from the four corners of the galley stove. They flattened as they reached the cabin headliner, and filled the cabin with acrid kerosene fumes. It was a terrifying sight," he noted later.[3]

Creamer had to empty the contents of a large Halon-filled extinguisher in order to get the fire under control, but for some time afterward, the red-hot metal of the stove kept reigniting puddles of kerosene that had accumulated in the bottom of the oven. Needless to say, the bread was a total loss, a forlorn, blackened brick that sat smoking in the burned-out oven. But the boat, smoke-stained as it was, survived, as did its crew.

Says Jeff Herdelin, who crewed on that first leg, "We acted quickly, as soon as we discovered the fire. Marv went to the stove and I went forward to the vee berth area to look for a second extinguisher. (It was early in the trip, so we still had some equipment piled up there.) I was a little less worried than I might have been in a fiberglass boat; I had seen at least one glass boat on fire as a kid and they go quick."

"Marv got the fire down and I don't think we needed to use the second extinguisher. I'm thinking the loaf of bread was the biggest loss."[4]

Today's kerosene stoves are safer and more efficient, but it's entirely reasonable to blame Marv for the fire in the first place, at least partly. To begin with, his rush to depart Cape May in December meant that there were no shakedown cruises. That's a dangerous—perhaps *foolhardy* is not too strong a word—thing to do, and it seems at odds with Marv's reputation as an almost-obsessive planner. He provisioned and launched his vessel in a mere twenty days or so; many sailors would prep, provision, test, run sea trials, and do shakedowns for as much as a full year before embarking on that long of a voyage. It's very possible that his many stove-related problems (and several other belatedly discovered issues too) could have been revealed and mitigated during one or more shakedown cruises; that is, after all, the purpose of such preparatory cruises. Then there's the unattended stove itself. Few sailors would leave an unattended oven in the galley, especially a kerosene-fired oven. (Today's propane stoves are undoubtedly safer, but most sailors would nonetheless be loath to leave even a propane oven running unattended.) Entering the saloon to find the galley ablaze was undoubtedly an unpleasant surprise, but it really shouldn't have been that much of a shock.

In any case, Marv loved to bake, and the loss of that loaf of bread really was felt by the crew. In fact, it seems that almost all sailors relish fresh bread at sea. It tastes wonderful, of course (or it does most of the time, at any rate), but aside from that there's something about the smell of

Figure 03.01. Jeff Herdelin (*right*) on a visit to Marv (*left*) in 2016.
(IMAGE COURTESY OF JEFF HERDELIN.)

fresh-baked bread—perhaps it reminds sailors, cold and wet and isolated as they may be, of home and safe harbor.

Jeff Herdelin really loved that bread. "If there's anything that picks up your spirit, it's when some of that bread comes out. I mean, when *doesn't* fresh bread coming out of the oven sound good? And after being at sea for days, it was *especially* good."[5]

Globe Star's kerosene stove was not at all uncommon at the time, and not unknown even now. Such appliances are often used because they're inexpensive and simple to operate, and because the fuel is cheap, efficient, and readily available. Even today, many world travelers utilize kerosene (often called *paraffin* outside of the United States) for light or heat because there are places in the world where diesel, propane, and gasoline are hard to come by, while kerosene is almost always available. Creamer would have chosen a kerosene stove simply because fuel would be easy to find, if for no other reason.

Kerosene, oddly enough, does not burn readily. You could strike a match and douse it in a can of kerosene, if you had a mind to and if you moved quickly enough. Kerosene *vapor*, on the other hand, burns extremely well. (Which is why you should not try the match-dousing trick at home; the kerosene might not burn, but you could set off the fumes, which would burn explosively.)

To use a kerosene stove, one simply pressurizes a fuel container, which emits vapor that is sent to a burner and ignited. A kerosene stove is a fairly uncomplicated, straightforward mechanism. But as Marv knew well, even simple devices can exhibit unanticipated behaviors. In the case of the *Globe Star*'s stove, it turned out that when the oven door was opened, the edge of the door nudged the control valve, leading to droplets of kerosene being collected under the burner before the kerosene vapor actually ignited.

In addition to that, though, it appeared that more kerosene was collecting in a reservoir beneath the burner even after ignition. It turned out that beneath the burner platform, sandwiched in between the burner platform and the bottom of the compartment, was a piece of insulation that, however good at insulating it might have been, turned out to be even better at collecting and absorbing stray kerosene. The heat of the burner

Figure 03.02. A modern kerosene stove, much safer and more efficient than the one Creamer installed in *Globe Star*'s galley some forty years ago, though they work in roughly the same manner. (PHOTO COURTESY OF SEA SURE LTD.)

eventually forced the fuel out of the insulating material and into the surrounding compartment, where it caught fire. Creamer was well aware of the irony: the insulation, installed to prevent fires, turned out to be the very same thing that ended up causing them. This was not the last time that this stove would bedevil Creamer and his crew.

In the meantime, ruined bread notwithstanding, the voyage continued. About three weeks into the one-hundred-day leg to Cape Town, the first big storm hit. Wind speeds of forty knots produced waves twenty-five feet high, one of which swept overboard one of the boat's two fifteen-gallon drums of kerosene, which could have been used for cooking or as emergency fuel for the diesel engine.[6]

Gales continued for four days, and at first it was difficult to determine a wind direction, so the boat ran under bare poles until the crew could get a good look at the sky and determine the direction of the wind.

Most of us would be uncomfortable bobbing about during a storm and its aftermath, but Creamer was used to it, and even found the motion fairly pleasant. The exasperating part, he said, was the fact that he had little idea *where* he was drifting and was unable to set a course without seeing the sky. Thus, he was reduced to helpless waiting, even as potentially helpful winds rattled the halyards and whined through the rigging.

Being battered by gales and heaving seas while dancing in place is downright frustrating. Time seems to stand still. On deck, you search the sky for the break that might provide a clue to direction. You feel the tremendous power of the gales and wish you had the way-finding ability of the migrating birds. With safety harness tether sliding on cabin-top safety cables, you crouch and inch your way around the cabin hand over hand along the grab rails looking for signs of line chafing or gear failure. Below, you cock an ear to pick up the hint of letup that never comes.[7]

When the winds abated and the skies cleared, *Globe Star* could once again set a course to South Africa. As the boat neared the vicinity of Cape Town, though, danger lurked. This first leg was intended to be in three parts, each portion representing a segment of the Z-shaped sailing route used for hundreds of years by trading vessels of old. The first segment was to the vicinity of the Cape Verde Islands, the second southeast to the latitude of southern Africa, and the final segment was to see the boat head almost due east to Cape Town.

But a problem loomed. Because *Globe Star* was restricted to latitude sailing, Creamer and crew did not dare dip into the higher latitudes of the southern Atlantic to pick up the steadier trade winds as the old sailing ships did. To do so would have risked missing the southern tip of Africa altogether. If that happened, the crew would run out of water long before they raised the next continent—Australia.

That sort of risk was ever present, of course, as were many others, and as we hear of Creamer's journey, we begin to wonder about some of the chances he took. We speak of some types of risk as being "calculated," but in truth, *all* risks are calculated. There is an equation, a calculus—sometimes so subtle as to be almost subconscious—by which people determine the amount of risk with which they're comfortable, their level of risk tolerance. Psychologists refer to this level of comfort as *risk homeostasis*, and they note that it changes, sometimes moment by moment. According to psychologist Rüdiger Trimpop, of the University of Jena,

> *We compensate constantly. If it starts raining on the highway, we slow down; if it stops, we speed up. With driver assistance features, we pay less attention . . . [and we may] play on the mobile or read the newspaper.*[8]

Trimpop, author of *The Psychology of Risk Taking Behavior*, says that *without* risk taking, there is no progress. He feels that Creamer is definitely more of a risk taker than most, though that's probably true of any blue-water sailor. But the successful risk takers who sail are usually also very careful planners. They calculate the amount of risk with which they'll be comfortable and act to mitigate those risks. They may set out on a short jaunt to a nearby island, but not without at least some planning. A transoceanic crossing occasions a great deal more preparation.

Figure 03.03. Dr. Rüdiger Trimpop is the chair of industrial and organizational psychology at the University of Jena. (PHOTO COURTESY OF DR. RÜDIGER TRIMPOP.)

And a circumnavigation, of course, requires more organization or preparation still. A circumnavigation *without instruments* requires not only a great deal of planning but also a certain amount of faith in your methods because those methods are not backed up by the modern technologies most of us use to ensure that we'll make it safely from one place to another. Naturally, there are people who undertake long voyages with very little planning; some of those are surely successful, but many eventually require rescue and some are simply never heard from again. Creamer was a very careful, perhaps even an obsessive, planner, but he was known to be an impatient man.

Kathleen Saville knows about both planning and risk taking. The author of *Rowing for My Life*, Saville and her husband rowed across both the Atlantic and Pacific Oceans, feats that required a great deal of advance planning and that naturally involved a great deal of risk.

"Marvin was definitely into risk-taking, though he might try to take the so-called high road and intellectualize all the decisions he made on his voyages without instruments," she says.

Ironically—but perhaps not surprisingly—it was Marvin Creamer on whom Saville and her husband called when they lost their sextant midvoyage. Having met Creamer at a boat show before the Savilles began their voyage, they contacted him via ham radio for help.

"He walked us through the steps of navigating with stars at their meridian points and specific latitudes," says Saville. "His method and kind help saved our lives, I believe."[9] (In a tragic irony that later led Kathleen to study risk-taking herself, her husband, Curt, walked into the Egyptian desert some years after their rowing voyage, woefully unprepared for a long desert hike. He died of thirst and exposure in the Cairo hospital to which he had eventually been transferred.)

In Creamer's case—and this is undoubtedly true of many adventurers—the risks involved may actually have been part of the appeal. As Julian Sancton says of polar explorers in *Madhouse at the End of the Earth*, "The perils involved were not a deterrent but rather an inducement: the more harrowing the story, the more people would want to read it, and the more publishers would pay for an exclusive account."[10] Creamer did have a book in mind, after all, and he relished the danger—provided he could survive to tell (and perhaps sell) the tale, of course.

Risks notwithstanding, Creamer and crew decided to turn abruptly eastward after reaching the latitude of Cape Town and to hold that latitude as best they could until they ran into (not literally, one hopes) the African land mass. This meant missing the trade winds, and it also presumed that the sailors could hold the vessel on course even absent those favorable winds. It further supposed that Creamer's latitude calculations were correct and that he would head *Globe Star* east at the right time.

But that was a set of problems that would be dealt with at a later time. For now, the first order of business was to find Cape Verde, a string of volcanic islands in the central Atlantic, located west and slightly north of Dakar, Senegal.

Figure 03.04. Kathleen Saville rowed across both the Atlantic and Pacific oceans and is the author of *Rowing for My Life*. She is associate chair of the Department of Rhetoric and Composition at the American University in Cairo. (PHOTO COURTESY OF KATHLEEN SAVILLE.)

CHAPTER 4

HEADED FOR AFRICA,
IF ALL GOES WELL

It is good to have an end to journey toward; but it is the journey that matters, in the end.

—URSULA K. LE GUIN

RUNNING LIGHTS HAVE BEEN STANDARD ON BOATS OF ALL SIZES FOR many years. (Very small boats, such as rowboats, are allowed to run without lights, but boaters on board are required to have a flashlight or lantern handy after dark.) In the United States, the Coast Guard stipulates that boats of various sizes must display lights of a specific intensity and angle of visibility, and most of these rules are identical internationally. Thus, *Globe Star* possessed the requisite set of lights for a sailboat her size. In 1982, Creamer's boat would have been subject to the nautical "rules of the road" contained in Rules 22 and 25 of the 1972 International Regulations for Preventing Collisions at Sea (aka COLREGS). These mandate specific types and placement of lights for specific conditions and are aimed mainly at safety. Among other things, they ensure that another vessel can not only locate your boat at a distance but can—by virtue of the stern light and colored port/starboard lights—determine your heading. More than one collision has been averted by a knowledgeable skipper spotting another vessel and knowing at a glance where that vessel was headed and if the paths of the two boats would at some point cross.

Marv Creamer, however, had been known to flout the occasional rule, and he chose to flout *these* rules. While *Globe Star* had the required lights, using them ate up battery power, and running the engine to recharge those batteries used up valuable fuel. In Marv's mind—and many other sailors would have performed the same calculus—it was actually *safer* to conserve fuel, which might be needed when docking or maneuvering, to make forward progress in the absence of wind, or simply in order to get out of the way of an obstacle or of another vessel. Not using running lights, thought Creamer, was the safer course of action, especially because, offshore, the odds of collision with another small boat were infinitesimally small.

> *Collision, if it comes, will be with an oceangoing ship. Ships must avoid each other and do not dare to disregard international regulations, therefore they carry all required lights. These are hundreds of times brighter and can be seen many miles farther than those required for small boats. My practice has always been to keep lights off until we see the lights of a ship and then if it appears that there will be an approach within a few miles to turn them on. By maintaining a careful, all-night watch a considerable amount of fuel is saved. There is another safety factor involved also. Unless a separate battery is maintained to start the engine for emergency use, it is very difficult to use a battery for lights and at the same time be sure there is enough of a charge left to get the engine started. Not having enough charge to crank the engine that is needed to restore the charge is a dilemma that no safety-minded sailor wants to face.* [1]

The key, of course, is the maintenance of an all-night watch. If you're sailing solo, you may be unable to maintain such a watch, or may choose not to; instead a solo sailor, if he or she is smart, will turn on the boat's lights and heave to, or set the self-steering mechanism in order to continue forward movement while heading belowdecks for some (usually fitful) sleep. Marv felt—and many would agree with him—that so long as someone was on watch, running without lights was quite safe. (This in spite of the fact that many large ocean-going vessels, especially freighters, although they may display the required lights, leave no one on watch; smaller sailboats have been run down by ships so large that the impact with a sailboat does not slow them down in the slightest. Many large vessels also seem quite lax about keeping an eye on their radar, even though most small boats used, as *Globe Star* did, radar reflectors to enhance the radar profile of their vessels.)[2]

It's important to note that today's low-power LED lights have been a bit of a game changer in situations like this. Their low power draw means that in many cases it's perfectly possible to display the required lights without worrying too much about running down the vessel's batteries. In 1982, though, affordable white LEDs were still a decade away, and LEDs that produced in excess of one hundred lumens would not become common until the mid-2000s.[3]

USCG CDR John Harrington (Ret.) says that on his boat, *Tango*, a Tayana 52 sloop, LEDs have made a major difference: "The brightness and low power consumption are really amazing. The old lights on *Tango* were all 10–20-watt lights (navigation, internal, instrument, etc.). Today my power draw, including a monster autopilot, is only about 10A day or night."[4]

In *Globe Star*'s case, there was always a series of night watches, the last of which was usually taken by Marv himself, so that he could note the first hint of dawn and perhaps get a position fix or gauge the coming day's wind and weather.

At this point, *Globe Star* had been at sea for almost a month, and Marv and the crew were watching for indications that they might be approaching the vicinity of Cape Verde. The first such clue arrived in a surreal fashion. During Jeff Herdelin's nighttime watch on January 24, the masthead lit up with an eerie glow, presaging the appearance of St. Elmo's fire, a soft, yellow-greenish light that, in this instance, spread from the masthead to the deck. The phenomenon was named after St. Elmo, the patron saint of sailors. Elmo was also known as Erasmus of Formia. (Oddly, he was also the patron saint of abdominal pain. In fact, he is often represented with his entrails wound around a windlass, a simple machine used to pull heavy objects or large ropes under tension, such as those used to move freight or to haul large sails up a tall mast. Apparently, the windlass served to signify—in a particularly gruesome fashion—his connection to and patronage of sailors.)

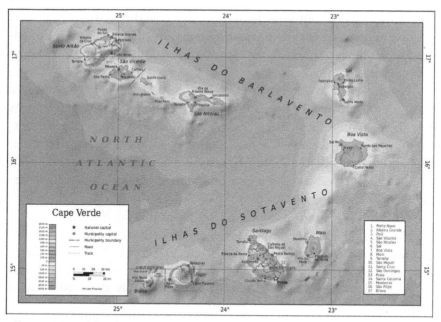

Figure 04.01. A topographic map of the Cape Verde Islands. (USED UNDER THE TERMS OF THE GNU FREE DOCUMENTATION LICENSE, COURTESY OF USER: *MYSID*.)

The ghostly light of St. Elmo's fire was followed by a spectacular display of lightning and ear-splitting thunder. This went on for hours and, in spite of Creamer's many years of sailing experience, he had never seen anything like it.

St. Elmo's fire is not lightning, though it is sometimes accompanied by lightning. Instead it is a coronal discharge, basically glowing plasma. It glows—sometimes brightly—but it does not burn, and it does not float around, as ball lightning often does; instead St. Elmo's fire remains attached to some prominent, normally metal, protrusion. A sailboat's metal mast is ideal, but in the days of wooden masts, those too were sometimes the locus of St. Elmo's fire.

The fact that St. Elmo's fire often occurs under heavy cloud cover and that heavy cloud cover itself often occurs over or near large land masses constituted a clue to *Globe Star*'s location, but by itself, it was a very tenuous clue indeed; after all, St. Elmo's fire also occurs far out at sea. Creamer needed more evidence in order to determine his location.

Two days later, some of that evidence appeared. First, a school of porpoises visited, surfing along in *Globe Star*'s bow wave and gamboling about beside the boat. Then the crew caught a glimpse of a large land bird, just before fog closed in. The fog itself was still more evidence that they were in the vicinity of land because fog forms near cold water. Were they near a demarcation site in which warmer water transitions to cold? That would explain the fog, and Creamer was well aware of what is known as the Canaries Current, a colder current that flows past the Canary and Cape Verde Islands. That current, flowing clockwise around the Canary Islands, cools the surrounding warmer water, creating an area of excellent fishing grounds—hence the porpoises, and hence the fog.

During the night of January 27, the final piece of the puzzle fell into place.

Says Creamer, "When daylight came, our sails bore reddish-brown streaks where fine red dust and sand had been turned to mud by the dew-dampened sail cloth. The fabled Sahara had dropped by during the night and left its calling card. The maroon grit not only tie-dyed our new white sails but found its way into the cabin and even got inside our circuit breaker panel box!"

There was no doubt about it. *Globe Star* and her crew were very close to the Cape Verde Islands. Long-distance sailor Naomi James had written about the Saharan dust in *Alone Around the World*, and Creamer himself had encountered it on the way home from Dakar in 1980. Once again, the Saharan "calling card" had helped Marv deduce his location—or at least his proximity to Africa.

Now began a tense period of watching for the huge black rocks that guard the entrance to the chain of islands. At night, when keeping an eye out did little good, the crew was reduced to straining their ears, listening intently for the chilling sound of breakers booming on the rocky shore. When time allowed, the crew rehearsed procedures for quickly shunting *Globe Star* safely away from the danger they expected to encounter at any moment.

Data provided later by the ARGOS tracking system on board the boat showed that Creamer and crew had passed just thirty miles west of Santo Antão, the westernmost island in the Cape Verdean archipelago.

At this point, *Globe Star* had spent thirty-six days at sea and traveled 2,693 nautical miles. ARGOS data would later show that Creamer had underestimated their speed somewhat, and that *Globe Star* was thus about forty-four miles south of her predicted latitude. After almost 2,700 miles of travel, being forty-four miles off was not bad at all. Not surprisingly, though, their longitude showed a much greater disparity, about 432 miles. But when "sailing down the latitudes," one's longitude is generally less important; if *Globe Star* was at or near her estimated latitude, she was in a good position to raise the coast of Africa when (and largely where) expected, especially given that Africa is a *very* large target.

This was the point at which Creamer had expected to pick up the northeast trade winds, but they failed to materialize, leaving *Globe Star* bobbing gently in a weak breeze, with her largest head sails out (and held open with poles because the wind wasn't stiff enough to open and fill the sails) and the crew more or less marooned in a variable haze with, at that equatorial latitude, no real sunrise or sunset.

Creamer and his crew slogged, very slowly, though the flat seas. The only relief was an encounter with bands of riffled water, equatorial countercurrents that flowed against the main east-to-west equatorial current. The riffles were tantalizing; they seemed to promise—but never did deliver—some decent wind, and *Globe Star* slid sluggishly, agonizingly, east toward Cape Town, South Africa.

CHAPTER 5

HEADING FOR CAPE TOWN

Travel is glamorous only in retrospect.

—Paul Theroux

Unlike the western equatorial Pacific, the western equatorial Atlantic is not surrounded by islands, rocks, and dangerous shoals. Nonetheless, Creamer worried about the several small islands and rocky outcrops that could have brought the voyage to an abrupt—and possibly deadly—end. Two of these in particular loomed large in Creamer's mind as the *Globe Star* crew headed east.

The first hazard was the St. Paul Rocks, outcroppings that were part of the St. Paul and St. Peter Archipelago. These are unlighted rocks that jut dangerously into the central equatorial Atlantic about sixty miles north of the equator and about five hundred miles from the nearest land in South America, Piaui, Brazil.

The other potential danger was the Arquipélago de Fernando de Noronha, part of the state of Pernambuco, Brazil. The archipelago lies about 230 miles south of the equator and 130 to 200 miles off Brazil itself.

The risk, especially at night, was an unintentional grounding at either of these places, or for that matter, on other such rocks and outcroppings, including Ascension Island (in about mid-ocean) or St. Helena, or on Ilhas Martim Vaz and Trinidade, 630 miles from the Brazilian shoreline.

Certainly, accurate information on either latitude or longitude would have been very helpful in avoiding such hazards, but the *Globe Star* crew made do, as best it could, by keeping a close eye on the horizon and on the color and surface of the water. At night, the best that could be done

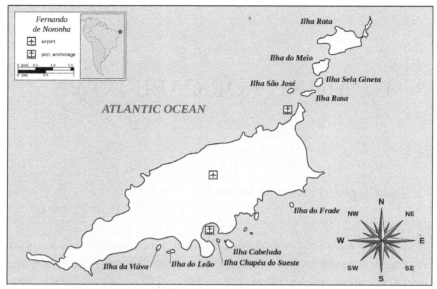

Figure 05.01. Map of the Arquipélago de Fernando de Noronha.
(IMAGE PLACED IN THE PUBLIC DOMAIN BY USER ANTONSUSI.)

was to remain alert for any change in the boat's rhythm or motion that might provide a clue that she was encountering reflected waves or shoaling water. Of course, it was entirely possible that such changes, subtle as they were, might remain unnoticed until it was too late to do anything to save the boat from grounding on rocks or, if they were very lucky, washing up on a sandy beach.

Occasionally, the absence of good information about longitude resulted in ludicrous scenarios: At one point while heading for Africa, Creamer's estimated longitude seemed to indicate that the vessel was sailing *over* South America. Because the boat was obviously not sailing on dry land, it was clearly time to fine-tune their estimated position, and Creamer noted that the best adjustment they could make was to "intersect their estimated latitude with the coast, find the longitude of that point, subtract the angular distance represented by visibility to the imaginary coast, and adopt that longitude as our estimated longitude."[1]

Worried about being thrust too far west by the current, Creamer and crew struggled to maintain an easterly heading. (As it turned out, the ARGOS positioning data later showed that they were in no danger of sailing too far west, and thus ending up north of the "bulge" of Brazil. In fact, they probably wasted time and effort in a needless attempt to stay on an easterly heading.)

By this time, *Globe Star* having approached the equator, Polaris—the star on which the crew had relied greatly for direction finding—had mostly disappeared, sinking toward the northern horizon. The crew had to find a new directional lodestone. Using star charts, they began acquainting themselves with the stars of the Southern Hemisphere, finally settling on the stars of the Southern Cross as their new direction finder. "By going beyond Acrux four and a half times the distance between Gacrux and Acrux we were able to establish a crude but satisfactory polar point," says Creamer.[2] (Later in the journey, with the help of an Australian Boy Scout troop, of all things, Creamer would be able to refine considerably the accuracy of his south-of-the-equator direction finding.)

By now, *Globe Star* was in the doldrums, more properly known as the Intertropical Convergence Zone (ITCZ). This is the area where the northeast and the southeast trade winds converge and, near the equator, the result is an almost complete absence of wind. The weather is hot and muggy, and a sailboat could find itself becalmed—and its crew miserable—for weeks. Creamer described the zone as "a watery desert."

From January 25 to March 19 we did not see a single ship in the sea, jet in the sky, nor, after crossing the equator in mid-February did we see birds, porpoises, or flotsam of any kind—not even an oil slick. Our last contact with visible life for a long period was a lone brown shark that inspected Globe Star's *bottom minutes after George had spent two hours scraping away masses of gooseneck barnacles. Jeff and I speculated on whether the shark homed in on the trail left by the barnacles or George but gave him the benefit of the doubt inasmuch as he was out of the water before "Jaws" appeared.[3]*

While the doldrums are often confused with the so-called horse latitudes, they are not the same thing. Both zones are near the equator, but the former are located at about 5 degrees north and south of the equator (roughly where Creamer now found himself), while the latter are located at 39 degrees north and south of the equator. The doldrums are also associated with severe thunderstorms, which are much less common in the horse latitudes. (The story that horses were thrown overboard to lighten the load in becalmed sailboats is disputed these days, though it is recounted—and noted as a "legend"—on the NOAA website.)[4] Note that, while Creamer's experience in the calms of the doldrums is typical of the way we think of the region, the ITCZ also plays host to some truly horrific weather: CDR John Harrington, USCG (Ret.), describes his knockdown experience approaching the southern edge of the ITCZ with crewmates Paul and Janet aboard *Tango*, a fifty-two-foot Tayana sloop:

> *It was ugly and we could have had a real problem.* Tango *is a big, tough, blue water sailboat. Paul was steering as Janet and I were cleaning up supper and BOOM . . . over we went. A squall had snuck up behind us and we had "all sail set" due to the previously calm winds. It took me about an hour to get* Tango *under enough control to let Paul and Janet above decks to help me change the sail plan. Ugly, ugly ITCZ day.*[5]

Harrington, who, during his USCG career has commanded USCG vessels, performed search and rescue operations and taught navigation and other subjects at the Coast Guard Academy, says that the ITCZs (north and south) drift over time, changing how they interact. Usually, the ITCZ location can be predicted by the warmth of the waters (as in El Niño and La Niña). Sometimes the interaction causes doldrums in which days of light air can persist due to the rising air. However, sometimes interactions create thunderstorms and squalls that are equally persistent.[6]

In *Globe Star*'s case, calms predominated, and she worked her way, very gradually, east and south. The crew measured their longitude by estimating their speed—which they approximated by watching the vessel's

Figure 05.02. CDR John Harrington, USCG (Ret.), and his wife Janet aboard *Tango*, their fifty-two-foot Tayana sloop, shortly after crossing the equator in April 2019. (PHOTO COURTESY OF JOHN HARRINGTON.)

wake—and their latitude by the stars. Each day the crew would determine which stars to look for that night, and each crewmember would be on the alert for those stars that would make meridian transit during his watch. (One watch consisting of three turns of the custom-made hourglass that hung in the cabin.)

Back in New Jersey, Blanche Creamer was following the ARGOS reports closely. She wrote to Lynn on March 22 that *Globe Star*'s position was "584 miles below the equator and about 270 west of the Ascension Islands" and that the crew had averaged about one hundred miles per day.

She went on to note that the ARGOS signal was, as expected, weakening, "and will probably go down fast."[7]

The goal was to reach 33°54', the latitude of Cape Town. "Sailing down the latitude" meant that, once the appropriate latitude was reached, *Globe Star* would head east until they "ran down" the coast of South Africa. The technique was simple in concept but devilishly difficult to achieve. If one's estimate of latitude were off, it was possible to miss your target and sail off into the ocean, eventually to run out of food or water. Of course, in this case, latitude sailing to South Africa was a bit safer than, say, attempting to run down a small island. Africa is a *very* large continent, with an area of almost twelve *million* square miles and with almost twenty thousand miles of coastline; even if *Globe Star* missed Cape Town, she should be able to locate herself based on which part of the coast she sighted and then sail down to the capital of South Africa. Of course, if she found herself *south* of Cape Town, she was in grave danger: the next landfall after missing the southern tip of Africa could very well be many thousands of miles distant.

When *Globe Star* finally made her way out of the doldrums and began making some real progress, the crew was elated, but at sea, every positive has a potential negative; in this case, three months of bouncing about in rough weather meant that the boat was beginning to show some wear and tear. In late February, a toggle connecting a headstay on the vessel's bow gave way.

That a toggle might give way is not at all surprising. The stress on a sailboat in use is tremendous. Incredible pressure is exerted on the sail itself, and that pressure is transmitted to other parts of the standing rigging—including such small but essential components as toggles.

Just how much force a sailboat endures can be calculated using a formula: wind pressure per square foot = (0.00256) × (wind speed in mph).[2] Professional rigger Herb Benavent says, "The bigger the sail, the more force on it as the wind builds. This is why we reef: it makes the sail smaller, so that the absolute value of wind pressure on the sail is the same as on a full sail on a nice day. As for the force being transferred to the boat via the rigging, that is shown by how far the boat is heeling. The further over it goes, the more force is being put on the boat in the form of torque to heel it over."[8]

Figure 05.03. Herb and Maddie Benavent on board *Wisdom*, their 1968 Morgan 45, off the coast of Puerto Rico. (IMAGE COURTESY OF HERB BENAVENT.)

The theoretical greatest strain occurs at 30 degrees of heel. After that point, the sails start to lay flat to the wind, so they are effectively presenting less area in that calculation. A boat that is knocked all the way down to 90 degrees of heel has no sails presented to the wind and therefore there is no pressure on the sails. Of course, as the boat tries to right itself (by virtue of the ballast in the keel), the wind may catch the sails and lay them back down.

Globe Star's design specs stated that she could carry 649 square feet of sail. In the (unlikely) event that she were carrying a full set of sails in a 25 mph (about 22 kt.) wind, that would mean that at 30 degrees of heel, the force on the sails would be roughly 1,038 ft. lbs. That's a half ton of force trying to knock down the boat. (Of course, wind also strikes the hull, which adds still more pressure, and the sea itself can contribute to the forces attempting to heel the boat.) Much of that pressure is ultimately transferred to the standing rigging; the result is that the rigging—especially connection points and small pieces that are meant to move—takes a beating. It is not surprising at all that, after almost one hundred days at sea, Creamer was starting to deal with some deterioration of his vessel and its rigging. Sailing is tough on both sailors and sailboats. (For more information about *Globe Star*'s sail plan and specs, see appendix D.)

Toggles are relatively inexpensive, and *Globe Star* carried several spares. But a few weeks later, when the portside toggle broke, the genoa's tack grommet also gave way; this released the headstay and the stay and its turnbuckle thus flailed about in the wind. The turnbuckle was heavy enough that, swinging wildly about, it became a potentially lethal weapon. If a crewmember were to be struck in the head by that turnbuckle, the result would almost certainly be death or serious injury.

It was time to act quickly, and Creamer and crew released the halyard to calm the gyrating stay, managing to drag the whole mess—sail and all—onto the deck. The flailing was so wild that the sail itself had torn; it would remain torn until the boat docked in Cape Town, where it would be repaired. At that time, a more careful look would reveal twenty-five or more foot-long tears in the Dacron sail; under pressure, and released from its forestay, the sail had begun to rip itself to pieces.

But sails were not the only problem Creamer had to deal with. By the end of February, he had noticed a weakening of the green light on the ARGOS transmitter, which was supposed to blink every minute as the device sent data to an orbiting satellite. By March, the device had quit altogether. The crew installed a new bulb, but that did nothing. Nor did

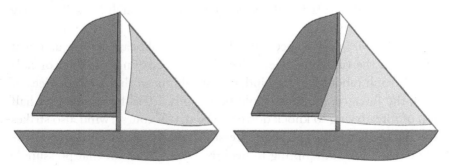

Figure 05.04. For nonsailors, here's a representation of a jib (*left*) and a genoa (*right*). Note that the genoa overlaps the mainsail, while the jib does not. (IMAGE PLACED IN THE PUBLIC DOMAIN BY WIKIMEDIA COMMONS USER *CUMULUS*.)

cleaning a corroded antenna connector or even connecting the emergency antenna solve the problem. Later Creamer and crew would learn that the transmitter was simply draining the lithium batteries far more quickly than anticipated. (Early 1980s lithium batteries were not rechargeable and had nowhere near the useful life of today's lithium-ion batteries, the first commercial versions of which were released in 1991.)[9]

ARGOS transmitters, such as the one on board Creamer's vessel installed by the Smithsonian as part of a data-collection experiment, send short bursts of data to satellites passing some five hundred miles overhead. The geographic location of the specific (usually mobile) ARGOS platform is derived on the basis of Doppler effect measurements and the repetition period—in this case, one minute.

The failure of the ARGOS transmitter had little effect on the crew or on *Globe Star*'s mission; after all, Creamer and his colleagues did not have access to the location (or any other) data gathered or computed by the ARGOS system. (ARGOS, by the way, stands for Advanced Research and Global Observation Satellite. The organization is a cooperative endeavor involving several nations and organizations, among them NASA, NOAA, and the French space agency Centre National d'Études Spatiales. Not at all coincidentally, Argos also happens to be the name of Ulysses's loyal dog in Homer's *The Odyssey*.)

Nonetheless, the lack of ARGOS data did cause some consternation back home in the United States. Absent any location data, the press reported the vessel and crew missing, and some families and supporters back in the states expected the worst. (Not Creamer's wife, though. Throughout the voyage, although Blanche worried about her husband, she never believed any of the dire reports from the press or from ham radio operators who passed along information, sometimes laced with supposition and rumor.)

The day that the ARGOS transmitter died, it gave *Globe Star*'s location as 17°34'S; 21°52'W, or about 1,100 miles due east of Cumuruxatiba Prado in Bahia, Brazil. This did not accord with Marv Creamer's estimates, which listed their (presumed) position as 19°37'S; 37°07'W, some 876 miles west/southwest of their actual position. *Globe Star*'s estimated latitude was in variance with the crew's actual latitude by a distance of

2°3', or about 123 miles. Still, that was not a bad margin of error considering that by then they had sailed some 2,500 miles or more.

The error in longitude, though, was much greater, about 872 miles. This is what happens when "sailing down the latitude": One's latitude is assumed to be fairly close, but longitude, which cannot be deduced without a sextant, sight reduction tables, and an accurate clock, is always dicey, unless there is some handy landmark along the way. In the middle of the Atlantic Ocean, however, landmarks are few and far between.

Obviously, finding one's longitude is important. In fact, it is *so* important that some very smart people worked very hard for hundreds of years trying to find a way to determine longitude while at sea. In 1714, the British government offered a £20,000 prize (equivalent to millions of dollars today) to whomever could find a way for ships at sea to determine their longitude. (Leaders of other countries offered similar prizes, feeling that accurate navigation in pursuit of trade and colonization was worth every penny.) In Dava Sobel's illuminating and entertaining book *Longitude*, she explains just how imperative it was to find a way to determine longitude and just how difficult it was to do. (The answer, as noted, was to invent a chronometer—a clock—that would keep accurate time even on the pitching, rolling deck of a ship.) Like sailors of old, Creamer—who did not have a clock on board, and who had no sight reduction tables and no sextant, in any case—was forced to estimate longitude by interpreting clues from the shape and direction of waves, the clouds and weather, the color and temperature of the water, and the flora and fauna sighted nearby.

With the loss of the ARGOS transmitter, Creamer worried about what the folks back home would think, especially Blanche. He fretted that headlines reading "Creamer Missing at Sea" were bound to worry and infuriate her. He was right to worry. In fact, she was so incensed by that particular headline that she tracked down a Miami-based Coast Guard technician, who told her that there was a 40 percent failure rate on ARGOS devices. (These days, the devices are much improved, but in 1982 they were largely experimental.) After that, Blanche got out charts and a calculator and worked out where she thought Creamer's vessel was, reassuring herself that her husband knew what he was doing and would bring *Globe Star* into port safely. (In the end, it turned out that Blanche's figures were quite accurate; so accurate, in fact, that she correctly estimated the exact day Marv would reach Cape Town and calmly told him so when he called her after his arrival.)

CHAPTER 6

LANDFALL IN SOUTH AFRICA

Just because you're lost doesn't mean you can't explore.
—CLARA BENSEN

ESPECIALLY ON A SHORT-HANDED YACHT, A SELF-STEERING MECHANISM of some sort is almost a prerequisite; it would require a superhuman effort, especially in heavy seas, to man the tiller or wheel (*Globe Star* had a tiller, rather than a wheel) twenty-four hours a day for months at a time. Creamer had equipped his vessel with a mechanical vane steering apparatus, which uses a wind vane attached to a trim tab and adjusted such that it uses the force of the wind itself on the vane to move the trim tab and rudder to keep the boat on a given course.

These days, self-steering mechanisms are quite high tech, often incorporating electronic controls and hydraulics or gear-driven tiller systems; some integrate with GPS devices that can keep a vessel dead on course in most conditions.

In the early 1980s, Creamer's self-steerer was nowhere that sophisticated, of course, although it was a clever enough arrangement of gears, levers, and pushrods that converted the force of wind on the vane to pressure on a trim tab that acted as a small rudder.

However, like all mechanical devices—indeed, like entire systems—aboard a sailboat, the vane steerer was prey both to the slow, grinding wear and tear of the sea and the wind and to sudden damage caused by unanticipated extreme forces acting upon the boat.

This became distressingly apparent around midnight on March 7 (all times are estimates; no one aboard *Globe Star* carried a timepiece of any

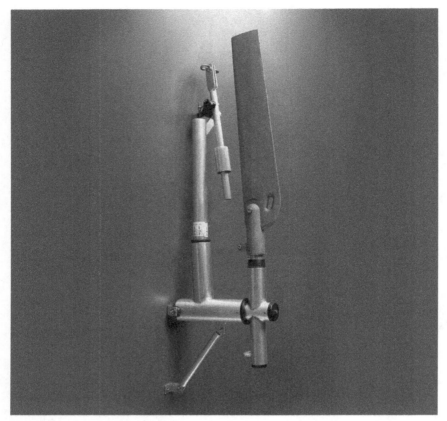

Figure 06.01. This South Atlantic wind vane steering mechanism is similar, functionally, to the Fleming gear that Creamer carried on *Globe Star*. (IMAGE COURTESY OF PAUL ELMERS AND MORGAN WHITTALL, SOUTH ATLANTIC WINDVANES.)

kind) when George Baldwin, on duty in the cockpit, yelled for help: the vane steerer's independent rudder had slipped out of its retaining bushings and was banging ineffectually against the transom. Closer examination revealed that it was being held only by a badly twisted piece of aluminum strap that, under ordinary circumstances, connected the end of the vane shaft to the trim tab. Twisted as it was, the strap was bending back and forth and quickly becoming fatigued. Within minutes, it would simply snap, and the steering rudder would float away.

With his legs dangling in the warm water, Creamer, holding a wrench in each hand, checked each nut and bolt. As he worked, the boat rose and fell in the heaving sea, and water was repeatedly forced up to his armpits. It was a wet, uncomfortable, and, in the end, fruitless effort.

By morning, it was obvious that a temporary repair would be impossible. "The aluminum end cap that held the steering rudder's solid nylon supporting shaft in place had been worn and battered through. We would have to hand steer to Cape Town—an added incentive for finding it," noted Creamer.[1]

By mid-March, well out of the doldrums now, *Globe Star* was making respectable time. On some days, the boat traveled as much as 142 nautical miles. At that rate, they should make the coast of Africa within a couple of weeks.

And they were definitely closing in on land. On March 24, Creamer noted green water (a sign that the sea was getting shallower), and a pod of seemingly companionable pilot whales swam nearby for several hours. Pilot whales feed largely on squid, octopus, and fish such as mackerel and herring, all found more readily in shallower waters such as Creamer believed the *Globe Star* had now entered. (Note that pilot whales are so called not because they pilot boats into harbor—though that would certainly be rather charming—but because the pod is thought to follow a member of the group that acts as a "pilot." Pilot whales, in fact, have been known to act quite aggressively toward human swimmers.)

Once they did reach the coast, Creamer hoped that they would get a respite from the powerful southwesterly swells that, though occasionally uncomfortable, had actually aided in direction finding in cloudy weather: long-distance swells are directionally constant for quite a while, so they can often be used for direction finding long after the storm that produced them has moved on, and for the several days that the stars had been hidden by clouds, Creamer and crew had been able to (roughly) estimate their direction based on the swells.

Even more importantly, reaching the coast would provide relief from having to worry about the boat's dwindling supply of fresh water. Creamer had no extra water with him, no jerry-cans stashed belowdecks or lashed on deck. His entire water supply was in the seventy-five-gallon tank built into the boat itself. Once that ran out, there was simply no more available and, at the time, "water makers" were in their infancy; no small vessel would have carried a unit capable of creating enough pure water to sustain a three-person crew for days, let alone weeks or months. Sailors today, on the other hand, can carry a variety of very efficient water makers on board, most of which work by desalinating seawater. (Note that in the case of a desalinator, the term "water maker" is something of a misnomer; it's not really *creating* water, it's purifying it, extracting drinkable water from seawater.) There's really nothing new about desalination; it goes back at least to Aristotle, and even the Bible speaks of "bitter waters made sweet." Today most marine desalination units for smaller cruising vessels use reverse osmosis to remove salt and other minerals from water by using a powerful pump to force salt water through a semipermeable membrane; the salt is trapped in the membrane, while fresh water passes through. This requires a fair amount of power, which means that large power vessels are better equipped to house and power such units, although smaller devices can be carried aboard sailboats. While a "water-maker" on a large motor yacht might process two thousand gallons of fresh water per day, a unit suitable for a small sailboat can produce in the neighborhood of two hundred or so gallons per day. (These units are not inexpensive—a small one can easily cost several thousand dollars—but they can literally be lifesavers on a blue-water voyage. If efficient desalinators had been

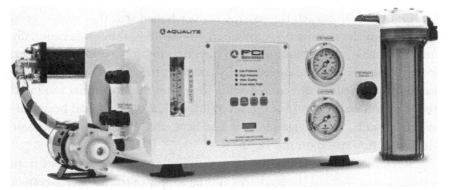

Figure 06.02. This Aqualite reverse osmosis unit is typical of the efficient water makers available today for smaller vessels. (IMAGE COURTESY OF FCI WATERMAKERS.)

available in his day, we can be pretty sure that Creamer, having shown that he would not skimp on such things as survival suits and on the boat itself, would have been sure to carry a desalination unit. Having one would have alleviated the need to find or buy—potentially skunky—water at some far-off port.)

There was another reason that Creamer and crew looked forward to a landfall on the South African coast: They would then finally be able to contact family and friends who might have become apprehensive when the boat "disappeared" from the ARGOS tracker. It's true that Blanche was pretty sure that her husband and his boat were safe, but she couldn't *know* that. And like any spouse left at home to ponder the fate of a loved one somewhere in the mid-Atlantic, she must have fretted some. As Lynn Creamer Borstelmann says about her mother, "She had confidence, but by nature she was a worrier. It took a heavy toll on her, I think, to have [Marv] out there. Well, there was certainly plenty to worry about!"[2] Marv Creamer wanted to make landfall, if for no other reason, so that he could reassure friends and loved ones that the crew was safe.

While Creamer knew that he was closing in on the South African coast, he could not tell how close he actually was, and that was a problem. In fact, it was a looming and grave danger. He did not dare approach the menacing coast at night; with no landmarks to guide him and few lighted navigational aids nearby, *Globe Star*'s best course (quite literally) was to stay out to sea, loitering offshore far enough to ensure that she did not end up being driven onto the rocky shore or onto a sandbank in the dark.

This was not at all an idle fear. Several ships had in fact been wrecked on the South African coast, beginning with a Portuguese vessel, the *Bom Jesus*, which left Lisbon in 1533 and was not seen again until it was discovered on the bottom of the sea off the coast of Namibia in 2008, 475 years later. Four more ships ran aground between 1909 and 1955. Creamer was undoubtedly familiar with these wrecks, and well aware of the risk of skirting the coast too closely in poor visibility. (Two more ships would be wrecked on the South African coast after Creamer's circumnavigation, one in 2008 and one in 2013. Creamer, who lived until 2020, passing away at the age of 104, would have noted these newer wrecks with knowing interest.)

Figure 06.03. As of 1998, this was all that was left of the ship *Eduard Bohlen*, a 310-ton cargo vessel that ran aground on the South African coast in 1909.
(IMAGE LICENSED UNDER THE TERMS OF THE GNU FREE DOCUMENTATION LICENSE, VERSION 1.2.)

Creamer and crew treated the rocky, reef-strewn coast with the respect due any powerful predator, aware that it might spring on them at any moment. Not for nothing is this area of the African coast known as the "Graveyard of Ships."

Finally, about 1:00 a.m., George Baldwin, on watch in the cockpit, spotted a flashing light that *might* be a lighthouse or lightship.

It took George most of an hour to decide that this really was a legitimate aid to navigation. The Cape Agulhas Lighthouse is, of course, located at Cape Agulhas, at the extreme southern tip of Africa. It's visible for some thirty nautical miles and gives off one white flash every five seconds.[3]

After George observed the light—taking some time to ensure that it wasn't simply the lights of another vessel, being interrupted by waves—the crew tentatively identified the light as that of Cape Agulhas but waited about four hours until daylight so that they could make a positive identification.

Figure 06.04. The Cape Argulhas Lighthouse as it stands today. The light is actually about one-third of a mile inland of the promontory it protects.
(SCREENSHOT VIA GOOGLE EARTH.)

Once they were sure that what they were seeing was indeed the Cape Agulhas light, they knew they were only one hundred miles from Cape Town. Unfortunately, it might be the most dangerous one hundred miles of the entire voyage. As Creamer notes, the mellow atmosphere provided by the sudden profusion of bird and sea life, and by the passing landmarks they could see on the coast, vanished when the sun set and the wind rose:

> *It was a long, arduous night paralleling the steep, rocky, reef-strewn coast in near gales without the benefit of [a] compass, depthsounder, radar, or radio direction finder. . . . We doubled the watch and exercised extreme caution.*[4]

It was a tedious and nerve-wracking night, watching for lights in the distance, trying to determine if *Globe Star* was handling differently, perhaps in the grip of wave surges reflecting from an unseen shore. Above all, they listened for the unnerving sound that no mariner wants to hear at night off of an unknown coast: the boom of surf on the rocks or on the shore. That would indicate that they were *much* too close to the shore, and it might well mean that it was too late to do anything about it.

The tense night passed without incident, and with the men who were not on watch dozing only fitfully. Just after daybreak, the winds let up, and they turned the boat to starboard to enter the harbor at Cape Town, searching for the Royal Yacht Club, where Creamer hoped to berth and repair his boat before setting out for Australia, *Globe Star*'s next port of call.

CHAPTER 7

FINDING YOUR WAY

Travel makes one modest. You see what a tiny place you occupy in the world.

—GUSTAVE FLAUBERT

WHEN MARV CREAMER AND CREW SAILED *GLOBE STAR* INTO THE harbor at Cape Town, they had just spent one hundred days at sea and traveled 7,800 nautical miles, wending their way from Cape May, New Jersey, to South Africa. Creamer, George Baldwin, and Jeff Herdelin had sailed through all kinds of weather, fighting their way through stormy seas and enduring maddening calms, and managed to find their target: Cape Town, South Africa. And they had done it all without the use of a single navigational instrument, other than their brains and their five senses.

It was a journey fraught with danger and plagued by equipment failures. The people themselves fared well enough, but the boat was battered and burned, her self-steering was inoperable, and parts of her rigging and sails were in tatters. They had made port just in time.

But they were not the first to mount a long ocean voyage without instruments. Far from it. Creamer believed that others had accomplished this before, thousands of years ago. Part of the point of his journey was to show that ancient peoples—the Norse, the Polynesians, and others—might in fact have navigated the seas, crossed oceans, and perhaps even circumnavigated the globe many years before. If he could do it without instruments, he thought, then there's no reason not to suppose that ancient sailors might also have crossed the seas. Creamer's intent was not

Figure 07.01. Trade routes of the Phoenician civilization in the Mediterranean Sea. (IMAGE USED UNDER THE CREATIVE COMMONS ATTRIBUTION-SHARE ALIKE 3.0 UNPORTED LICENSE, COURTESY OF USERS: *RODRIGO* AND *REEDSIDE.*)

to show that he had discovered these technologies but that he had *rediscovered* them.

So how did ancient people, working with rudimentary and often flawed maps and charts, manage to cross oceans—including the Pacific Ocean, the largest ocean in the world—in small ships lacking modern equipment and instruments? Could the Norse really have discovered America? Could East Asians have sailed to Polynesia, and the Polynesians in turn sailed the Pacific, four thousand miles from Hawaii to what is now New Zealand? How did the ancient Phoenicians establish trade routes with Greece, Egypt, and Mesopotamia? And how could these ancient civilizations have achieved all of this without such tools as the sextant and compass?

The Phoenicians

We can find answers to these questions by examining how ancient peoples navigated the seas, beginning with the Phoenicians, whose civilization lasted from 2500 BC to 64 BC. Sailing from the eastern Mediterranean (from the area in and around what is now Lebanon), the Phoenicians used the sun as a directional beacon: knowing that it rose in the east and set in the west, ancient Mediterranean sailors used that knowledge to fix their sights on distant lands. Modern voyagers, on land and at sea, still do much the same, of course. At night, the stars guided the Phoenicians, who used techniques not far removed from those employed by Marvin Creamer and his crew. PBS writer Peter Tyson describes the Phoenicians' method of determining latitude by stars:

> *At any one time in the year at any one point on the globe, the sun and stars are found above the horizon at certain fixed "heights"—a distance that mariners can measure with as simple an instrument as one's fingers, laid horizontally atop one another and held at arm's length.*[1]

You'll note that this ancient navigation technique is quite similar to Creamer's method of finding a star's meridian (see chapter 1) and using that as a guide. It's a mistake to think that Creamer was sailing off into the unknown without any tools; it's just that the tools he used were quite ancient and required some knowledge to put to use. In this particular case, his toolkit comprised his senses, his fingers, and his brain. Ancient sailors used the same tools.

The Norsemen

The Vikings, a fierce, seafaring Scandinavian nation—a collection of tribes, really—were known to have ventured far from their native land, discovering what we now know as Iceland and Greenland in the process.

In fact, Greenland may have been among the first land scams in history. Norseman Erik the Red attempted to start a colony on the land mass he called "Greenland," some 1,500 miles or more from his embarkation point in Norway. The name was a lie, and a purposeful one: Erik was attempting to make the journey sound modest and the land to which the colonists were headed appealing. It was not. The journey was brutal, the weather harsh, and the land largely unattractive. Greenland, the world's largest island, is anything but green; much of it is covered with ice for most of the year. The temperature rarely exceeds 50 degrees Fahrenheit even in midsummer. In the winter, it can drop to a stunning −58 degrees Fahrenheit. In any case, the expedition was ill advised; of the twenty-five ships that sailed west from Norway in the year 990, only fourteen arrived.

(Even today, only about 56,000 people live there, on an island that measures some 836,000 square miles.)[2]

But Erik and his fellow hardy Norsemen did indeed sail far from their native land, and Erik's son, Leif Erikson, may have discovered, completely by accident, the North American continent while doing so. (Whether they were the first to do so is still being debated, and of course, the people already living there had "discovered" it long before that.) Other accounts say that it was a kinsman, Bjarni Herjolfsson, who actually first viewed the coast of what is now Canada. If so, then Leif sailed more than two thousand miles *back* to this new land after Herjolfsson was mocked for having found, but not bothered to land in, this new world.

Whichever story is true (the history is a bit murky), it's almost certain that a Norseman beat Columbus to the "discovery" of America (in this case, the discovery of what is now Canada) by some five hundred years. (Remnants of a Viking settlement were found in Newfoundland in 1960.)

How did the Norse manage to find their way across the vast ocean? Well, one technique may have involved the help of birds. Specifically, ravens—or so the story goes.

Ravens—and crows, their not-so-distant cousins—are very smart birds.[3] Some investigators have reported that crows have the intelligence of a typical seven-year-old, and ravens are said to be even smarter. They are known to play, use simple tools, remember how specific people treated them, and imitate the calls of other birds. Ravens can even plan for future events, a feat that often eludes both seven-year-olds and teenagers.[4]

Ravens were esteemed by the Vikings and were, in fact, pictured on the banners of various early Viking tribes. That may have been as an homage to Odin (known to Anglo-Saxons as Wōden), the Norse god of war and of the dead, among other things, who was often pictured as being accompanied by two ravens. The ravens were said to bring Odin information from far-flung regions of the world.

This sort of mythic information gathering turns out to be quite appropriate because, as it happens, ravens really may have brought "information" to Norse sailors trying to find their way across vast reaches of featureless ocean.

Figure 07.02. The distinctive bill and tail of this raven are easily visible as it flies. (IMAGE USED UNDER THE CREATIVE COMMONS ATTRIBUTION-SHARE ALIKE 3.0 UNPORTED LICENSE, COURTESY OF COPETERSEN/COPETERSEN.COM.)

In the ninth century, a Viking named Floki (real name: Hrafna-Flóki Vilgerðarson, which is why we simply call him "Floki") is said to have used ravens to help find land. Ravens, especially hungry ones, can be a reliable source of direction for sailors seeking the nearest land: The men would starve a cageful of ravens and then, when in doubt as to the direction of land, release the hungry birds. If no land was near, the birds would tend to circle the ship confusedly, but if land was nearby, they would almost always head directly for it, and the Norse ship would simply head that direction. (Ravens, it turns out, are both fast and hardy travelers. One study showed that they could fly at speeds up to 25 mph and could easily cover more than thirty-seven miles in a day.[5] It must have been difficult to keep a speeding flock of hungry ravens in sight.)

The Vikings were certainly familiar with the stars and would have used them much as the Phoenicians did, but at that latitude, there are long periods when the stars do not appear because it stays light for many weeks at a time. Thus, other clues were useful in direction finding.

The Vikings also knew that the behavior of birds other than ravens could be helpful. They realized, for instance, that a clue to the direction of land could be found by noting what—if anything—a bird carried in its beak. Auks, for example, are not only powerful long-distance fliers, they are also excellent swimmers, so they sometimes hunt far out at sea. If an auk was sighted carrying food, it was probably flying back to its nest (on land) to feed its young; the Viking ship seeking land might therefore head in the same direction as the bird. If the bird's beak were empty, on the other hand, it might be heading out to sea, hunting. (Even then, the sighting might offer a clue, given that one might assume that there could be land in the direction from which it flew.)

Birds played—and still play—an important part in navigation, ancient and modern. Creamer, for example, could tell by the type of birds he was seeing whether *Globe Star* was close to land. His sighting of a terrestrial bird when trying to determine if he were close to Cape Verde was a clue that land was indeed near. On later legs of the voyage, Creamer's sighting of an albatross seemed to suggest that they were some distance from land. An albatross is a very large bird, and it can glide for many miles, soaring through the sky on updrafts and thermals. They often feed in very deep waters far out at sea, so the presence of an albatross could mean that the *Globe Star* was far from land at the time of the sighting, while the presence of terrestrial birds would normally mean that land was close.[6]

The Compass

Things have come a long way since the days of using one's fingers and the stars as a sort of compass. We now walk around with digital compasses in our pockets, tied to GPS smartphone applications. With satellite transmissions, we could tweet and post photos on Facebook from mid-ocean. Using such tools, we can easily find our way almost anywhere, but one wonders what would happen if (when?) those technologies fail us. Will our reliance on these new tools be so profound and so complete that we'll discover that we've lost the ability to find our way around? Bob Rout, an irrigation engineer who crewed on *Globe Star* on a later leg of the voyage, wonders that too. "Everybody's got all the toys now," he says. "And I think that's the general trend. You know, if the GPS system stopped working, a lot of people couldn't even navigate their way home from work."[7]

Long before we carried around a smartphone with a built-in compass, the first real compass was utilized not at sea but in a land war by the

Figure 07.03. From the Song dynasty, 960–1279, a figurine of a man holding a compass. (IMAGE USED UNDER THE CREATIVE COMMONS CC0 1.0 UNIVERSAL PUBLIC DOMAIN DEDICATION, COURTESY OF DR. GARY TODD, PROFESSOR OF HISTORY, SIAS INTERNATIONAL UNIVERSITY, XINZHENG, HENAN, CHINA.)

Chinese, who used a floating lodestone to find direction during battle.[8] The first use of a compass at sea, as far as we know, was by the British. In 1187, Englishman Alexander Neckham wrote of sailors who "use a magnetic needle which swings on a point and shows the direction of the north when the weather is overcast."[9] Despite its usefulness, the compass took a long time to come into wide use, perhaps because many seamen thought it operated by black magic. (Thus, some have reported that the binnacle was invented so that captains could hide the "magical" instrument from their superstitious crews.)[10]

Like Creamer, though, sailors often used their senses to help navigate. Their eyes noted and tracked clouds: What form did they take? In what direction did they move? At what speed? They often formed over bodies of land, so sailors took that as a clue as to the location of landmasses.

But sailors, even sailors with compasses, also used senses other than their eyes to aid in navigation. A seasoned sailor could *taste* whether the water was more or less saline than it had been. If it was less salty, perhaps bordering on brackish, one could deduce that they were near a spot where fresh water flowed from a river into the sea. They also used their sense of smell. An experienced sailor could (and still can) smell land from miles off, and many a ship navigated toward land by following the nose—so to speak—of a knowledgeable sailor.

Winds and Currents

Early voyagers noticed that certain winds were reliable: They would blow in a specific direction for a specific amount of time; at other times of the year, they would reverse direction. Either way, sailors could use those winds to sail to new lands, sometimes for colonization, but often for trade. Not surprisingly, they came to be called "the trade winds." If you've ever seen a facsimile of an old map, complete with a cartoonish head blowing puffs of wind, it may surprise you to find out that those heads were not mere decoration; they pointed out the direction of the prevailing winds near the lands depicted on that map.

If one looks at a map of Creamer's voyage (see appendix A), one can see that, as far as possible, he stuck to the trade winds to help him sail *Globe Star* across the oceans.

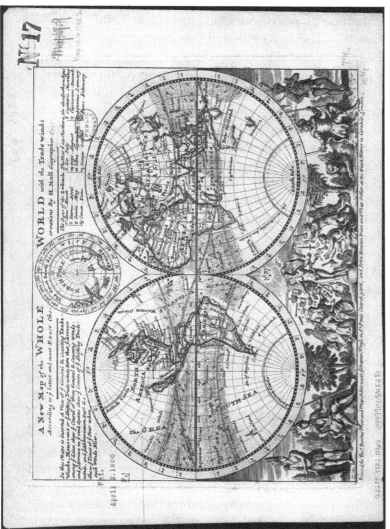

Figure 07.04. There are four sets of arrows in this image. The top and bottom sets of arrows (blue, if viewed in color) are the westerlies—that is, they blow consistently from the west toward the east. The middle sets of arrows (yellow above and then brown below, if viewed in color) are the trade winds that blow mostly from east to west. (IMAGE IN THE PUBLIC DOMAIN, COURTESY OF USER: KVDP.)

Wind is not the sailor's only friend. There are also *currents* that are just as reliable as the trade winds. For instance, the western-trending currents of the Indian Ocean are likely responsible for the Indonesian-based race that inhabits Madagascar, an African island more than 3,500 miles from Indonesia. Boats from Indonesia followed that current, taking natives to what was to become their new home in Africa.

The Gulf Stream (named, oddly enough, by the indefatigable Benjamin Franklin) is a powerful current that sweeps northeast into the Atlantic Ocean, eventually becoming what is known as the North Atlantic Current. (That clockwise current in the North Atlantic was, in fact, one of the reasons that Erik the Red's previously noted Greenland colony failed: the Viking ships sailed against the current, and many of them foundered or turned back.) The warmth of the Gulf Stream influences climate, contributing, for example, to the relatively comfortable climate in England, which—as cold and misty as it often seems—is much warmer than one might expect given its latitude.

In effect, there are winds both above and beneath the sea, and sailors have for thousands of years made use of them to aid their travels and to help them navigate safely.

The Polynesians

No discussion of early navigators would be complete without including the Polynesians, perhaps the masters of ancient navigation.

Most people are familiar with Thor Heyerdahl, the Norwegian explorer who sailed *Kon Tiki*, a raft built using ancient native materials and building techniques, five thousand miles from Peru to French Polynesia. Heyerdahl was attempting to prove that ancient peoples could have crossed the Pacific Ocean in a primitive craft, using rudimentary tools and taking advantage of the prevailing wind and currents. He wrote a book about the experience, and a few years later a 1950 documentary film about the expedition won an Academy Award. (There was also a somewhat melodramatic 2012 commercial film that was shot simultaneously in English and Norwegian and was a minor success in both languages.)

Controversy about the voyage erupted because Heyerdahl argued that the inhabitants of Polynesia originated in South America, migrated to

Asia, and eventually populated what is now British Columbia; he felt that the contemporary tribes of that area were descendants of those migrants. Few anthropologists today support that notion, though the question remains somewhat unsettled.

What is undisputed, though, is that the Polynesians—whatever their origins—were master mariners. Their large, double-hulled canoes crossed the Indian and Pacific oceans, settling Hawaii, Easter Island, and parts of New Zealand. But how did they navigate?

Luckily, we have near-contemporary sources of information about the Polynesians' navigation methods to help us answer that question.

Pius "Mau" Piailug was a Micronesian sailor who, in the 1970s and beyond, taught traditional wayfinding methods. He had been taught by elders who were taught by *their* elders and so on, back through many generations. Mau was concerned that the ancient practice of traditional Polynesian navigation would disappear as his people became acculturated. To help prevent that, he worked with the Polynesian Voyaging Society (PVS) to utilize ancient Hawaiian navigational techniques on *Hōkūle'a*, a traditional catamaran meant to be used as both a floating laboratory and classroom and as an ocean-going ambassador, carrying information about the Polynesian people (and about conservation in general) to other countries. The large (sixty-two-foot) seagoing canoe is a floating platform dedicated to education and to keeping Hawaiians in touch with their cultural heritage. (The boat's name means "Star of Gladness.") PVS sailed *Hōkūle'a* to Tahiti in the 1970s, and in 2014 undertook a three-year around-the-world voyage aimed largely at educating people about the Polynesian experience and culture. Part of PVS's goal was to support the idea that Polynesians originated in Asia and that Polynesia was *intentionally* populated by those Asian wayfarers. (Mau, prior to his death in 2010, passed along much of his knowledge to another crewmember, PVS president Nainoa Thompson, who is in turn teaching other PVS navigators.)[11]

Author and sailor Patricia Wood, who wrote the best-selling novel *Lottery*, taught marine science for many years in Hawaii, where she and her husband berth their forty-eight-foot sailboat, *Orion*. She has toured *Hōkūle'a*, attended presentations by her crew, and has studied their

Figure 07.05. A US Coast Guard boat escorts *Hōkūleʻa* upon its 2017 return to Oahu. (IMAGE IN THE PUBLIC DOMAIN.)

navigation techniques. In an interview with the author, she described one ancient tool used by the Pacific Islanders.

> *They have very few navigation accoutrements, but one thing they do have is the wayfinder, a wooden construct—mine was made by Micronesians—parts of which represent atolls or reefs. The bigger pieces of wood show current patterns, and they would have this wayfinder on the boat with them to kind of remind them, "Oh, to go from here to here, I aim this direction." So, what Creamer was doing was very much what the South Pacific Islanders did—navigating without a sextant, without GPS, without those tools.*[12]

Polynesian navigators, who for centuries passed their knowledge on to younger generations, read the waves and the clouds. They made their elaborate wayfinder maps, such as the one Patricia Wood describes, out of sticks, palm twigs, and cowrie shells. These ingenious "charts," carried on board their double-hulled boats and that exist today mostly in museums,

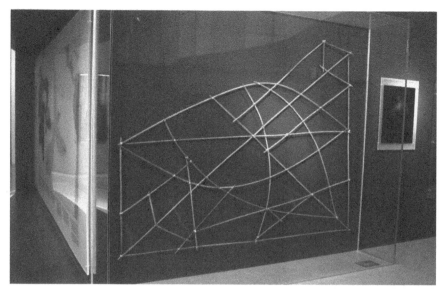

Figure 07.06. The Polynesian wayfinder was used to show waves, currents, and land masses. (IMAGE USED UNDER THE TERMS OF THE GNU GENERAL PUBLIC LICENSE.)

denoted everything from the position of islands to the prevailing direction of the swell.

The Pacific Islanders also used a mental construct, the Star Compass, which lists the names for the "houses" of the stars—that is, the places where they rise from the ocean and then go back in again. Ancient Polynesian navigators memorized the stars as they rose and set—no mean feat, considering the number of visible stars in the sky—and thus were able to find direction.[13]

Like these ancient navigators, Marvin Creamer used simple tools and his piercing native intelligence to find his way across the seas and around the world, first landing at Cape Town, South Africa. But he was not prepared for the cool reception he would encounter on arriving at Cape Town's Royal Yacht Club.

CHAPTER 8

A COLD SHOULDER AT CAPE TOWN

An explorer cannot stay at home reading maps other men have made.
—Susanna Clarke

After one hundred days at sea, Creamer and crew were looking forward to some rest, and *Globe Star* was in serious need of repair. Yet while everyone was elated to finally get to harbor, Creamer noted that, as tough as it was sailing the open sea, being on land offered its own challenges:

> *You have been looking forward to arrival and then, suddenly, you get a feeling of being suffocated and hemmed in. The pitching, rolling, and yawing creature that has carried you safely in its bosom for months is about to be tethered and you are going to have to deal with fenders, dock lines, dockmasters, documents, immigration, health, and customs officials, and other impedimenta associated with making a landfall.*[1]

Suddenly, the crew, which had become used to being alone and working as a team, was thrust into the real world of banks, buses, shops, ringing telephones, crowded streets, and occasionally bad-mannered shopkeepers. It was a rude awakening, but one that Creamer had experienced on earlier journeys. Unfortunately, their jangled nerves were set even more on edge by the cool reception they received from the Royal Cape Yacht Club (RCYC) docking supervisor.

Figure 08.01. The burgee of the Royal Cape Yacht Club.
(IMAGE PLACED IN THE PUBLIC DOMAIN BY WIKIMEDIA USER *I. BANDERAS.*)

A word about yacht clubs: Some of them are . . . well, it may be a bit much to call them *snooty*. Perhaps *staid*. Maybe *stuffy*. At any rate, many of them are decidedly old school, steeped in tradition. This was even more true some forty years ago, when *Globe Star* showed up in Cape Town. The RCYC advertises itself as "Cape Town's premium yacht club," and it lives up to that claim in terms of the privacy, luxury, and the many amenities it provides to members. (The RCYC is fairly expensive, but to be fair, there are many such clubs that cost a great deal more.) It is a first-rate institution, one that has provided top-notch amenities to the Cape's well-heeled residents and to visitors who take advantage of its reciprocity agreements with other such clubs, since 1905, and it is very exclusive: it's not enough for prospective members to apply; they must be *proposed* by a member, and that proposal must then be seconded by *another* member. It, like many yacht clubs, caters mostly to the well-to-do, and it provides first-rate services for its members.

But snobbishness was only part—and perhaps a very small part—of Marv's problems upon arrival at the RCYC (and later at other clubs). While some yacht clubs cater largely to an exclusive clientele, many are often quite welcoming even to visitors who are not members and who show up on short notice. But few clubs will cater to uninsured, transient boaters who show up without having made *any* prior arrangements, especially when they—wittingly or unwittingly—disregard the rules, written or unwritten, by which the club operates. In their view, Creamer and his crew were representative of the arrogant and entitled Americans they had come to view with suspicion. (These days, one *cannot* simply show up unannounced, so most radio ahead or make other arrangements prior to arrival. Also, few harbors or marinas these days would allow an uninsured boat entry at all; the liability would be too great if the boat sank or if it damaged harbor facilities or another boat.)

Irritated by the untimely and unannounced arrival of the battered and begrimed *Globe Star*, the docking supervisor directed Creamer forward through what looked to the *Globe Star* crew like an impenetrable wall of very expensive yachts moored gunwale to gunwale in front of him. Having no insurance, and being in a foreign country where any accident would surely cause no end of trouble, financial and otherwise, Creamer declined that invitation. He was then banished to "the wall," a solid concrete corner of a ship repair yard. The wall rose an imposing fifteen feet above the water, which made it difficult to scramble from the deck of the *Globe Star* up to the top, where there was a walkway. This was further complicated by the fact that Creamer was forced to tie up in the third row of boats from the pier and then climb a rickety ladder to get to the top. It was not the best of arrangements.

The inadequate berthing arrangements were indicative of their cool reception from RCYC officials. The RCYC attitude was made clear later in their stay at Cape Town when the commodore of the club brushed by Creamer on his way to a meeting and, rather shortly, commented, "I guess you'll be leaving soon," and continued on his way. No, "It's been a pleasure having you here," "We've heard so much about your voyage," "Thank you for stopping in," or "Hope you enjoyed your stay." Just, "I guess you'll be leaving soon." One assumes that the commodore followed up with a snippy "harrumph" as he turned to go.

Creamer—perhaps not always the most self-aware of men—was at a loss to explain the unpleasant attitude of the RCYC officials. He wondered if some of it might stem from the fact that his very presence might be judged an affront to the club membership given that the club was involved in certifying boaters:

> *The club had taken responsibility for testing would-be skippers of small craft and issuing licenses, called "tickets" and required by law, to those who meet preset standards. How to use a compass is a vital part of the club's educational and testing program and here we were, iconoclastically, suggesting by deed, if not by word, that the magic magnetic direction finder was not altogether essential for the safe operation of a yacht.*[2]

Creamer professed to be unworried about the unenthusiastic attitude of the RCYC because it meant not having to deal too often with the officers, which left him and the crew more time to work on *Globe Star*. The rank-and-file members of the club, as it happens, treated Creamer and his crew well, sharing drinks and conversation with them.

One thing that Creamer and crew discovered while at Cape Town was that disbelief in the particulars of their journey was quite common. George Meeks, an RCYC member, was typical. Invited to dinner at the Meeks home, Creamer found himself peppered with questions—some quite blunt—that made it obvious that Meeks, an experienced long-distance sailor himself, doubted very much that the *Globe Star* crew had in fact journeyed from the East Coast of the United States without instruments, and further, that they intended to continue around the world that way. However, Meeks was eventually convinced and became a staunch supporter during their time at Cape Town.

The nay-sayers became even more strident when it became obvious that Creamer intended to take *Globe Star* across the Indian Ocean in mid-winter. Historically, most yachtsmen avoid the Indian Ocean at that time of year, subject as it is to squalls, snow, sleet, and frequent gales. One RCYC member, an experienced sailor named Bob Deacon, summed it up simply: "You fellows haven't done your homework." Crossing at that time was, according to Deacon, a foolhardy decision.

But Creamer *had* done his homework. It's true that the Indian Ocean is subject to winter storms, but Creamer also knew that a summer crossing would subject *Globe Star* to tropical cyclones; in his mind, the winter storms were less of a danger than the cyclones.

This debate was no minor matter. The Indian Ocean is regarded by sailors with a good deal of respect and more than a little trepidation. One author characterized the area as "notorious: it oscillates between bland and twinkling affability and violently destructive turbulence. . . . A phenomenon referred to by some local oceanographers as the rogue or killer wave is not uncommon . . . [and such waves have] broken or buried not a few ships."[3]

Still, Creamer was an experienced long-distance sailor, perhaps more accomplished than many of the RCYC members realized. Prior to this voyage, he had sailed more than thirty thousand nautical miles and had crossed the Atlantic nine times. He had been through six hurricanes, a neutercane, and countless North Atlantic storms. He was adventurous, perhaps even fixated, and he was sometimes impatient, but he was not a foolhardy man.[4]

To reassure himself, Creamer took another look at the *Pilot Charts*, those mini-atlases, collections of charts that show average wind and current speeds and directions and also make note of typical air and sea temperatures, visibility, barometric pressure, and the presence of rocks, shoals, and other hazards. They are an invaluable aid to navigators, and Creamer pored over them, looking for reasons *not* to make the crossing on which he had been planning. He saw nothing in them to suggest that they should abandon their plan to make a winter crossing. In fact, he expected less severe conditions than he thought he would encounter on later legs of the trip. "If eventually we would have to endure the gales and high seas around Cape Horn," he said, "then the seas of the Indian Ocean would provide us with a challenging practice arena."[5]

What did concern him, though, was the upcoming Australian landfall. He knew the boat would need more repairs, water, and provisions. It would be wisest, he knew, to depart for the Horn from a spot as close to the Pacific as possible so that they could start out fully provisioned and with the boat in good repair.[6] Thus, it was smartest to choose a port in eastern Australia as their next landfall—perhaps Hobart in Tasmania, or Sidney on the mainland of Australia.

And yet Creamer wanted to see Perth, which is located on the *western* side of Australia; it is, in fact, the capital of Western Australia. It's a beautiful place, boasting majestic parks and gardens, opera houses, and galleries. Hobart, also beautiful, but on the far eastern edge of the country, is the capital of Tasmania, an island state some one hundred or more miles from the Australian mainland; heading for Hobart would mean that *Globe Star* would be that much closer to the *next* anticipated landfall, across the Tasman Sea, at Whangaroa, New Zealand.

Of course, no matter what, Tasmania represented a problem. *Globe Star* would have to go around or past Tasmania one way or another, and the shortest route around Tasmania led through Bass Strait, a 250-mile stretch of water that is dangerously shallow and strewn with rocky shoals and small islands. It would be a dangerous crossing, and especially perilous during the evening hours. Accurate position information would have made the passage fairly straightforward, but accurate position information is exactly what the crew of *Globe Star* lacked.

Bass Strait is an unforgiving body of water, a relatively narrow channel, really, through which the sea surges and huge waves build up; those waves can easily overwhelm a vessel, and the wind, waves, and currents can combine to drive even large ships onto the rocks. One writer recalls a shipwreck that occurred in August 1845.

> *The* Cataraqui *was a ship of 800 tons, out of Liverpool for Melbourne, Captain Finlay, master. A crew of forty-six and 369 emigrants . . . including seventy-three children. The seas were monstrous, no observations had been possible for some days. Despite arguments, the captain was obstinate. The* Cataraqui *ran before the gale and at 4:40 a.m., without even a warning cry of "breakers ahead!" crashed and crunched onto the west coast of King Island, where her remains lie to this day with those of sixty other vessels. A couple of days later, David Howie, who bore the title of Constable of the Straits, found 401 bodies on the beach, and nine survivors. The dead were buried in four mass graves.*[7]

King Island lies midway between Tasmania and the Australian mainland, basically blocking the west end of Bass Strait. If Creamer were to choose that route, he would have to thread *Globe Star* through the strait, dodging King Island, and avoiding any reefs, shoals, or rocky outcroppings he might encounter along the way. This would be extraordinarily difficult. The *Cataraqui* at least had a sextant and a good chronometer; Marv Creamer had neither.

The alternative course would be to steer south to attempt a landfall at the south end of the island. The risk there was that, not knowing their precise position or course, they might *miss* the island altogether. That would have meant facing the wild west coast of New Zealand at a time and place famous for its wild winter storms.

For now, Creamer decided, they would aim somewhat north of the southwest portion of the Cape in order to ensure that they did not miss the island. This too had its drawbacks: they would be sailing toward a rocky, largely uninhabited coast with few navigational aids and only two safe inlets.

The decision could wait, of course, until they had a better idea when they might arrive off Tasmania, and *that* would depend on when they departed Cape Town and when they arrived in Australia.

The Cape Town departure, meanwhile, hinged on two things: how long it took to effect repairs to *Globe Star* and how long it took to find new crew.

Creamer's crew was about to change. George Baldwin had committed only to the first leg, Cape May to Cape Town, and would be flying back to the United States shortly after they arrived in South Africa. He had turned out to be an excellent crewman, and Marv was sorry to see him go. Jeff Herdelin was staying on for the second leg, Cape Town to wherever in Australia Creamer finally decided to head. (This turned out to be Hobart, meaning that the next leg would be about 7,800 or so miles, almost as long as the first leg, although it would take less time, mainly due to favorable current and wind conditions.)

The first problem, though, was repairing *Globe Star*. That required someone conversant with not just sailboats but with the Cape Town area itself: Creamer needed to find a person who was familiar with the range of services that could be found in the area. Otherwise, too much time (and possibly money) would be wasted going in circles and dealing with services and providers that might in the end be unable to deliver what was needed. (Marv was not, of course, alone in finding himself far from home with a vessel in need of repair. As many have noted, "Yachting is about finding ways to repair a boat in exotic locations."[8] Creamer would not have disagreed with that assessment, nor would most blue-water sailors.)

He found his man in Stanley Gordge. Gordge was the port cocaptain for the local Slocum Society.[9] The captain of the local chapter was hospitalized when *Globe Star* arrived, so Gordge, acting in his stead, offered his help to Creamer. Gordge, an experienced sailor and a member of RCYC, was also familiar with the Cape Town nautical scene. He ended up being of enormous help to the *Globe Star* crew, acting as companion, tour guide, and driver.

The first thing Gordge did was to take all of *Globe Star*'s sails, some of which were by now quite tattered, to a local sailmaker's loft. That done, he proceeded to cart the crew around to chandleries, markets, the post office, and many other places. There was time for some sightseeing, including a memorable visit to a nearby baboon colony, during which Creamer was somewhat nonplussed when a nursing mother baboon jumped up on the hood of the car and peered inside.

The necessary repairs were neither simple nor inexpensive. Australia was a long way off, and *Globe Star* needed to be hauled out of the water and her hull scraped to remove barnacles and then painted.[10] Repairs to the tiller and vane steering were also required, and the two headstays needed to be secured in such a way as to preclude—or at least mitigate—further damage to toggles.

One other major task was the design and fabrication of a dodger. *Globe Star* had set sail without one, partly because Creamer was not expecting too much bad weather on the first leg and partly because, after the rushed delivery of the boat, he simply hadn't had time to have one made. (At any rate, the builder, Bob Patterson, felt that the aft end of the cabin top was "too busy" for a dodger.) Dodgers often have to be custom made for the specific boat, so it's not as if Creamer could just pop on down to Massmart (South Africa's version of Walmart) and pick one up.[11]

Finally, the crew needed to restock their provisions and get water and fuel for the little Volvo diesel.

Repairing the vane steering took a great deal of time and effort. Creamer was determined to replace the worn-through bushing cap with one made of stainless steel. This would seem to be a minor job, but he had difficulty finding anyone to take it on. It wasn't that it was too large and complicated a task, it was that it was deemed too minor for anyone to bother with; larger jobs made more money for suppliers, so they were reluctant to waste time on this tiny—but to Creamer very important—chore.

At the same time, Creamer really wanted to find a way to avoid the headstay-toggle problem that had vexed him so on that first leg. He felt that the issue arose in the first place because the tang to which the toggles were attached had been welded to the hull at an incorrect angle. Creamer felt that the angle at which they were currently welded introduced an unusual side load, which caused the toggle to fracture.

Interestingly, this issue with the tangs was not due to a design flaw. Ted Brewer had designed *Globe Star* with a single headstay, but Creamer had insisted that the boat be equipped with twin headstays, feeling that the redundancy added to the vessel's reliability. He was undoubtedly correct, but the addition of the extra stay meant that a tang was added to each side of the forward bow, and it was these new tangs that had been welded incorrectly.

Creamer's solution was to bolt a half-inch-thick, six-inch-wide piece of stainless steel to the original plate, "leaving the new piece to stand two inches above the old so that the two stays could be attached to the stainless plate in a fore-and-aft arrangement."[12] Creamer was an experienced machinist himself and knew that shaping a thick stainless steel plate was beyond his capabilities, so he made a mockup of the plate out of plywood and turned it over to a machine shop to be duplicated in stainless steel.

There were plenty of other repairs and modifications to be made before *Globe Star* headed for Australia. The cap screws fastening the tiller to the rudder post had worked loose; the crew had been regularly retightening them mid-ocean, but that was neither a safe nor satisfactory solution to the problem, and Creamer imagined the joint falling apart at the worst possible time. Also, the stop on the forward end of the teak hatch had split; Marv had fashioned a makeshift stop out of a right-angled piece of metal, but again, that wasn't a permanent solution.

All of these problems were eventually solved, although a frustrating discovery was made along the way: All of *Globe Star*'s fittings were in English measurements, while South Africa had gone determinedly metric years before. The crew had to scramble to find metric nuts and bolts that were close enough in size to work with US hardware, and they became very careful about tossing away or losing overboard any fasteners because there were few to spare and even fewer appropriately sized replacements readily available.[13]

Another discovery turned out to be important, but the crew would not realize it for many weeks. When repairing the errant hatch, Creamer noticed that the new plywood hatch cover he had made to replace the splintered teak cover screeched loudly when moved along its stainless steel runners. This was a minor annoyance, and it turned out that it was intermittent: It occurred only when the air was dry. When there was enough humidity, the moisture dampened the runners, lubricating them enough that the noise disappeared. Oddly, this "feature" would eventually save the crew a great deal of sailing time on their Pacific leg.

Time passed on "the wall," as Creamer and crew worked on the boat and waited for the outside repairs to be completed. (The dodger took an especially long time, and eventually it was the delivery of the dodger that would determine their departure date.) There were plenty of local workmen working on boats docked or moored nearby, and the *Globe Star* crew had ample time to chat with them and with the crews of other boats. Once Jeff Herdelin mentioned to a South Rhodesian skipper that they had found their way to Cape Town from New Jersey without using any navigational instruments; completely missing the point of the voyage, the bemused skipper responded, "Why doesn't one of you learn how to use a sextant?"

But not all of their time was spent working on the boat. Marv managed to have lunch with a colleague's wife and son at a luxurious hotel restaurant (the colleague, fellow sailor John Hartman, was traveling at the time and couldn't be present); the hotel dining room and the sumptuous food were in sharp contrast to the cramped quarters and tasty but unsophisticated food on *Globe Star*. A few days after that, Chris Neethling, a local insurance consultant, invited Marv and Jeff (George had left by then) to a "braaivleis," a picnic featuring an open barbecue. These Sunday

Figure 08.02. A South African *braai* (barbecue grill) of the type often used at a braaivleis, such as the ones attended by Creamer. (IMAGE PLACED IN THE PUBLIC DOMAIN BY WIKIPEDIA USER *BOTHAR*.)

lunches became a regular occurrence, and the hillside setting at the Neethling home provided a breathtaking view of the harbor, with Chris's wife, Leo (Leonora), taking a motherly interest in her globetrotting charges. *Her* mother, Max (Maxine), also watched over the pair of sailors, cautioning Marv when she thought he'd been eating or sleeping too little. Some eight thousand miles from home, Creamer was being mothered by locals and feted by other guests, many of whom were dignitaries, writers, and artists, which provided for vigorous discussions of many interesting topics. Creamer, in his element and able to expound on the virtues of instrument-less sailing, among many other things, likened the gatherings to a modern-day Chautauqua; he enjoyed himself immensely.

In 1983, times were changing in South Africa, as evidenced by Leonora herself, who served as the first woman on the Supreme Court of South Africa. Other changes were also occurring. Almost to the day that *Globe Star* made port there, the South African government, headed at the time by President Marais Viljoen and Prime Minister P. W. Botha, announced that "blacks paying income tax in South Africa would no longer have to do so at higher rates than whites." (Nonetheless, the same article reported that, while pension payments for whites would rise by $12.80, to a maximum of $138.70 per month, black pensioners would see a rise of only $7.30, to a maximum of $52 per month.)[14] Why Black residents were paying higher income tax rates than white residents in the first place is unclear, although the rationale may have had something to do with the fact that Blacks worked mostly at lower-paying jobs and therefore paid less in taxes in general—albeit at a higher rate. Keep in mind that this was during the zenith of apartheid, institutionalized South African segregation that lasted until the 1990s. *Apartheid*, meaning *separateness*, was the official—and undisputedly racist—government policy that ensured domination of the Black majority by a white minority. It included an act (the Population Act of 1950) that categorized all inhabitants of the country into one of four classes. Other acts prohibited marriage between people of different races and forced people of certain races to live in designated areas.[15] It was not a good time to be anything but white in South Africa. Marv Creamer, who was something of a progressive, must have cringed to see it in action, but there is no evidence that he publicly objected.

In addition to the various gatherings, Jeff and Marv were able to take in a concert, a movie, and a rugby game. (Jeff, who had played rugby at Washington and Lee, especially enjoyed that; Marv was less enthralled.) The two sailors reciprocated by inviting the Neethlings and some friends of theirs for a Saturday sail and a picnic lunch. The sail did not go as planned. The winds were inconstant, the seas lumpy, and the temperatures low. Creamer cut the sail short, started up the engine, and headed back to port, where all enjoyed a meal prepared in *Globe Star*'s tiny galley. (Marv loved to cook, of course, and the meal was tasty and varied: It included rolls, cold cuts, cheese, baked beans, deviled eggs, potato salad, hot tea and coffee, and sodas. The potato salad, one of Marv's specialties, was made with mayonnaise, diced boiled potatoes, chopped olives, sliced sweet and dill pickles, and sprinkled liberally with small chunks of freshly boiled ham. That was especially well received, and Marv beamed at the praise from his guests.)

Figure 08.03. Nelson Mandela, pictured in 1994 on a trip to the United States. A committed anti-apartheid activist, Mandela was repeatedly arrested and spent twenty-seven years in prison, from 1962 to 1990. He was elected president of South Africa in 1994. When Creamer arrived in South Africa, Mandela had just been transferred to Pollsmoor Prison, in Tokai, Cape Town. (IMAGE USED UNDER THE TERMS OF THE CREATIVE COMMONS SHARE ALIKE 2.0 LICENSE, COURTESY OF KINGKONGPHOTO AND WWW.CELEBRITY-PHOTOS.COM.)

Sailing into foreign ports is always fraught with danger: In an unfamiliar harbor, one may not know where to dock or moor, and it can be difficult to steer clear of obstructions, other vessels, or ongoing work. Often enough, though, the danger is of the bureaucratic sort. Creamer managed to avoid a $370 fine (that's about $1,100 in 2021 dollars), though his supposed offense was, he felt, no fault of his own. When *Globe Star* had entered the harbor, she had hoisted her yellow flag, as required. The yellow flag, or "Q" flag, is a declaration that the boat is free from quarantinable disease; in effect, it is a request to port officials to board the vessel and declare her free of such disease. Until they're cleared, no one from the quarantined boat is allowed to leave the vessel except the captain, and he or she is only allowed to leave in order to complete official customs- or quarantine-related business. Although Creamer had his flag up, no one from customs showed up, so after a week, he took it down. A month later, when he saw officials checking in a French yacht, he asked them why he had been ignored. The response was a bureaucratic brouhaha that required *Globe Star*'s skipper to traipse all over town being interviewed, signing statements, and generally sitting around wasting time in offices while he waited to be seen by various functionaries. Luckily, instead of the $370 fine with which he had been threatened, he was let go with a warning, even though, as far as he could tell, Creamer had done nothing wrong.

While in Cape Town, Creamer was also able to trade his nonfunctional ARGOS transmitter for another one furnished by the US Coast Guard. In the end, this was wasted effort. The problem with the original transmitter turned out to be faulty batteries, and the new transmitter contained the same type of batteries; the transmitter would die just four days out of Cape Town, meaning that for ten weeks, families and supporters had no idea where *Globe Star* might be as she trekked toward Australia.

Marv and Jeff were almost ready to set sail again, this time across the Indian Ocean, but Creamer really wanted a third hand on board, and crew seemed difficult to find in Cape Town. Blanche, back in the states, had gotten in touch with potential mates whose names Marv had collected, but there didn't seem to be anyone available for this leg of the trip. The most likely prospect seemed to be a young man who was attracted to the idea of shipping out on *Globe Star* but who was slated to enter South

Africa's Merchant Navy Academy in a few months. He was interested but worried that he might not get back in time to begin classes at the academy. (Privately, Marv thought that the young man might have been influenced by the doomsayers, who were many and vocal.)

Of course, Marv himself might have been partly to blame for the paucity of potential crew members. He was in the habit of posting "help wanted" advertisements prior to the voyage and at the various ports he visited. They might not have inspired much confidence or enthusiasm. One of Creamer's efforts, this one aimed at finding a videographer for the expedition, read as follows:

> *WTD: Filmmaker-sailor for pre-Viking-style circumnavigation. Long hours. No pay. Prefer non-smoker with gear.*

It's difficult to think of a less enticing advertisement. And yet while applicants seemed in short supply in Cape Town, there had earlier been, in spite of such want ads, no shortage of applicants. Creamer's personal papers contain dozens of letters, scribbled notes, and résumés entreating him to allow their writers to work "Long hours. No pay." just for the chance to sail the world. Unfortunately, none of them were in—or available to travel to—Cape Town.

As it happens, the academy-bound prospect had a friend: Canadian adventurer Rick Kuzyk, who was looking for his next challenge. Kuzyk simply showed up at the *Globe Star*'s dock, looking for details. Kuzyk, nineteen years old at the time, eventually signed on to the second leg of the voyage because, he said, he felt that the *Globe Star* crew had a better sense of humor than the other boat on which he had been considering shipping out.

The fact that Rick had never been on the water in anything larger than a canoe didn't bother Creamer. Marv was impressed by the young man: "He was short, stocky, and mentally tough. He had worked a forty-hour week in a supermarket during his four years of high school and when he graduated at eighteen, he traded a large chunk of his savings for travelers checks, bought a round trip air ticket to London, and set out to see Europe via his thumb."[16] Creamer admired the fact that Kuzyk was

Figure 08.04. Rick Kuzyk works on *Globe Star*'s boom.
(PHOTO COURTESY OF THE CREAMER FAMILY.)

healthy, strong, and had a keen zest for life. He was also strong willed, with an independent, self-determined streak that had served him well during his travels. In Marv's eyes, the young man was tough and resourceful, two qualities valued in crewmen on blue water.

The only worry, given that Rick had never been to sea, was that Marv and Jeff didn't know if he could handle the turbulent passage without getting seasick. A minor bout and a rapid recovery would be one thing, but nursing a sick—and essentially useless—crewmember across an ocean was not something they wanted to deal with.

However, the dodger had taken so long to finish that the southern winter was at hand; they had no time for sea trials of any sort, least of all to find out if Rick's stomach was too sensitive for the job at hand. They decided to take a chance—the kid seemed robust enough, after all.

The new dodger finally arrived and was installed on May 25, so Creamer and crew began getting ready to head to sea. This involved installing the dodger (for which Creamer paid US $200—a bit over $500 in today's dollars), finishing up the provisioning, and topping off the fuel.

Marv and Jeff had spent almost two months at Cape Town. Their initial chilly welcome had for the most part turned into a pleasant reception, with many of the town's inhabitants offering good wishes—and the occasional lunch or dinner—to the *Globe Star* crew. Relations between the Creamer crew and some of the RCYC officers were still frosty, but no real antagonisms developed. Creamer felt relaxed and renewed by his time in South Africa, and the boat was once again in good shape for a long cruise. That turned out to be a good thing because the next leg, Cape Town to Hobart, was going to be another long one: almost seven thousand miles over a period of seventy-seven days, a trip that included forty-five-knot winds, heavy seas, and more than a few harrowing moments.

CHAPTER 9

HEADING FOR AUSTRALIA

The gladdest moment in human life is a departure into unknown lands.

—Sir Richard Burton

GLOBE STAR BEGAN HER JOURNEY TO AUSTRALIA BY LEAVING ON THE wrong day.

As noted, sailors are a superstitious lot, and hundreds of nautical superstitions have developed over the years. Some actually have their basis in fact, while there are others that may have made sense at one time but whose origins have now been lost.

One of the latter superstitions has to do with departing on a Friday. No one is quite sure why a Friday departure is considered bad luck, unless it has something to do with the fact that the crucifixion of Jesus is said to have taken place on a Friday. This allegedly ill-omened departure day for sea voyages has, over time, become more generalized: some feel that *all* journeys, not just sea voyages, ought to start on a day other than Friday. (One assumes that a voyage that begins on Friday the 13th would be *especially* bad luck. Sunday, in contrast, is said to be a lucky day to begin a journey.)[1]

Marv was familiar with this superstition, but it had slipped his mind; at any rate, Creamer, being a confirmed rationalist and not a particularly patient man, was not big on superstitions, especially ones that led to delays. But he did note that Jeff, who had been pushing hard to get going, was suddenly finding reasons not to leave until Saturday. The real reason for Jeff's reluctance to leave on Friday would not dawn on Marv for weeks, by which time *Globe Star* was well out to sea.

At any rate, they were off, and Marv noted that it was a thrill to start off on the next leg, even though, as he noted, "it may seem hard to get excited about a trip that begins at five miles per hour."[2]

The excitement was intensified by the fact that *Globe Star* was immediately in danger: they were heading out on a journey of some seven thousand miles and, according to the locals, they were starting at the worst possible time of year. After they exited the harbor, they found themselves paralleling a rocky and hazardous coast until they were far enough offshore to head east, across the Indian Ocean toward Australia. Creamer was delighted to be out at sea and away from the dangers of the coast:

Standing free of the land brings a deep satisfaction. You are finally doing what you have spent weeks, perhaps months or years, preparing for. But by nature sailors are a restless lot. On land they have a single-minded urge to get back to sea and when they get offshore think constantly of returning to land. The most enjoyable parts of any long voyage are, therefore, the beginning when you are flushed with the glow that comes with finally getting off and the end when you are pumped up by the impending landfall.[3]

Most of us know that the Atlantic Ocean is often cold and storm-tossed, huge and dangerous. And the Pacific Ocean, the largest in the world, is daunting in its immensity and by no means always peaceful, in spite of its name. But the Indian Ocean is nothing to be trifled with.

The Indian Ocean is the third-largest in the world. It is relatively warm and the oxygen content of its waters is low; as a result, the water there is low on nutrients. Thus, there is less sea life—and therefore less readily available food for voyagers—than in other oceans. The region is subject to monsoons, creating a great deal of wind during the winter and torrential rains in summer. In the southern portion of the ocean, tropical cyclones occur in both May/June and January/February, and mariners must watch for occasional icebergs. Creamer knew that this would not be an easy voyage.

In spite of Rick's unfamiliarity with the sea, and contrary to Creamer's worried expectations, the new crewman acquitted himself well in the

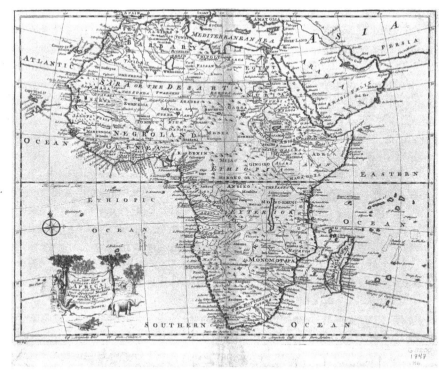

Figure 09.01. A 1747 map depicting the Indian Ocean, to which it refers as the Eastern Ocean. (IMAGE IN THE PUBLIC DOMAIN.)

seasickness department. He was a bit queasy the first day and then, a day or two later, survived a wild night of building seas as *Globe Star* sailed downwind. Rick, it turned out, had an iron stomach—always a good thing for a seaman.

At first, though, he seemed to be not at all fond of some of the food. The second dinner at sea included grilled cheese sandwiches, boiled cabbage and potatoes, apple salad, and pumpkin bread. Rick made it clear that he was not thrilled about the cabbage, purchased during a drought in South Africa, when other vegetables were in short supply. Jeff and Marv felt that the cabbage was a great addition and welcomed the chance to integrate it into the shipboard menu, but Rick, not shy about sharing his opinions, turned his nose up. Marv wondered what to do about the problem and came up with the idea of adding chopped apples and nuts to very finely chopped cabbage. When he asked Rick later how he liked the cabbage, the new crewman protested, "We didn't have cabbage!" The culinary disguise had worked, and Creamer discovered that Rick actually wasn't that picky about cabbage or fussy about food in general: he simply didn't like *boiled* cabbage. He ate almost anything else, especially if it contained ketchup or a variety of spices he had brought on board. Perhaps fortuitously, his only real dislike had been discovered at the beginning of the journey.

The crew's food preferences probably sound like minor issues, niggling matters that ought not have much of an impact on such a long and important voyage. But any long-distance sailor will tell you that food is *very* important aboard ship. In the first place, there are sometimes hours spent waiting for a fair wind. While waiting, there may be long periods of sitting around with little to do *except* eat. (Or at least *think* about eating. Provisions have to be conserved, after all.) Mostly, though, sailors undergoing the hardships and privations of a grueling sea voyage—often having spent many hours in wet and freezing cold or hot and humid stickiness—very much look forward to a good meal. As one sailing magazine noted, "On an offshore passage, food is more than just sustenance. It can mark the passage of hours, become a highlight of an otherwise unexciting trip or be a life-sustaining force shared with good crewmates."[4] Creamer knew this well and had made a heroic attempt to provision *Globe Star* with a wide variety of foods; he also made every effort to cater to each crewmember's particular preferences, knowing, of course, that he could never make everyone happy all the time. But Creamer himself loved good food while sailing, and he enjoyed cooking that food and trying to create interesting, tasty, nutritious meals for himself and his shipmates.

So far, so good: Marv's new crewmate was not fussy about food and he was not prone to seasickness. Now if Marv could just teach the young man how to sail, everything would be good. As it turns out, though, Creamer need not have worried about Rick learning to sail; he was a natural. At first, the younger man sat watches with Marv or Jeff, but it didn't take him long to learn to interpret ships' lights and how to handle the boat in the heavy following seas they were encountering. Rick was learning to be a sailor; perhaps most importantly, he could now judge accurately when he was ready to take on a new responsibility.

Globe Star was now sailing through the shallow and turbulent waters of the Agulhas Bank and on into the Indian Ocean. As expected, they were alternately battered by nerve-wracking gales and beset by frustrating calms. During the gales, Creamer and crew experienced forty-five-knot winds and seas approaching thirty feet as they sailed under bare poles.

Given that the wind was actually pushing the boat in the direction Creamer wanted, he opted to lie under bare poles rather than heave-to—a maneuver that would have almost stopped the boat but might have let it drift some to leeward. Sailing under bare poles meant that the sails were safe and the boat was making headway, but it was mostly uncontrolled headway, with the boat rolling and pitching. The result was a very rough ride:

> *Downwind under bare poles is most uncomfortable. . . . One wave sent me, opened eggs, loose tea, oil and coffee jars, etc. sprawling into the chart table and my bunk (quarter berth). What a mess!*[5]

Getting bounced into the chart table was exactly how George Baldwin had split his head open early in the voyage, so Creamer was lucky that he was uninjured. Chart tables, or any furniture with sharp corners, can be very dangerous in a boat, as Creamer knew all too well.

By June 5, the weather had turned warm and the sea was calm, except for a rhythmic heaving that sometimes made the boat roll uncomfortably. Of course, a calm sea reflected a lack of wind, and that is always frustrating to sailors anxious to be making progress toward their next landfall. On the plus side, in the warmer weather the crew was able to wash up in the cockpit and tackle minor repairs. Jeff made lemonade and, seasoned sailmaker that he was, repaired the storm jib. The calm weather also allowed the crew to track down a foul odor that had been emanating from the refrigerator: it turned out to be due to a broken egg, probably dislodged by a large wave back on June 3. This meant spending several hours emptying the fridge, cleaning it out, washing and drying all of the contents, and then putting everything back in the fridge.

In Marv's notes there is a scrap of paper and the beginnings of a poem, one that might well have described the feelings shared by the three *Globe Star* sailors—or *any* sailors—becalmed on a long journey:

My world is a circle,
Ever-changing, ever the same,
We stay at the center,
My two shipmates and I.
We've been here forever,
Or was it yesterday we departed Cape May?
Time has little meaning; we sail on and on,
Yet stay at the center of our circle.[6]

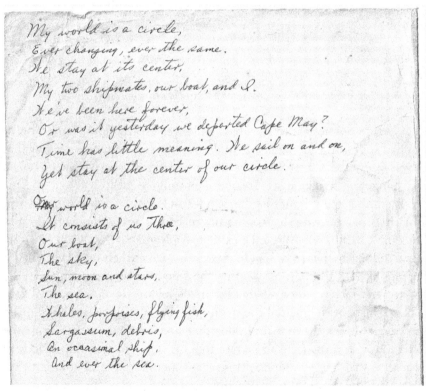

Figure 09.02. This is the poem that Marv wrote on the back of a 1982 Index to Stations page. (IMAGE COURTESY OF THE CREAMER FAMILY.)

The becalmed sailors longed for wind, and they more than got their wish later in the week, when the wind—and consequently the seas—both picked up. By June 9, a twenty-knot wind on the port beam made for a jarring ride, and Creamer managed to lose his footing, banging his head and glasses on the molding above the chart table, this in spite of having just warned Rick to be careful.

The next night brought heavy squalls and twenty-foot seas, leading to an uncomfortable downwind sail. As always, the bouncy ride managed to shake things loose no matter how well they were secured, and the crew had to put up with items in the cabin banging against lockers or against each other. In the midst of squalls and heavy seas, though, there was no time to find and secure the items; the best they could do was hang on, hope that nothing was damaged, and trust that things wouldn't get any worse.

Things got worse. By June 11, they were once again down to bare poles, and the working jib was damaged as a result of a violent jibe in heavy seas and high winds.

Really, there's nothing inherently bad about a purposeful jibe, that is, changing tack such that the stern of the vessel, rather than the bow, turns through the wind. Sailors often jibe when the situation demands it. In this case, Creamer's jibe may have been purposeful. If so, it may have been ill advised; in heavy winds, the motion was forceful enough to damage his working jib.

One might wonder how a jib could get damaged this way because it's normally rigging or spars that get abused during a jibe. Professional rigger Herb Benavent comments that such damage might occur if the sail were older, but we know that's not the case here. Otherwise, he says, "If the jib was a large overlapping genoa, it could have snagged on the spreaders, making part of it stay behind while the rest moved to the other side. Normally [in this scenario] . . . the sail will rip the spreader forward, taking out the now-windward cap shroud and leading to a dismasting. If it was the sail getting hooked on the rigging situation, [Creamer] was lucky that the sail tore and spared his mast!"[7]

Because Creamer gives no further specifics in his journals or logs, we can't know exactly how the sail was damaged.

By now, winds had increased to forty-five knots, and the seas were a daunting (and to most terrifying) forty feet high. Under bare poles and sailing downwind once again, the boat's motion was more than a little uncomfortable. Sleeping was difficult for the crew, and the force of the seas and winds drove water into the closed hatch and even into tightly buttoned rain gear. A Japanese tanker surprised Jeff on his watch, appearing seemingly out of nowhere and wallowing badly in the heavy seas, startling Jeff with its horn. It was a wet and miserable twenty-four hours.

Sleeping in such conditions is almost impossible, but the crew needed rest in order to stay alert. When sailing downwind, the boat rolled from side to side, tossing bunk occupants from the cedar planking on one side to the lee cloths on the other. Even though bunks on a sailboat are purposely kept narrow so that occupants simply don't have the *room* to get tossed around much, Creamer and crew still found it necessary to make allowances for the boat's motion as they tried to get some sleep:

> *Even with the narrow width, it was necessary to bend at the waist and thrust your back against the cedar lining and your knees into the canvas to wedge your body into a position that would resist the lateral "G" forces. The best approach was to become aware of how close you were to dropping off and rehearse tensing and relaxing in rhythm with the boat's rolling motion. With practice you learned to slip quickly into the arms of Morpheus when the boat was level between its port and starboard motions. After that the tensing and relaxing became automatic as you slept.*[8]

Creamer's description of sleeping during a storm makes it sound even more exhausting than simply staying awake, but it is a skill that sailors learn, much as members of the armed forces learn to sleep anywhere, at any time, whenever they get the chance.

As always, food played an important part on this leg of the voyage. When weather permitted—and Creamer had mastered the art of cooking complete meals in all but the worst weather—the crew found a good meal an effective antidote for the cold, wet conditions. A gift of lemons back in Cape Town provided the opportunity for Jeff to make lemonade, one of his favorite drinks, and Marv used them both as an ingredient in salad dressing and to make lemon butter to top off a sponge cake. (This in spite of the fact that his first attempt at making a sponge cake didn't turn out well. His subsequent attempt at making bread—using flour picked up in South Africa and a fast-acting yeast that had been the gift of an acquaintance at the American Embassy—went much better.)

Marv's seagoing culinary legerdemain relied on a particular (and perhaps peculiar) approach to working in *Globe Star*'s tiny galley. He didn't care for the time-tested approach used by many other cooks, that of using a body restraint while cooking; he felt that, while it was a way to avoid getting thrown across the galley or into a hot stove, it was too restrictive. Instead he preferred to use what he referred to as cooking "one-," "two-," or "three-step" meals:

> *In moderate conditions I put my left foot on the bottom step of the ladder and as conditions deteriorated my foot went alternately to the second or third step. Breakfast prepared in the forty-foot seas of June 11 was a three-stepper.*[9]

Few people would have even attempted a breakfast of pancakes and fried eggs while traversing forty-foot seas, but Marv was not most people, and a few swells—even forty-foot ones—were not going to deprive him or his crew of a good breakfast. Still, even Marv admitted that "some acrobatics were needed" for this particular breakfast.[10] Creamer was occasionally given to understatement.

Creamer's stove had gimbals and a fiddle, which made it a bit safer to use in rough weather. Between the two, at least items were less likely to go sliding off the stovetop when *Globe Star* pitched or rolled—that is, when the stove worked at all.

When it did work, Creamer made impressive use of it, and the mealtime miracles continued: chicken and dumplings with salad on June 7, a pumpkin pie on the 13th (made with butternut squash instead of pumpkin, but without nutmeg, much to Marv's disappointment), spaghetti on the 20th, fresh bread for grilled cheese sandwiches served with canned soup on the 25th. No one on *Globe Star* was going to starve if Creamer had anything to say about it, and few would complain about the meals.

By the end of June, it was time to make a decision about where to land in Australia. Marv had really wanted to see Perth and then Hobart, but that would have entailed sailing down the rocky coast of Tasmania during a very stormy season. As the southern winter deepened, he knew that the frequency and intensity of storms would increase as time went on, and he knew just how treacherous the west coast of Tasmania could be. Creamer decided that the safest thing to do would be to approach the lee shore as soon as possible; thus, they determined to make directly for Hobart, near the southeastern edge of Tasmania, an island that comprises Australia's easternmost state.

Globe Star thus altered course to move fairly quickly into the latitude of Tasmania so as not to accidentally enter turbulent and rocky Bass Strait if it turned out that they were farther east than the boat's daily log indicated. This quick course change reminds us of a crucial point: Creamer and crew were sailing without any way to know exactly where they were. They could certainly find latitude with a fair degree of accuracy, but longitude was basically guesswork. It might have been well-informed and intelligent guesswork, but it was still a guess; if they guessed wrong, they could all die.

One result of working their way into higher latitudes is that the weather worsened considerably. Creamer's log showed gales on July 3, and even heavier gales the night of the 4th, and then again on the 5th, on which day Creamer estimated winds of sixty knots. (One consequence of the continual bad weather was a minor flood that soaked Creamer's bunk mattress. A trivial irritant, perhaps, but one that would result in several wet, miserable nights.)

By July 8, the weather had eased, and the *Globe Star* crew switched from the storm jib to a working jib and began to dry out their possessions (including the wet mattress) and themselves. After three days of gales, the crew could finally rest a bit.

As they moved south, another issue arose. Instead of a one-man nighttime watch, the shorter daylight period meant a two-man watch during the dark hours, and the crew had some trouble adjusting to the change. Sleeping periods were altered, as were eating times. At the same time, as they moved closer to land, two-man watches would help them keep a sharp eye out for rocks, shoals, and other vessels.

On the plus side, the weather was getting warmer. (Creamer told Jeff that he looked funny without his ski mask.) With calmer seas, Creamer baked bread and made a supper that only starving seamen could love: baked potatoes and SPAM.

They were still sailing downwind, and manning the tiller became an increasingly demanding task:

For the most part the seas and winds were dead aft or on the quarter which called for a lot of tiller action to hold Globe Star on a downwind course in seas sometimes as high as forty feet. The physical strain of pushing and pulling to prevent backwinding sails and what could be a disastrous broach was matched by the mental stress of deciding which way to push or pull. Not only did the helmsman have to anticipate from the feel of the helm as a pooping wave slid under the keel whether the boat was about to lurch to port or starboard, he had to be engaged in a continuous second-by-second process of deciding which way to steer.[11]

There were few directional clues, as the stars remained hidden by cloud cover. The result was that a five-hour stint of sailing left the helmsman in a state of physical and mental exhaustion.[12] This was exacerbated by the fact that, after changing sails in response to a wind shift, the boat would still be reacting to a sea state generated by the previous wind conditions. Thus, while the sails and rigging were driving the hull in one direction, the water would be attempting to propel it in another. If the helmsman didn't react quickly enough, the result could be an accidental jibe that could be dangerous to both crewman and the boat. (Nowhere do Creamer's notes or journals mention him having rigged a preventer from the boom to the toe rail to prevent such accidental jibes. This isn't all that surprising. Although a useful safety tool, they can be a pain to rig, use, and maintain. Many sailors—even on blue-water cruises—eschew their use.)

Figure 09.03. Jeff Herdelin in 2017. (IMAGE COURTESY OF JEFF HERDELIN.)

One thing that couldn't be avoided under such conditions was the risk of damage to the sails. Such strain often caused damage that had to be repaired before the sail could be used again. Luckily, Jeff had spent time at a sailmaker's loft. Creamer came to appreciate both Jeff's expertise and his work ethic.

It was a real joy to watch him go to work with sail cloth, sailor's palm, needle, and thread. When he was finished the neat patches and reinforced areas became the sail's merit badges for a job well done.[13]

Unfortunately, the onboard sail repair kit lacked replacement grommets for the luffs of the headsails. That meant repairing and then reusing the existing grommets, a painstaking and frustrating exercise given the lack of a swaging tool to mate the two sides of the thin metal piece. Creamer took on the task of attempting to repair the seemingly impossible-to-repair grommets, using a utility knife, pliers, screwdriver, hammer, and a tapered drift pin or punch. It was meticulous work, made worse by the fact that he couldn't afford to damage any of the precious grommets. It took hours to do the first one, and the rest were only marginally faster.

As it happened, the sails were not the only things in need of repair.

No matter what precautions one takes, sailors know that water *will* get on board a boat. That water (along with a lot of other scummy, grungy materials) collects in the bilge and must be pumped overboard. *Globe Star* carried on board an automatic bilge pump that proved itself unreliable almost immediately; luckily, there was a backup pump, one that operated manually. It was a simple, rugged device, not prone to failure. And yet it failed. When Creamer tore down the manual pump, he found that, of all things, a toothpick stuck in one of the valves had completely disabled the device.

The list of infuriatingly wayward mechanical items went on. Over the next several days, Creamer and the crew:

- replaced the main halyard winch drive shaft with a spare after the original one broke;
- fashioned a bearing out of epoxy, so that they could use an eggbeater someone had given them. (Eggbeaters can't possibly be that important at sea, but Marv was constitutionally unable to resist a challenge.);

- repaired the heater locker door against which Rick had fallen when the boat lurched unexpectedly;
- repaired the galley stove burner;
- made a drying rack for gloves, etc.;
- fixed the wind vane, which had not worked since leaving Cape Town (A loose screw was the culprit.);
- bolted down the galley table, which had worked its way loose;
- repaired the clutch in the self-steering vane; and
- fixed the stove, after getting water in the fuel lines, by pressurizing it and letting the water flow out of a dismantled burner. (The stove was driving Creamer crazy. He said that the continual problems with it reminded him of Franklin Roosevelt's story of the man who bought a boomerang and spent the rest of his life trying to throw it away. The stove—with its waterlogged burners and other problems—would plague the crew for the remainder of the voyage.)

None of this is at all surprising. The wear and tear on a boat at sea, especially in rough weather, is astonishing. It would be quite unusual if mechanical items *didn't* break down; Creamer expected problems and was prepared to deal with them. A long sea voyage—like any large project, from building a house to writing a complex piece of software—is a succession of problems and obstacles; it was part of Marv's nature to overcome such obstacles. Any skipper worth his salt knows how to repair, or at least jury rig, his boat, and Creamer was especially suited to such mid-voyage repairs. His years on the farm, in construction, and in his basement machine shop back home had always paid off on his earlier transoceanic passages, and they paid off handsomely on this circumnavigation too.

No amount of mechanical ingenuity, however, could prepare him for his next task: inching his way around the treacherous Tasmanian coast, simultaneously dreading finding it yet terrified of missing it in the dark.

CHAPTER 10

CAN THEY FIND *AND* AVOID TASMANIA?

Exploration is really the essence of the human spirit.
—Frank Borman

By mid-July, overcast nights and drizzly days had become the norm—but at least the weather had warmed to the point that the *Globe Star* crew could no longer see their breath. However, everything was wet: clothes, mattresses, pillows, and sailors were all sodden and uncomfortable. Even the stove—the accursed stove—joined in the fun, with the burners refusing to light or, if they did light, refusing to burn cleanly. By pressurizing the tank somewhat more than normal, Creamer nonetheless managed to make a loaf of bread, "great for morale on a dismal day," he said.[1] Note, though, that overpressurizing a kerosene stove is neither safe nor recommended. The excess pressure could cause the relief valve in the pressure cap to open and gas to escape; the escaping gas could then flare up. Creamer was quite literally playing with fire.

As the boat slogged on toward Australia, tension was mounting. Their presumed longitude was pure conjecture: a dead-reckoning position deduced from estimates of speed based on little more than observation of the boat's wake. (Creamer and his crew were very good at dead reckoning, but it is by its nature an imperfect—though long utilized—method for determining one's position.) Their educated guesswork indicated that they should be approaching western Tasmania, and this was seemingly confirmed when Rick spotted a plane flying back and forth, apparently killing time while waiting for weather to clear, perhaps headed to a Tasmanian airport. (This presumption turned out to be in error.) Two days later, in a gale, sailing in the pitch dark, with rough seas and water coming aboard even through the closed hatch, things were looking—and the crew was feeling—pretty gloomy.

Part of the reason for that gloom was the fact that, according to their calculations, they should by now have found Tasmania. Their log showed that they were somewhat south and well east of the southern tip of the Australian island state and, with a dropping barometer, they knew that they could expect more southwest gales and rough weather. They actually hoped that they *had* missed it; one possible alternative could be that they were so far off course that they would never see it (that could mean dying of thirst and hunger) or that they'll "find" it by crashing into it (which could also mean dying, this time by being crushed against the rocks on the shore). Any situation in which two of the diminishing number of available options result in death can't be a good one, and Creamer's grim mood reflected that somber reality.

On July 27, though, we can see Creamer's confidence returning. In his log, he writes,

> *Sea and sky evidence continue to support our hypothesis that we are moving toward Sydney, e.g., no SW gales, moderate south winds as shown on the* Pilot Charts, *fairly warm nights in spite of south wind. . . .*[2]

The next day, the crew was excited when Jeff sighted land on the port bow. However, the two islands they passed did not match the notations on their small-scale chart. (Which they were lucky to have at all, given that the wind had earlier swept it overboard and that it took some doing to retrieve.) But since the scale was so small, the sodden chart was not terribly helpful in any case.

It was even less helpful sometime later, when what had begun as a feeling of relief for the sailors turned into a desperate attempt to avoid disaster. As they neared what they thought was land, they discovered that the "land" was in fact a small island surrounded by even smaller islands, scattered in a sea of what Creamer called "spouting, geyser-like plumes of water."[3]

This was a very dangerous place to be. The underwater obstructions creating these "fountains" could have dealt *Globe Star* a fatal blow. They wanted to reverse out of the area, but there was no good way to do that against both the wind and current and with their tiny engine. By late afternoon, it was obvious that they were not going to be able to sail their way out of the maze of islands, rocks, and reefs; the alternative was spending the night in a terribly dangerous situation. They couldn't anchor because getting close enough to find shallow water in which they could anchor would mean facing the very rocks that threatened them. Besides, Marv thought that the seabed—if they could find a seabed—would probably not hold their anchor well enough.

In any case, Marv had a personal bias against anchoring. He felt that a sailboat was made to sail and therefore would be most likely to survive danger when underway. He thought that a tethered sailboat, relying on a steel hook to protect her, is actually far more vulnerable than one free to sail. Opinions differ on this, but Marv was not always willing to hear differing opinions.

And yet sailing through the rock-strewn labyrinth seemed suicidal. In the end, they decided to lie ahull, furling the sails and simply letting the boat drift. They tested the engine to be sure that it would start quickly in an emergency and rehearsed plans to try to work their way into the islet's lee if a squall should blow up.

The weather gods were with them. As unpredictable as the weather had been up to this point, the night passed without a hint of nasty weather. It was a tense several hours waiting in the dark, but in the morning, *Globe Star* continued her run among the breakers, rocks, and scattered islands. That evening, the sun appeared to set over solid land; the Australian mainland? Creamer couldn't tell for sure, so they spent several hours paralleling the forbidding coastline without seeing any signs of life: no navigational aids, no telephone poles, not even a fencepost. They finally concluded that they had sailed through part of the Recherche Archipelago and stumbled onto the western edge of the Great Australian Bight—they were a long way from southeastern Australia.[4]

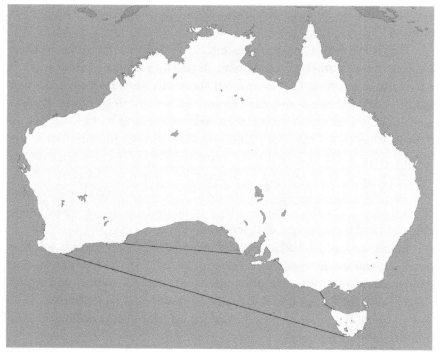

Figure 10.01. The outer line on this map depicts the limits of the Great Australian Bight, as determined by the International Hydrographic Organization. (USED UNDER THE CREATIVE COMMONS ATTRIBUTION-SHARE ALIKE 3.0 UNPORTED LICENSE. IMAGE COURTESY OF USER: *URHIXIDUR.*)

On July 30, the dejected crew turned southeastward into a brisk onshore wind. By dark, the winds were at gale force; the crew was mentally and physically drained. To make matters worse, they had wasted time, possibly as much as two weeks, on the northwest jaunt during which they had sought to determine their location. The lost time wasn't a big deal in and of itself. But the *Pilot Charts* indicated that the later they approached the west coast of Tasmania, the more likely they were to encounter severe storms.

At least they had been able to get a good latitude sighting and had finally established what they thought was a decent working longitude, based on the northwest trending coast on the western edge of the Great

Australian Bight. Even the weather cooperated. On August 21, Creamer wrote,

> *Took a long nap this morning and am feeling fine. We were all a bit tired after our encounter with the islands. . . . It was not the kind of atmosphere conducive to relaxation and sleep. According to our noon position we have about 1050 miles to round Cape Bruny in south-western Tasmania.*[5]

Still a thousand miles to go, and now it was time to face the problem of preparing to make a landfall on one of the worst lee shores in the world: the west coast of Tasmania.

Western Tasmania is, even now, rough, isolated country, devoted mainly to mining and wilderness tourism. In the early 1980s, when *Globe Star* was headed there, the 180-mile-long coast was steep and rocky, mostly uninhabited, and boasted only three short-range navigation lights. Only two inlets allowed access, and both of those required—so said the charts—local knowledge for entrance. The ideal landfall would be at Southwest Cape, lying on Tasmania's extreme southwestern corner, which would allow Creamer and crew to avoid the forbidding west side of the island. But without instruments, aiming for the southern tip meant taking the risk of missing it altogether. Yet they had to make landfall. After 6,000 miles of rough sailing, they needed to put in for fuel, water, repairs, and provisions; this put them in the dubious position of having to simultaneously find *and* avoid the western Tasmanian coast. In some ways, thought Creamer, this was worse than rounding the Horn:

> *There it would be necessary only to avoid it. Finding it would be nice but not required for our safety. In Tasmania our safety demanded both finding and avoiding [it] at the same time.*[6]

Their options were limited. One possibility was to heave-to at nightfall to preclude sailing into the rocky shore during the fifteen-hour night. This, however, would mean using only three-eighths of the twenty-four-hour period to move eastward. Given the increasingly bad weather, this was not an attractive choice.

Another possibility was to proceed at night, but under reduced sail, hoping that they could detect a change in the boat's motion as it entered shoaling waters—or that they would hear the sound of breaking surf, and that they would hear it in time to sail out of danger. This, Creamer felt, was too risky: by the time they had determined that they were in danger, it might be too late to turn to windward and claw off.

Basically, they needed to find a way to maximize eastward movement during the twenty-four-hour period, while at the same time minimizing the risk of running aground at night. Given the southeast trending coastline, Creamer came up with a third option:

Why not make the final approach near the southern end of the island and sail northeastward straight toward the unseen coast in the daylight so as to close the coast as rapidly as possible by day, and sail southeastward parallel to the coast at night so as to minimize the possibility of contact in the dark hours? The zigzag course would not advance us as speedily as a straight, eastward heading but would be greatly superior to heaving to at night. Assuming the angles involved to be 45 degrees, the daily eastward advance would be comparable to running two legs of a right triangle as opposed to running the hypotenuse.[7]

A bit of math showed that, using this technique, the daily eastward achievement would be equivalent to that accomplished in seventeen hours of straight eastward sailing—almost double what they would accomplish by heaving to at night. Reading Creamer's notes and journal, one gets the idea that Marv was quite proud of this elegant solution to a sticky problem. The approach didn't eliminate the risk of making the difficult landfall on Tasmania, but it did reduce it to something they could live with.

On August 6, a succession of squalls hit, and over the next several days, the delicate sailing intended to help them find Tasmania and maneuver around the southeastern tip into Hobart was made more difficult by squalls and gales, some of the latter lasting as long as twelve hours. As near as they could guess—and it really *was* a guess, though an educated one—land was now about 380 miles away, and the atmosphere on board *Globe Star* was tense as they headed toward what they hoped was Tasmania.

Creamer grew philosophical during those last dangerous miles. He made a sincere effort not to wallow in the fear that such a situation must necessarily produce, instead trying to acknowledge the danger they were in while not letting it permeate his every thought. The thought of dying at sea did occur to him though. He did not fear death, or so he said; he had lived a full life, and he would die doing what he loved, but he did worry about Jeff and Rick:

> *Jeff at twenty-four and Rick at nineteen were entitled to a longer stay on planet earth. I would have died a "thousand deaths" if, like the Pied Piper of Hamelin, I became responsible for their untimely demise. But when an occasional crashing wave reminded us all of our mortality my philosophical stance weakened and I would find myself shouting above the roar of the storm, "I don't know about you guys, but I'm too young to die."*[8]

As they neared their destination, the higher latitudes in which they were sailing brought new problems. Low temperatures plagued them, and Rick had frostbite on the backs of his fingers. Jeff had chilblains on his face from the cold.[9] To top it off, sailing southeastward exposed *Globe Star* to heavy seas generated by southwesterly gales.

It was at this point that a near disaster occurred. Jeff had gone forward, shouting that he was going to add the staysail to the storm jib because the single sail alone was not allowing them to maintain steerageway. As he positioned himself on the foredeck, a towering wave crashed into *Globe Star*, rolled her on her port side, and sent her scudding to lee. It was a knockdown; the sea and wind had driven the boat on its side, taking the mast down to the water. Jeff disappeared from view. Marv yelled for Rick to check on Jeff, but when he looked, all Rick could tell Marv was that he couldn't see his crewmate.

For a few moments, the two men feared the worst. Jeff may have been washed overboard. He should be tethered, so they thought that at least

Figure 10.02. Samples of Marv Creamer's logbooks.
(PHOTO COURTESY OF ROWAN UNIVERSITY ARCHIVES.)

they might find him trailing overboard by his safety line—if he had in fact been tethered, and if being knocked off of the boat and then dragged through the water hadn't injured and perhaps drowned him.

A moment later, Jeff raised his head above the cabin top. He had flattened himself between the dorade vents and hung on for dear life. He was drenched, but okay.

The boat, however, was not okay. A winch handle had flown across the cabin and broken one of the stove grates and water had poured in and soaked charts, records, the tape recorder, and Marv's gun. (Marv carried a .357 revolver and a semiautomatic rifle on board. These were meant mainly as protection from pirates, many of which were active in coastal waters at the time.) In addition, glass jars containing spare parts were broken and strewn about.

Because Jeff had been unable to add the staysail, Marv suggested that they gain more steerageway by running the engine—but as soon as they started the engine, BOOM! They were knocked down again. Once again *Globe Star* was on her side and her mast was in the water. Something—possibly a freon air horn—flew across the cockpit and struck the engine's Master switch while it was running, which put the engine's alternator out of commission. (It's difficult to understand how something striking the engine's Master switch might burn out the alternator, but that's what Creamer's notes say. One possibility is that the metal horn struck the switch with such force that it *shorted out* the switch, which might have resulted in damage to the alternator. In any case, the switch itself would have, for the time being, been useless.)

Globe Star was now limping toward Tasmania, but she *was* at least headed toward Tasmania. At noon on August 10, they estimated their latitude at 43°37' based on an observation made using theta Scorpii during the dark hours of August 9. (Theta Scorpii is a very bright star in the southern constellation of Scorpius, Latin for *scorpion*.) *Globe Star* continued on a port tack until nightfall, then, with a west wind blowing, Creamer changed over to the starboard tack so that they could sail southeastward during the night. As usual, Marv was on watch when the first blush of dawn appeared in the northeast. He switched back to the port tack and within an hour had Southwest Cape, Tasmania, in view. Its latitude is 43°34'; they were just about spot on, and Creamer knew that their plan had worked:

> *It was apparent that we had sailed almost within sight of the coast during the night and in all probability would have made an unwanted nighttime landfall if we had not been following our plan by sailing parallel to the coast at night.*[10]

This was pretty good unaided celestial navigation. Each minute of latitude is equal to one mile, so they were only about three miles off. It also speaks well of Marv's geometrically devised "daily eastward advance" plan, as Creamer no doubt made sure to point out.

Figure 10.03. *Globe Star* sailing in Tasmania.
(PHOTO COURTESY OF THE CREAMER FAMILY.)

Still, they looked for confirmation. The presence of the Maatsuyker Island lighthouse (the last manned lighthouse on the Tasmanian coast, or in Australia, as it happens) provided a measure of that, but they really wanted to see something with a name on it, something that literally said "Tasmania" or at least "Australia." A helicopter circled overhead, but it had no identifying marks except "Hookway Rescue Service" painted on the side. The crew cursed good-naturedly at the lack of information on the side of the chopper. (Amazingly, two days later, the pilot of that helicopter, along with his wife, stopped by to say hello at the dock in Hobart.)

After a rollercoaster ride on forty-foot swells, they identified the entrance to the D'Entrecasteaux Channel and turned sharply northward toward Hobart, where they were guided into port by a cray fisherman and his son. It was pitch dark by the time they got to their anchorage, where they were invited to raft up on one side of fisherman Bill Wignall's boat. Within minutes, the greeting had turned into a party, with several other boats joining in. (Most sailors know that a raft up can be a convenience or a safety measure when there aren't enough slips available, with the heaviest boat in the group setting the anchor, but it's also pretty much a recipe for a party.) Marv, Jeff, and Rick had made it safely across some seven thousand miles of often stormy ocean. They were, for the time being, safe, and they were definitely ready for a party.

CHAPTER 11

SIX WEEKS IN TASMANIA

So much of who we are is where we have been.
—William Langewiesche

The get-together at Bill's raft up was a welcome diversion for the tired *Globe Star* crew. The food was wonderful: crayfish hors d'oeuvres, delicious hot broiled fish, and French fries. The newly arrived sailors contributed an aluminum foil "goatskin" of wine, and the boisterous camaraderie helped temper the recent memory of the cold, wet, tense hours in *Globe Star*'s cockpit.

One thing Creamer and crew needed to do as soon as possible was get in touch with family in order to inform them that everyone was okay. Bill helped them route calls through a radiotelephone operator on the Australian mainland, but the connection was not always good. Jeff's parents misunderstood him when he told them that they were tied up to a larger boat. As a result, Blanche received garbled information, and when Marv called her, she was wondering why they'd been towed by a ship. (Blanche, as it happens, would soon arrive for a three-week visit.)

The new ARGOS transmitter that the crew picked up in Cape Town had failed four days out, meaning that their friends and families had not known of their whereabouts for ten full weeks. In spite of that, Blanche had faith in Marv and had not wavered in her belief that they would make it to Australia—or so she said. Years later, Creamer's children noted that Blanche *did* worry when he was on a sea voyage. Even if she had all the faith in the world in Marv's ability, how could a wife *not* worry when her husband is at sea, sailing without instruments, and is not heard from for over two months?

Blanche was not the only family member to worry about his safety. In fact, prior to the voyage, the family pleaded with him not to go. He was adamant about taking on the challenge though, saying (as he often maintained) that he "had been taken prisoner by an idea" and simply had to go. As sure as he was that he would survive the journey, his family was not as confident. His daughter Andra says now that she figured at the time that his chances were about 50/50, and that Creamer's son, Kurt, felt the same.

> *That his grandchildren might not get to know him, or that my siblings and mother would lose him did not seem to persuade him at all. I recognized that if anyone could accomplish such a feat, it would be Dad, but he wasn't young and he wasn't immortal.*[1]

The next day, *Globe Star* caught a tow to Hobart, passing under the tiny drawbridge that guards the entrance to Constitution Dock about 4:30 in the evening.

This time, Creamer's "Q" flag was noticed promptly by the authorities, and they came by to inspect *Globe Star*. As usual, though, the bureaucracy was problematic: Quarantine Officer Roger Norton knew that *Globe Star* had spent the night before tied up in the lower part of the channel and wanted to know if they had been part of the raft up. If they had been rafted up with any Australian boats, Creamer knew, that would mean that those boats would *also* have to go through quarantine. Creamer did what any self-respecting contrarian would do: he lied.

The reality, though, is that Norton was no fool. He knew full well that they had been rafted up with the Australian boats all night, and he knew that Marv was being disingenuous; he was just doing his duty as the law prescribed. And to prove that he was an upstanding guy, he loaned Marv $20 AUS because the quarantine had prevented Creamer from changing money before the weekend.

The "Q" flag issue taken care of, the crew was now free to take care of their portside business, the first example of which was getting Rick's fingers attended to. Creamer and Rick visited an emergency treatment center, but that did little good: In spite of the fact that near-constant immersion in saltwater during the voyage had actually exacerbated his problems, the doctor there prescribed—of all things—soaking his fingers in a saltwater solution until they healed. Eventually, Rick began soaking them in *fresh* water, and they slowly mended.

By now, *Globe Star* was halfway through its journey around the world, and Creamer was looking forward to rounding the Horn—although perhaps "looking forward" is not the correct term. Cape Horn, at the southernmost tip of South America, is the point at which the Atlantic and Pacific oceans meet, and they meet with terrific force. Low pressure systems abound in the area. The region is often stormy, but even when it appears peaceful, violent storms can blow up quickly and seemingly out of nowhere. Huge waves are common, and the area is considered home to some of the roughest waters in the world. Rounding the Horn is not an enterprise to be taken lightly. Some eight hundred ships have sunk in the area, and thousands have died attempting to round the Horn.

Creamer was definitely *not* taking the Horn lightly. Even though Tasmanian friends had assured him that, having made a wintertime landfall on Tasmania's west coast, he had weathered conditions at least equal to those he would encounter at the Horn, Marv was determined to make substantial preparations to ensure the safety of his boat and crew as they rounded the Horn.

The first thing he needed was a new vane steering system. That would be a major project, but the crew would need help keeping their vessel on course in the rough waters. Manning a tiller on a boat as large as *Globe Star*, especially day after day in high winds and rough waters, can be incredibly exhausting; a working vane steerer would be a great help.

Then there was the matter of the boom, which Creamer felt was too long and too heavy for the sort of waters they might encounter. His answer was to shorten the boom. That wasn't terribly difficult, but it meant that it would also require some trimming of the mainsail and, while they were at it, some alteration of the genoa and drifter to eliminate chafing on the bow pulpit. Meanwhile, the luffs of other sails had to be reinforced and regrommeted. All in all, some serious time (and expertise) at the sailmaker's loft was required.

When new crewman Jesse Edwards arrived from Maryland (Jeff Herdelin and Rick Kuzyk had departed), Marv put him to work sprinkling ground cork into a film of clear epoxy paint on the deck to eliminate slipping. Also it was time to replace the sacrificial zinc anodes that protected the boat's dissimilar metal fittings.[2]

But the biggest job of all remained: *Globe Star* needed to be hauled out of the water for inspection, for barnacle removal, and for the reapplication of antifouling paint. Luckily, Muir Engineering, which operated a Hobart branch, had purchased the rights to the Fleming steering gear, one of Creamer's favorites, and offered to remove the original steerer and fit a new one to the boat's transom while she was hauled out. Even better, the same branch operated a sail loft that could take care of both the boom and sail alterations, *and* the same company provided a man to remove the propeller so that Creamer could install a new cutlass bearing for the propeller shaft. (The old bearing, which holds the prop shaft in place, had worn, but Marv had been unable to remove the prop in order to replace the bearing. It turned out that someone at the manufacturing plant had coated the parts with a "locking" compound, an error that had occasioned no small amount of sweat, skinned knuckles, and what Marv termed "a torrent of expletives" when he attempted to replace the worn bearing himself.[3])

While *Globe Star* was out of the water, Nick Gill, a maintenance man for the University of Tasmania, showed up at the dock. He chatted with Creamer about long-distance sailing in general and offered to do just about any type of job in exchange for information and advice about sailing. Marv put him to work restoring some badly rusted tools, and Nick impressed Marv with his work ethic and his thoroughness. When the cleanup was through, the younger man volunteered to crew the next leg, which at the time was assumed to be to Chile in South America. Nick seemed an excellent candidate and, his other possibilities having fallen through, Marv accepted Nick's offer. Nick was building a steel boat of his own, and when Marv and Blanche—she was visiting from the states—had dinner at the home of Nick and his wife, Marv had the opportunity to check out Nick's work on the steel hull he was welding together. Once again, he was impressed with Nick's workmanship; *Globe Star* had found its newest crewman.

The attitude at the Royal Tasmanian Yacht Club (RTYC) was, Marv thought, decidedly different than that of the RCYC in Cape Town, and his experience in Tasmania was much more cordial. He was invited to give a talk about noninstrument circumnavigation at the club and, while there was some skepticism, it was good-natured, friendly, and positive.

The positive reception continued. Marv and Blanche, the latter spending her "vacation" traveling to Tasmania and helping Marv provision and clean up the boat, were dinner guests of several RTYC members and even had an overnight stay at the home of one resident, whose mate provided Marv with both fishing advice and a huge lure that was "guaranteed" to provide a tasty meal of tuna. In fact, during the forty-two nights of their stay in Hobart, the Creamers and the *Globe Star* crew received thirty-six dinner invitations. If nothing else, they would head to Cape Horn well fed. In a letter to daughter Lynn back home, Blanche noted that the people in Tasmania "fall all over themselves to do things for us" and that the couple had been treated to several "overnights and dinners—fabulous meals."[4]

Blanche Creamer was something of an unsung hero in all of this. She had helped get the voyage underway in the first place, of course, but she also flew to Hobart—spending more than twenty hours in the air on five different flights to get there—to deliver gear and supplies to Marv and his crew. (Among other things, she brought with her survival suits that would serve the voyagers well in their crossing of the often-violent Tasman Sea.) Once in Hobart, she continued her labors, spending much of her time securing food and supplies for Marv and the crew and helping get the boat ready for the next leg of the trip.

Marv appreciated his wife's efforts. In a letter to Lynn, written just after he'd seen Blanche off on her trip back to New Jersey, he commented ruefully on how Blanche had spent her supposed vacation "working on the boat [and] doing inventories" and noted, "Whatta gal!" Of course, she *had* to be quite a gal to fly ten thousand miles just to deliver supplies, spend much of her visit working on the boat and its provisions, and then fly back home another ten thousand miles while her husband set off on another leg of what he termed, only half-jokingly, as "this foolish trip."[5]

As if meals from well-wishers in Hobart weren't enough, even more food made its way to *Globe Star* via some "surplus" goodies courtesy of the

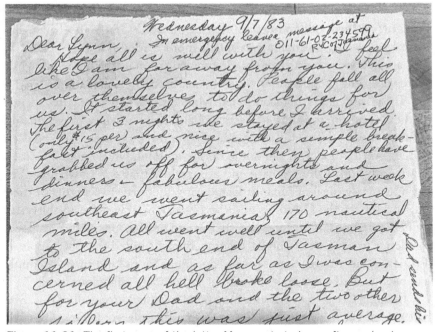

Figure 11.01. The first page of the letter Marv wrote to Lynn after seeing her mother off back to the States. (IMAGE COURTESY OF LYNN BORSTELMAN CREAMER.)

US nuclear submarine *Boston*, which was also at Constitution Dock. In spite of masses of protestors parading along the docks nearby (they were protesting both the presence of a nuclear vessel in the harbor—flyers labeled her a "KILLER SUB" and noted that her visit to Hobart was "not in the interests of humanity"—and American foreign policy in Central America in general), the Creamers' visit to the US Navy boat went well and they came away with more good wishes and, more importantly, more good food.[6]

Perhaps the most interesting thing, certainly one of the most *useful* things, that occurred in Tasmania was that Creamer received a lesson in navigation himself—from, of all things, a troop of Hobart Boy Scouts. Invited to give a speech about his instrument-free navigation, Creamer was happy to oblige, but he almost certainly got more than he gave. At one point, the boys in the troop asked how he arrived at a polar point in the Southern Hemisphere.

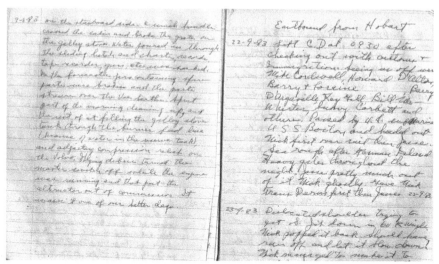

Figure 11.02. Pages from Creamer's log during his visit to Hobart. Note comments about the submarine *Boston*. (IMAGE COURTESY OF ROWAN UNIVERSITY ARCHIVES.)

Marv explained that he used the two bright stars, Gacrux and Acrux in the Southern Cross, as "pointers" to the South Celestial Pole, very much the same way that the stars Merak and Dubhe in the Big Dipper point to the opposite celestial pole in the north. But unlike the North Celestial Pole, which is marked by the bright star Polaris, the South Celestial Pole is just a blank spot in the sky. Marv had to draw a line from Gacrux through Acrux and extend its length about four and a half times, a tricky estimate.

The Boy Scouts had a better idea, one that increased the crew's direction-finding ability and cut many hours from their passages in the Southern Hemisphere. Said Creamer,

> The problem that we were having was in laying off the proper distance from Acrux. [The Scouts'] solution involves pure geometry. They use two bright stars positioned close to the Southern Cross. These stars, Hadar and Rigil Kentaurus, are of almost identical declination. Using earthly terms, they lie on about the same parallel of latitude. The Scouts erect a perpendicular at the midpoint on a line between these

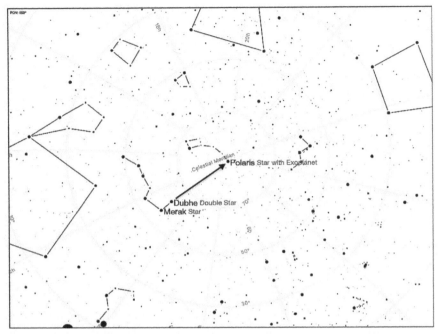

Figure 11.03. Here's an image showing how Creamer determined latitude in the Northern Hemisphere. Note that he was able to use two stars to point to Polaris, the North Star. (SCREENSHOT COURTESY OF RICK BROWN.)

two stars and extend it so that it crosses the line extended from Gacrux through Acrux and beyond. The latter line represents a meridian, and the line perpendicular to a parallel represents another meridian set at an angle to the first. The crossing point represents the polar point in the southern hemisphere. Because all of the stars involved are bright and their patterns easily identified, the method was usable in partial overcast and made direction finding possible when only some stars in the cluster were visible.[7]

Creamer was pleasantly surprised that these young men had come up with a much more elegant solution to the problem than he had, even with all of his experience. Of course, Tasmania is an island; many Scouts in Hobart would have spent a great deal of time and effort learning to sail

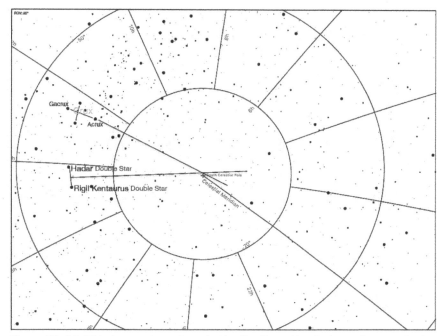

Figure 11.04. This image shows how, in the Southern Hemisphere, Creamer had to draw a line from Gacrux through Acrux and then *estimate* what it would look like if he were to extend that line 4.5 times. (SCREENSHOT COURTESY OF RICK BROWN.)

and to navigate. Knowledge of this nature would not be at all unusual, and it's possible that the young men wondered why Creamer hadn't come up with this on his own, unfamiliar though he may have been with the Southern Hemisphere. In his own manuscript and journal, Marv made a special effort to ensure that the Hobart Boy Scout troop got credit for this navigational innovation.

As far as the refit went, one irritating issue remained. The ARGOS transmitter had been nothing but trouble, with the major problems caused, it seemed, by battery failure. Ian Milne and John O'Brien, both of whom worked for the (now defunct) Australian Department of Communications, had heard about the transmitter failures and stopped by to see if they could help out. Given that the problem was the failure of the transmitter's own batteries, their solution was to wire the transmitter

Figure 11.05. Jeff Herdelin and Rick Kuzyk on board *Globe Star* in Hobart.
(PHOTO COURTESY OF THE CREAMER FAMILY.)

directly to the *boat's* onboard batteries. Marv gave his permission, and the pair made the switch. Ironically, the US Coast Guard had opted against precisely this approach because they feared that the boat's batteries might fail. (And yet *Globe Star* never experienced any problems with her solar panel–charged batteries or her alternator—except when the latter had been physically damaged during the previous knockdown.)

While Milne and O'Brien were aboard, they took care of another ARGOS-related problem too. *Globe Star's* ARGOS antenna was clamped to the bow pulpit, where it was constantly doused with saltwater. The pair suggested using the coaxial cable already in place inside the mast to feed the signal to a mast-top antenna. However, this would require removing the VHF antenna that they would need if they had to break out their radio in an emergency, so the pair came up with a novel alternative: leave the VHF antenna in place, but clamp a small transmitter antenna to the VHF antenna at a 45-degree angle. If they should have to break out the VHF radio to call for help, they would simply switch the coaxial cable over from the ARGOS transmitter to the VHF radio.

Jesse's tenure as a crewman was intended to be a short one—he was not terribly interested in going around the Horn—so the plan was to drop him off in Chile. However, US Naval attachés in both Washington and Canberra advised that the only decent place for a yacht to approach the Chilean coast was at Viña del Mar near Santiago, *not* near the central and most populated part of the country, which was Jesse's preference. Creamer did not relish making a landfall in a place other than where the military recommended.

The problem with a Viña del Mar landing, though, was that it made setting off for the Cape even more problematic. It added 2,400 nautical miles to the route and it led through the light winds of the southern Pacific subtropical high-pressure belt. Moreover, the final leg would then have to be made against an adverse current and into weak—and then strengthening—southwesterly gales. Tacking to the southwest toward a position from which it would be safe to head for the Horn would add another one thousand miles and two weeks to the voyage. Neither of these was a palatable option. From Creamer's journal:

> *Even if the restocking of fuel, water, and provisions could be accomplished in a week's time at Viña del Mar, the three months between the time of departure and the occurrence of the December solstice was scarcely enough time to make the trip under ideal conditions.*[8]

Expecting those ideal conditions to occur would have been foolhardy, and yet that's exactly what Creamer did.

CHAPTER 12

LEAVING HOBART

We were born to be free, to expand our horizons by going where we have never gone before, and not to hang out in the relative comfort and safety of the nest, the known. There is a place within us that is courageous beyond our human understanding; it yearns to explore beyond the boundaries of our daily life.

—DENNIS MERRITT JONES

JESSE EDWARDS'S PLANNED TENURE AS A *GLOBE STAR* CREWMAN WAS already intended to be brief, but it ended up being even shorter than anticipated. The original plan had been to sail northeastward across the Tasman Sea, graze the northern tip New Zealand's North Island, and then head straight across the Pacific to Viña del Mar in Chile.

That plan was turned topsy-turvy very quickly—and more or less literally. Within twenty-four hours *Globe Star* was violently knocked down, the wind and seas combining to thrust her mast some 45 degrees under the surface of the Tasman Sea, and Creamer's upper left arm had been wrenched out of its socket. Jesse, plagued with stomach trouble that seemed to worsen as they headed out to sea, had decided to withdraw altogether, and the crew's target port had been switched from Viña del Mar to Sydney, which was only 621 miles away, compared to 6,677.

Part of the problem was, not surprisingly, the weather. Creamer had been warned about the violent storms of the Tasman Sea, and sure enough a howler blew up, one that produced fifty-five-knot winds in Hobart and seventy-five-knot winds across the Tasman in Wellington, New Zealand.

Even under trying conditions, Marv was comfortable with his crew. Jesse was an experienced yard man and had skippered yachts between the Chesapeake and the Caribbean. Nick had a strong maintenance background, was knowledgeable about boat building, and was eager to get in some sea time. Things should have gone well, in spite of a severe battering by the storm.

However, both crewmen ended up seasick (few would *not* have become seasick given the incessant rolling motion produced by waves and wind), and Jesse's gastritis, which he had thought he had conquered, seemed to have been reactivated by the roiling seas.

At dusk, they reefed the main to its smallest size and bent on the storm jib. With the other two men out of commission for the time being, Marv stood the night watch. Around 8:00 the next morning, Nick relieved him, and Marv went forward to strike the storm jib, which Marv felt was in danger of flogging itself to shreds in the hurricane-force winds.

There was another danger here, but Marv didn't anticipate it. As he hauled downward on the leech with his left hand, the wind took the loose sail and carried it—along with Marv's hand and arm—past his left ear. He could feel the shoulder separate. He could also feel the pain but managed to push past it for the moment as he stood on the gyrating deck wondering how he could get the storm jib down with an arm that was suddenly and painfully unresponsive. Flexing his hand, he discovered that he had an almost normal grip with his fingers, and he found that by quickly twisting his body, he could fling his mostly useless arm upward so that his fingers slapped against the sail. After a few tries, he managed to fling his arm up and grab the leech with his left hand, securing the canvas to the deck with his feet.

Note that Marv's commentary may be in error here. Captain David Jackson, USN (Ret.), who teaches blue-water sailing at Annapolis and who is the maintenance director of the US Naval Academy Sailing Department, says, "An experienced sailor would never grab the leech to pull down the sail, always the luff. The leech would keep the sail full and give it more energy. The luff collapses the sail."[1] So either Creamer's notes are in error, or he made a—potentially calamitous, and certainly painful—mistake up on the foredeck.

Figure 12.01. Captain David Jackson, USN (Ret.), and his wife, Christine, aboard the schooner *Summerwind.* (IMAGE COURTESY OF DAVID JACKSON.)

Now Marv had another problem: How was he to repair the separated shoulder at sea, with no radio and thus no access to medical advice? His only option was to ask Nick to yank on his arm hard enough to snap it back into place. It took a couple of tries, but eventually Nick got the job done. Afterward Marv said, "[The arm] was usable immediately, but it was twenty-four hours before I could sleep and three days before I could raise my arm without wincing."[2]

Anyone who's had a separated shoulder knows how painful it is. And *reducing* it—the technical term that physicians use to describe the act of snapping it back into place—is just about as painful as separating it in the first place.

Daniel Schneider is a physician and assistant professor of internal medicine with the University of Michigan Health System. He says that a shoulder separation, which basically involves snapping ligaments apart and pushing them out of the way such that the shoulder is literally shoved out of its socket, is just as excruciating as it sounds.

Figure 12.02. Dr. Daniel Schneider is a physician and researcher with the University of Michigan Health System. (IMAGE COURTESY OF DR. DANIEL SCHNEIDER.)

"It would be exquisitely painful. The best apples-to-apples comparison would be a ligamentous injury in a different part of the body. So, it would be very similar to a football player tearing his ACL."[3]

Reducing the injury is also painful, as Creamer discovered, but the risk of leaving it separated for any length of time makes the pain of reduction worthwhile.

"If your arm is out of the shoulder socket," says Schneider, "that in and of itself would risk further injury because you've got a bone flopping in that upper arm area. If you left it alone, you could risk damage to nerves and vessels and muscles, and maybe other ligaments too."[4]

Creamer was apparently one of those people whom we tend to characterize as "tough" because they seem inured to pain, unaffected by it. In fact, most such people are not actually unaffected, but, says Schneider, they have the ability to compartmentalize their pain and carry on.

"Most people you would describe as having a high pain tolerance are people who have much more experience or practice, probably out of necessity, of being able to compartmentalize pain," says Schneider. "It's not that they don't *experience* pain, but they realize that it's just telling them what they already know—that they're injured and that they have to just power through."[5]

This makes sense, especially when considering occupations that demand that one continue working even while in pain or in severe discomfort. That would apply to a farmer digging a lamb out of a snowdrift in subzero temperatures or a soldier manning a position in spite of having been wounded; the work is, at the moment, more important than the pain, so they simply *ignore* the pain for the time being. Most people can do that to some extent, but some people are better at it than most.

In Creamer's case, says Schneider, "He engaged that compartmentalization activity in the brain and used that to suppress the pain, even while acknowledging it. That's a very powerful mechanism that exists in everybody; they just have to have the prior experiences and the tools to know how to engage those processes in the brain."[6]

Obviously, we can also see this compartmentalization at work on board a sailboat. In a storm or other crisis, lives are at stake. You may be cold, wet, tired, and hungry—you might even be injured—but emergencies won't wait; there are no time-outs at sea.

Two hours later, as Jesse lay in seasick misery on the starboard settee and Marv cast about in the quarter berth for the least painful position to rest his arm, there was a *crash!!* on the port quarter. It sounded as if a locomotive had slammed into a truck. It was another knockdown, and this time *Globe Star*'s mast actually ended up *beneath* the water; as near as Creamer could tell later, the mast had been submerged to the point that it was 45 degrees underwater. It took agonizing seconds for *Globe Star* to right herself, but she did.

Nick, who had been on watch in the cockpit, was jerked to a stop against his safety harness and tether; without them, he would surely have been washed overboard. He was tough though. He knew that in the heavy seas of the southern oceans, sailors can expect to experience knockdowns or even complete rollovers. "When I signed on, I expected worse than this," he said to Marv.[7]

Belowdecks, of course, the boat was a shambles. On deck, a solar panel had been torn loose and a section of the "H" track fastened to the underside of the boom had been snatched away by the attached vang-preventer. The mast, however, had come up undamaged, which was the most important thing; a dismasting at sea is not a pleasant thing to contemplate.

Many blue-water boats carry a keel-stepped mast, but Marv had insisted on stepping it on the cabin-top. (Which in fact is how it is shown in Ted Brewer's original design drawings.) The main reason he had insisted on a cabin-top-stepped mast was to reduce the constant leakage that he felt always occurs around a keel-stepped mast; Creamer felt that crew morale would suffer in a wet cabin.

> *To offset whatever disadvantage the cabin-stepped mast might have had, I increased the diameter of all stays and shrouds from ¼" to ⁵⁄₁₆",*
> *mounted double headstays and double backstays, selected what I considered the best wire available—Universal Wire Company's super nitronic stainless, used STA-LOK fittings on all wire ends, lowered the mast ten and a half inches to accommodate to a one-piece aluminum extrusion, and had builder Bob Patterson weld a strong compression post between the keel and cabin top and cap it with a heavy, welded, internal plug for the mast step.*[8]

These steps taken, Marv felt that the cabin-top-stepped mast presented few risks.

The near capsize was enough for Jesse. He asked to be dropped off as soon as possible. He would have preferred New Zealand, but Marv insisted on Sydney, in order to avoid sailing down on a lee shore.

In avoiding one danger, though, they came face to face with another. On September 27, they were able to identify Green Cape Light, then opted to lie ahull until daylight. The next morning, they set sail, making a heading of west-northwest, sighted the coast again, and arrived off Brash Island under power shortly after sunrise. The weather was good that day, but in the evening, as the sky clouded over, they were still some sixty miles from Sydney. Now they had a problem—or, more accurately, a series of problems.

First, as they were nearing Sydney and the coast, sea traffic was increasing. Also, they were sailing against an adverse current of maybe two knots. Finally, while their safety depended on being close enough to shore to recognize landmarks, this left them no sea room in the event of an evening storm that might reduce visibility and spawn dangerous onshore winds.

Their options were limited. *Globe Star*'s anchor rode was too short to hold in the 150-foot-deep water. If an offshore navigation light had been present, they could have used its fixed point to maintain a position during the night, but this stretch of the Australian coastline lacked any aids to navigation. Five and thirteen miles ahead, respectively, lay unlighted Bass Point and then, just to the east of Port Kembla, a series of small, rocky, and also unlighted islands. These represented dangers that lurked unseen in the gathering darkness.

The chart showed one possibility: a tiny harbor with a navigation light at Kiama, about fifty miles south of Sydney. If they were lucky enough to find it, they might have literally found safe harbor.

They got lucky. While they were trying to decide how to make a safe entrance to the narrow harbor channel, a local fishing boat swept past them, headed for the inlet. That was an invitation too good to ignore, and they followed the trawler into the harbor at Kiama.

The boat's skipper directed Marv and the crew to a space between two boats that he thought would be vacant for the night. It was a tight fit, but Creamer managed:

> *The space between two boats required stern-to mooring and was barely wide enough to fit Globe Star between them. The maneuver called for setting a bow anchor in the middle of a narrow channel at a spot that was in line with the middle of the docking space and then turning the boat ninety degrees clockwise and backing down between the two boats. What we needed was a shoehorn or perhaps a small tug but we managed to get lined up and backed in on the second try. A line*

on each quarter secured the stern to the quay while the bow was held more or less in place by the bow anchor. Fenders placed on the beams were an absolute must.[9]

Then came the delicate matter of tension adjustment on the three lines. The frequent surges from Tasman Sea swells were funneled into the tiny harbor and sent masts swinging discordantly from side to side, so tension adjustments were both necessary and demanding, frustrating and tedious.

Eventually, *Globe Star* was settled into her berth, and the crew could get on with their other duties, chief among which, for Marv, was calling Blanche and letting her know that they had made landfall on the Australian mainland and that Jesse Edwards would be flying home.

The papers in Australia were trumpeting the news of Australia's America's Cup win, which meant that Marv, as the token Yank in the neighborhood, had to good-naturedly congratulate just about every Aussie he encountered while at Kiama. Marv had always appreciated superior seamanship though, so he felt the congratulations—while they might have stung a bit—were well deserved.

What stung more was learning that he had once again broken the law. The municipality of Kiama, NSW, it turned out, was not an official port of entry. After being dropped off by a friend at the customs office in Port Kembla, officials there drove him *back* to Kiama for a review of this latest example of flagrant outlawry. There was some back and forth—this being a bureaucratic entanglement and all—but in the end, the officials decided that Marv would not be cited because he had entered under duress. The irony here is that the duress did not consist of having sought shelter from a dangerous situation but instead was the putting ashore of a distressed seaman—Jesse Edwards and his stomach issues. The double irony, though, was that Jesse was in fact on board *Globe Star*, relatively hale and hearty, the next morning as they headed for Sydney, after having served as their excuse for a breach of regulations.

The sixty-mile trip to Sydney offered the opportunity for some cleanup and repair after the near-disastrous knockdown. Marv was able to repair and restore the starboard overhead cabin handrail, crucial for maintaining balance; if it were weak (or absent, as it currently was after

Figure 12.03. Nick Gill exploring the coast and finding whale bones.
(PHOTO BY NICK GILL. IMAGE USED WITH THE PERMISSION OF THE CREAMER FAMILY.)

the knockdown), that could result in a crewman being thrown into the pilot berth, galley stove, sink, or chart table. It turned out that the screws mounting the handrail to the cabin had been stripped out of the wooden blocks that backed them. Luckily, Marv found some stainless steel screws of appropriate size and some new backing blocks; the repair was actually stronger than the original, which was Marv's goal.

Another item of concern was the boat's eight portlights. They opened inward, which presented the possibility that water, under the tremendous pressures found in rough seas, might be forced through the sealing gaskets. (Water on the outside of a boat, Marv noted, is a lovely thing. But when it gets inside the boat, as any sailor knows, it kills morale and makes life miserable.) Luckily, Marv found a shop that could make covers out of Perspex and had them in hand the next day. And as a bonus, the proprietor threw in a custom-made shaving mirror, having heard that Marv's had broken.

On October 1, 1983, *Globe Star* finally entered Port Jackson, Sydney's harbor. It's a very busy harbor, the principal port of New South Wales, Australia, and the crew found themselves wending their way among ships, ferries, and sightseeing craft. Heading into Rushcutters Bay, they tied up at the fuel dock of the Cruising Yacht Club of Sydney, safe for now in their new temporary home.

CHAPTER 13

ACROSS THE TASMAN SEA

Traveling—it leaves you speechless, then turns you into a storyteller.
—Ibn Battuta

That temporary home almost turned out to be even more temporary than they had thought given that the official reaction to their presence was less than enthusiastic. In fact, there was some doubt that *Globe Star* would be allowed to stay at the yacht club at all: Club officials routinely turned away boats that violated the mandate requiring a twenty-four-hour watch while at sea. This even included single-handed sailors in the 1983 BOC race (since single-handed sailors, by definition, could not post a twenty-four-hour watch), and Marv was afraid that, although the *Globe Star* crew normally managed an all-day/all-night watch, the CYCS might feel that they were treading close to the line given their unfamiliar and unorthodox approach to navigation.

Not surprisingly, the official reaction to Creamer and crew was muted and cool, much like their reception at Cape Town. They did find a friend, though, in local reporter Robin Copeland, who was keenly interested in their instrument-less circumnavigation. Copeland even invited Creamer to attend a meeting of the Australian Institute of Navigation to hear a lecture by Ron Ware, who told of his reenactment of a small-boat voyage made by his famous ancestor, Captain William Bligh. Bligh's epic voyage, 3,600 nautical miles in a twenty-three-foot open boat with only seven inches of freeboard, was occasioned by the mutiny of his *Bounty* crew, who cast Bligh and eighteen crewmen adrift in 1787.[1]

Ware had built a twenty-three-foot replica of Bligh's boat and selected a crew of nine people to crew it as they sought to re-create Bligh's journey. Interestingly, while the boat fared well, the crew did not. Irreconcilable differences arose, the crew dwindled to three, and Ware found himself in much the same precarious position as his famous ancestor—but instead of casting Ware adrift, the recalcitrant crewmen simply abandoned the voyage. However, Captain Ware, like his famous ancestor, successfully completed the journey.

Creamer also gave an address to navigation officers at the Watson's Bay Royal Naval Base in Sydney. His assigned topic, per Commander John Lord, who was in charge of navigation instruction at the time, was to tell the assembled naval navigators how he managed to get to Australia without navigation instruments and how he intended to get from there to New Zealand, around Cape Horn, and then back to Cape May.[2]

Creamer enjoyed speaking with the officers, all of whom were in a position to understand both the problems Creamer and crew encountered and the solutions they applied, but he had to smile inwardly at the irony: here was an audience made up of officers who were experts in modern navigation techniques, listening intently to a speaker who had never had a navigation lesson in his life.

Creamer's encounters with the yacht club officials continued to be awkward and contributed to the frosty relations between the *Globe Star* crew and Sydney officialdom. Encountering the club's navigation officer, Gordon Marshall, the day after his talk at the naval base, the two men exchanged greetings:

As we parted I turned and asked, "By the way, Mr. Marshall, do you have any scheme for finding the polar point in the southern hemisphere?" Without hesitation he shot back, "With our method of navigation, we don't use the polar point."[3]

It seems that relations between Creamer and the yacht club officers were to remain chilly, and this was confirmed when the Sydney club's secretary, Bernie Hammel, echoed the Cape Town commodore's exact words when the crew was readying for departure from *that* club: "Well, I guess

Figure 13.01. Marv and Bob Rout in the cockpit of *Globe Star*, while docked in Sydney. (PHOTO COURTESY OF BOB ROUT.)

you'll be leaving soon." Creamer, it seemed, tended to irk establishment bureaucrats. As he said about his earlier experience at Cape Town,

> *By arriving safely after [a long] voyage without the use of the compass or any other navigation instrument, I had not only shown a contemptuous disregard for the rules but had set a very bad example for would-be practitioners of the sailing art. I deserved to be a pariah.*[4]

Of course, it's also possible that the arrival of an uninsured and unexpected transient vessel upset the yacht club hierarchy just as much as—or possibly more than—Creamer's navigation methods.

For a man who reveled in his many accolades, and who unabashedly sought recognition for his admittedly impressive accomplishments, it's odd that his status as a pariah didn't seem to bother Creamer. Perhaps he cared more for the approval of what he considered "real sailors" than for that of deskbound officials. The reality is that Marv could be contrarian and delighted in being an iconoclastic outsider; many people loved him, and he simply didn't much care about those who found him off putting.

There were last-minute details to be taken care of in Sydney. Provisions (including oatmeal, which Nick loved) needed to be bought and minor repairs to sails made, fuel tanks needed topping off, and, following Ron Ware's advice, Creamer had procured some floppy-brimmed canvas hats with pale green underlining meant to reduce burn-producing reflections that came from the more common all-white hats.

When Creamer returned to the dock after running his errands, he was in for a shock, and that shock portended—though he could not know it at the time—difficulties to come. In his absence, Nick had removed most of the provisions and supplies and was in the midst of restowing them when Creamer arrived.

Marv was a stickler for organization—he might even have been a bit of an obsessive-compulsive—and he did not take kindly to his authority being questioned. Back in Greenwich, he had stowed everything according to weight, bulk, frequency of use, and accessibility in an emergency, and here was Nick, calmly and industriously putting everything "where it belonged."

This time around, Marv held his tongue (not something he was known for doing), though he did eventually convince Nick that it wasn't a good idea to store paints and thinners in the lazarette.

The thing is that Nick was unlike some of Creamer's other crew. He didn't simply bow to the older man's experience, nor did he always keep in mind the fact that this was, after all, Creamer's boat, and that he was sailing on an expedition financed by the older man. Nick was opinionated himself, highly intelligent, and not easily cowed. He wanted to know *why* those items shouldn't be stored in the lazarette. Marv explained, probably a bit frostily, that the containers were made of lightly tinned steel that would rust through very rapidly in saltwater. Creamer had seen cabin-stored evaporated milk cans rust through and leak onto the cabin sole in less than six weeks on a trip to Africa three years earlier. Because *Globe Star*'s galley stove required lighting with matches and burned with an open flame, volatile paint thinners, having made their way to the bilge, could have created a serious risk of explosion and fire.

Still, as author and liveaboard Patricia Wood notes, Nick *was* in the wrong here, even if he meant well.

> *Especially on passages, there needs to be consistent and logical storage of safety equipment, food, tools, and spare parts so that they can be accessed quickly and easily by all the crew. There is not a lot of rear-ranging on a boat. There are so many lazarettes . . . under settees and in nooks and crannies, that if one person starts changing things it can be a huge issue. Organizing was really Marv's prerogative as the captain. Once you are satisfied where things belong or are easily found, then you keep it that way. Nick was out of line to just reorganize without the whole crew and captain's input.*[5]

Nick remembers the incident differently, contending that he was only trying to make room for a (still hypothetical) new crewmate and his gear.[6] Even given that, Marv would have thought—and many would agree—that one does not move gear around the boat without the captain's permission. Nick, though, might not have sailed offshore enough, or under enough different captains, to realize that. In any case, he was rapidly losing respect for Marv and, given the younger man's cantankerous nature, he might have chosen to move the gear regardless, just to spite Creamer.

Nick somewhat grudgingly restored the inflammable items to their original locations, but it was obvious to Creamer that Nick was not afraid of being assertive and perhaps had become more so after Jesse's withdrawal. For now, the two men put this minor difference aside and continued to work toward getting *Globe Star* ready to embark for New Zealand.

Jesse's absence left only the two of them to crew *Globe Star*, which was not the most comfortable option for either man. Really, they both wanted to find a third crewman but were reluctant to rush the process; neither was willing to settle for someone who didn't fit in. In the end, they opted to sail double handed to Whangaroa, in the far north of New Zealand.

They didn't get far. Having cranked up the engine to motor over to the fuel dock about two hundred yards away, the engine started spewing diesel out of the fuel line and onto the engine. They were in a tight spot, having already left the dock. Sails would have been useless and anchoring was out of the question. They decided to try to push on, hoping that the engine would get enough fuel to get them over to the marina where the fuel dock was located. It did, just barely. Checking over the fuel line, it became obvious that the culprit was an aluminum banjo washer damaged by corrosion. Nick managed to replace the washer while Marv bought oil, changed money, and paid bills. This leg of the trip was almost derailed by the failure of a part that in 1983 cost about 38 cents and, even now, costs only about $1.[7] Such is the nature of complex mechanisms, the performance of which can be undone by the failure of seemingly minor components.

Globe Star departed the CYCS dock at 9:30 a.m. on October 7, pulling alongside the customs boat in Watson's Bay a half hour later to allow the agents to come aboard and complete exit formalities.

By 11:00, they were free of the harbor, setting a course south of east in a northeast breeze. With a full main, yankee, and headsail, the boat moved smartly along, and Nick almost immediately announced that he was feeling poorly. They engaged the vane gear and, while Nick rested, Marv hung laundry out to dry. They were on their way to New Zealand, via the 1,200-mile-wide Tasman Sea, the northern tip of New Zealand, and then a five-thousand-mile jaunt through the Pacific's Roaring Forties and Furious Fifties before rounding the major pylon of the voyage—Cape Horn.

The little crew was feeling good. Marv thought that actually sighting the northern capes of New Zealand's North Island would be good for their peace of mind but not essential in terms of navigation. Nick was feeling better and had managed a hearty dinner. They had achieved seventy-five miles by noon on the 9th and had installed the porthole covers that they had picked up in Kiama. They felt ready for whatever weather lay ahead.

Shortly before midnight, the steering oar of the vane gear struck an unknown object, and they replaced the shear pin with a spare (their only spare, as it happened). This was probably not a problem, Creamer assured himself, because floating debris is more common near land, and they would be far out to sea. In any case, they assumed that they could find some sort of substitute if they needed one.

Easterlies dominated the wind pattern, and their point of aim on the New Zealand coast lay only slightly south of due east, so *Globe Star* was close-hauled on long tacks. More often than not, the tacks lasted half a day or more.

Progress slowed. In spite of what the *Pilot Charts* said they would encounter, the easterlies continued. On the plus side, the long tacks meant that few sail changes were necessary, which at least freed up the two men for other tasks, the first of which involved rescuing the boat's solar panels, which were behaving erratically because corrosion had eaten away at the plug receptacle at the bottom of the mast. Cleaned and greased, full charging functionality was restored, but Creamer wondered how long it would be before they would have to repeat that process. Ironically, it was a similar corrosion issue nine years earlier, though one dealing with compass light bulbs, that had given rise to Creamer's original thoughts about noninstrument navigation.

Winds veered a few days later, allowing *Globe Star* to sail due east, although the crew eventually attempted to sail somewhat north of east in order to correct for an unwanted increase in latitude. Veering east, though, meant that the boat was sailing directly into dying waves generated by previous winds, resulting in a lumpy, uncomfortable ride, one that made Creamer and Nick both feel a bit off.

By October 18, their estimated position was at variance with the ARGOS true position by only 5.3 miles—their EP was two miles north and five miles east of where ARGOS put them. On that day, the winds picked up from a typical twenty or so knots to about thirty-five knots, and it rained on and off all night. The stormy weather made them concerned

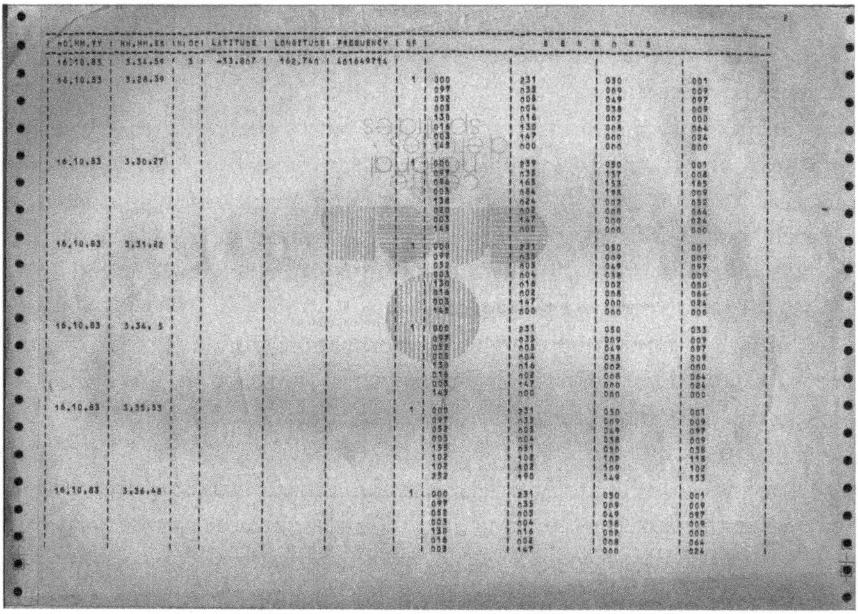

Figure 13.02. The ARGOS printout for October 13, 1983. It shows *Globe Star*'s location as −33.807, 162.740: in the Tasman Sea, just about midway between Sydney and Auckland, New Zealand. (IMAGE REPRODUCED WITH PERMISSION OF ROWAN UNIVERSITY.)

about their proximity to New Zealand. They should be getting close, and the continued turbulent weather—which went on all the next day—made visibility difficult. It would be nice, Marv thought, if the wind died down a bit and the water calmed so that they could see land approaching in the moonlight.

That didn't happen. Instead the winds picked up to about fifty knots on the morning of the 20th, forcing them to furl their triple-reefed main, which was the only sail they had up; they feared the consequences of another knockdown. They had escaped previous knockdowns with only minor damage, but both men knew that they'd been lucky; a knockdown in rough seas could result in injury and severe damage—perhaps even a dismasting, in spite of the pains Creamer had taken to make the somewhat shortened mast and accompanying rigging stronger than most.

Rigger Herb Benavent commented on *Globe Star*'s mast and rigging: "Having a shorter mast isn't really much of a hindrance because, at sea, it blows so much almost all the time. By having a shorter rig, it's less bendy, and being deck-stepped it's probably the equivalent stiffness that it would have been if it were full sized, but with fewer issues, since it's not keel stepped."[8]

Creamer had felt that a somewhat shortened mast—complemented by more stays and strong rigging—would enhance the boat's ability to withstand rough waters, and Benavent agrees. So far, he had been correct: neither strong winds, nor rough seas, nor multiple knockdowns had damaged *Globe Star*'s mast or rigging in any significant fashion.

By the 21st, winds were from the north, so, even though some rain continued, visibility was improved, and Nick and Marv were feeling a little better, knowing that it was less likely that they'd run into New Zealand, lurking in the mist.

When the sky cleared, they were able to hoist sails—triple-reefed main, staysail, and, in quick succession, a storm jib and then the working jib. They set a course for (as best they could tell) about 20 degrees north of east in winds of about twenty knots. Soon the water turned from blue to green, a sign that land was near. Sure enough, about 2:00 a.m., they spotted the Tauroa Point light near the northern tip of New Zealand, and their earlier gloom was transformed into euphoria: New Zealand was in their grasp.

Trying to get around North Island, about forty miles to the north, they motored northward. At first, the weather was fine, clear and moonlit. By daylight, though, they were groping their way forward in heavy cloud cover, rain, and mist, using swell and wind direction to maintain their heading. There seemed to be no immediate threat of gales, but they labored to get in the lee of the rocky headlands, just in case. As they moved closer to land, they were greeted by porpoises, petrels, shearwaters, and an occasional albatross, wheeling and diving as it hunted for food.

They opted for a quick stay at North Island: Marv wanted to see if there was a dentist available to check on a recurring toothache, and Nick was obliging, if for no other reason, just to see something other than rolling mountains of blue water.

Figure 13.03. *Globe Star* on the Derwent River in Hobart, Tasmania.
(PHOTO COURTESY OF THE CREAMER FAMILY.)

The two men piloted *Globe Star* around North Cape, looking for the sheltered harbor with the range lights that was noted on their charts, but couldn't find anything except an entrance blocked by sandbars and breaking surf. Given the calm weather, they didn't see any need to chance an entry there.

That evening, they were on the lee side of North Island and winds were gentle, but in the morning, a steady drizzle set in; it was not good weather for finding an obscure inlet. There were really two options: Whangaroa, which from Marv's reading of Eric Hiscock sounded like a paradise, and Russell, in the Bay of Islands. Nick preferred Russell, which was the harbor most used by small-boat sailors, but Marv pushed for Whangaroa because its location meant not having to spend another night at sea. They actually might have missed the entrance nonetheless had they not spotted another sailboat "that seemed to be sailing right out of the rocks."[9]

They motored idly along, taking in the luxuriant beauty of the vegetation on the steep hillsides, finally tying up at Fisherman's Pier about 11:00 on Sunday morning.

CHAPTER 14

TO THE HORN WITH A NEW CREWMAN, MORE CONFLICTS

Half the fun of travel is the esthetic of lostness.

—Ray Bradbury

GLOBE STAR MADE IT SAFELY TO WHANGAROA, BUT MANY VESSELS HAVE not. The seas are vicious there, with wind sometimes in excess of forty-eight knots (and with even stronger gusts) and waves well over fifteen feet and swells much higher than that. Even veteran sailors have come to a bad end near Whangaroa.

On June 6, 1983, not long before *Globe Star* made landfall there, racing yacht *Lion Heart* foundered in the heavy seas off Whangaroa, and seven people died. More recently (October 2019), a forty-seven-foot yacht sank in bad weather off of Cape Brett, killing the skipper. His wife and two crewmembers survived.

Nonetheless, Creamer and crew managed to find and enter the well-hidden harbor with no real problems, helped along by an outbound sailboat whose track they followed. But Creamer once again found himself battling officialdom. (He seemed always to be battling officialdom. Perhaps it was just something in his nonconformist nature.) Upon arrival, Creamer dutifully telephoned the authorities and was informed in no uncertain terms that he should seal *Globe Star*'s fridge—a measure that eventually resulted in some terrible odors permeating the cabin—and that it would take a while for customs officials to meet them, as they were some eighty miles distant.

Deciding to live with the sealed refrigerator, Marv and Nick got on with the business of restocking, provisioning, and refueling. The most pressing issue, though, was finding a third crewmember.

Against all odds, a potential crewman showed up at the dock, "just to chat." Bob Rout was an irrigation engineer whose wife, Val Robertson, was a teacher at a nearby school. Nick filled them in on the particulars while Marv was out running errands. An hour later, Rout showed up to invite them to dinner and treated the pair to much-needed showers.

It was definitely a change from sparse shipboard fare eaten in cramped quarters. Sprawling on thick carpets, listening to music on the stereo, helping themselves to seconds of roast chicken with all the fixings, the crew made themselves at home and enjoyed both the food and the conversation.

Early the next morning, Bob showed up at the dock and asked to join up. Marv looked at him and said, "Bob, you know we are sailing completely without instruments, don't you?" His response was immediate: "You got this far, didn't you?"[1]

Without even placing an ad or doing any formal interviews, *Globe Star* had found her third crewmember.

After feasting on crayfish (rock lobster) brought to them by neighborly fishermen, Marv was determined to have someone see to his painful tooth, so he ended up hitchhiking the twenty miles to a local dentist's office. The irritating cavity duly filled, Creamer splurged on a haircut, some long johns, some small tools, and some groceries.

One thing Creamer had neglected to do was to pick up oatmeal, Nick's favorite, so Nick took care of that when he went into town with Bob Rout—adding still more oatmeal to the ten gallons or so already on board. One gets the feeling from Creamer's notes that he felt ten gallons was more than enough, but, for a second time, he held his tongue.

However, he was unable—or unwilling—to hold his tongue when the next conflict arose. Since they had left Cape May, Marv had been sleeping in the quarter berth, a bit confining for him and certainly not the premium sleeping spot on a boat that, after all, he owned and skippered.

When Nick saw me moving my personal items, he told me that Bob should be assigned the pilot berth which was above and offset outward from the portside settee berth where Nick slept. He was afraid the quarter berth would be too wet. I had endured a few drenchings of salt water in it but felt that the plastic curtain . . . which we had installed on our way across the Tasman would shield the bunk in all but the most severe conditions. I felt we needed the pilot berth as a staging area because it was at eye level and well lighted. Moreover, almost all of our provisions, packed in heavy plastic five-gallon containers, were stored directly below. If someone were asleep in the pilot berth, he would have to be disturbed whenever we wanted to get at the provisions. To me it made much better sense to put Bob in the quarter berth and move him temporarily on occasion if conditions there became intolerable.[2]

Nick continued to argue, and Marv finally resorted to the "nuclear option." He said, "Nick, is this your way of telling me that you don't want to go any farther?"[3]

Nick said, no, that was not what he meant, and he stood down. He was simmering though. This was not the last time conflict would erupt between the two, and six weeks and five thousand miles later, Nick would remind Marv that the older man had "bludgeoned" him on that day.

About 1:00 p.m. the next day, the crew raised the yankee, cast off their lines, and glided toward the inlet, about six miles away. As they pulled away, a Maori man they had met earlier appeared in front of them in his outboard and made them a gift of a basket of freshly dredged scallops. Bob was an old hand at scallops; he had them cooked and on the table almost before *Globe Star* was out of the inlet. In the meantime, Marv and Nick set a course to the southeast in order to clear Taheke Rock.

Marv was feeling confident in his boat and his crew—notwithstanding a few contretemps with Nick. He felt that they should be able to sail the five thousand miles to Cape Horn with no major catastrophes, and given the longer (and warmer) days, they should be able to make much of it in daylight.

Figure 14.01. Bob Rout on the foredeck, handling sails.
(PHOTO COURTESY OF BOB ROUT.)

Then again, they had yet to encounter the Roaring Forties or the Furious Fifties, and they expected mountainous seas where the current runs strong over the shelf between Antarctica and South America. Of course, this was the trip that Nick and Bob had dreamed of: rounding the fabled Horn! Their dream was about to come true, assuming that all went well.

Although their primary aim was to clear the southern tip of South America, Creamer hoped that they'd be able to pick up some sort of longitudinal clues—steepening waves, bird or sea life, or water color—that would enable them to find the Falklands or make their way safely around Shag Rocks, six small islands in western Georgia.

The plan was to sail east until they had passed Cape Runaway and East Cape and then angle south into the Roaring Forties; that would, they hoped, give them steady winds for the Pacific crossing. They could always ease up on the southward dip if they ran into severe weather. "As we sensed ourselves nearing the South American coast we would move smartly southward and then level off to straight east for the run through Drake Passage past Cape Horn," Creamer said.[4]

Note Creamer's words: "As we sensed ourselves nearing the South American coast. . . ." These are the words of a man who is comfortable quite literally *sensing* where he is—using his five basic senses to locate himself in the world. This is a phrase with which most modern navigators, with their GPS, chart plotters, AIS, radar, and other electronic devices—let alone a sextant—would be most uncomfortable. But Creamer wasn't most navigators; he was a throwback, and purposely so. He aimed to find his way around the world the way he was sure the ancients had, using their brains, their eyes, their senses of taste and smell. He aimed to truly *sense* his way around the world, and he was now more than midway through proving that it could be done.

At the turning point, Creamer planned to find the required latitude by noting the intensity of twilight at the time of the December solstice: If they were far enough south to clear the Cape, the sun would set, twilight would occur, and the sun would rise with no intervening period of complete darkness. Creamer's task now was to develop a set of mental keys for judging the quality of twilight by observing the filling in of shadows in wave and wavelet troughs as the sun approached the horizon from below the surface. This meant judging twilight under deeply overcast, lightly overcast, and clear sky conditions.

The sail became what Creamer termed "a jolly romp on the ocean." In spite of a broken tiller and a damaged self-steerer, things went smoothly:

> *Life on board became a blending of rhythms paced by the rolling motion of downwind sailing. Light air and gales passed over us with predictable regularity and routines of cooking, eating, sleeping, watch keeping, and sail handling patterned our daily lives. We felt sorry for all the people on earth who would never know the sheer joy of a small-boat ocean crossing.*[5]

Bob was in his element. He was, according to Creamer, anyway, quite happy in the quarter berth "close to the hatch . . . near the sea that he loved."[6] During the first full day at sea, Bob caught a fifteen-pound black-fin tuna. Marv processed seven pints in the pressure cooker (the stove was apparently working at the moment), fried some up, and had a bit left over for tuna salad. Salad dressing on the tuna steaks acted as a marinade and spice, and the fried tuna that resulted tasted delicious—a lot like halibut, according to Marv's journal.

Bob was a deft hand—though lacking in blue-water experience—and an experienced loftsman, so he was a welcome addition to the crew. But he also served another function: Given the ongoing conflicts between Nick and Marv, and the explosive blowups that simmered just beneath the surface of both men, Bob acted as a buffer between the two. By this time, Nick was speaking to Marv as seldom as possible. Because Bob got along well with both Nick and Marv, he could often be counted upon to keep things running smoothly aboard *Globe Star*, even when tempers frayed.

The food adventures continued, with Marv making pancakes using baking mix, flour, baking soda, an egg, and some of the sour milk left over from their adventure with the sealed fridge. These were Bob's first pancakes, and he ate six. Nick loved them and ate at least a dozen.

The next morning Nick and Bob each landed a tuna, and Marv processed them in the pressure cooker again. Dinner was tuna dipped in

Figure 14.02. Marv and one of the many tunas the crew caught, November 1983.
(PHOTO COURTESY OF BOB ROUT.)

egg and bread crumbs and then fried. The same thing happened the *next* morning, when they landed another couple of fifteen pounders.

It was an embarrassment of tuna. What in the world would they do with it all? One answer had been provided by Ron Ware, William Bligh's descendent, during his presentation. Ware had mentioned that tuna were easily caught in the Pacific, and he recommended cutting the meat into strips and drying it in the rigging. Bob and Nick thought that was a fine idea, and for the next several days *Globe Star* was gaily—if somewhat mal-odorously—festooned with strips of tuna strung between the two backstays.

Some confusion ensued when the crew realized that they had crossed the International Date Line, ending up with two November seconds. They were at a bit of a loss until someone suggested labeling them November 2A and November 2B, and that's how they were recorded in the log.

Back home, Blanche's brother, who had access to the ARGOS data, noted with consternation that *Globe Star*'s longitude was *decreasing*. Panic stricken, he called Blanche and told her that Marv must be in trouble and heading back to New Zealand. Blanche in turn called Lee Houchins, the Washington coordinator and Smithsonian project manager, who explained what had happened: *Globe Star* had run eastern longitude up to the maximum of 180 degrees and had begun a traverse of western lon-gitude that *decreased* daily from a maximum of 180 degrees as they sailed eastward. Panic was averted, but there were undoubtedly some sheepish looks back home.

Everything was going smoothly, except that the crew now had a toilet problem. Earlier, a wad of toilet paper had gotten stuck in the marine head and then eventually jammed such that the seacock would not close completely. There was no immediate danger, but it did introduce the pos-sibility of flooding the bilge, or worse. Bob, being an irrigation engineer, had given the matter much thought, and he proposed connecting the intake line from the manual bilge pump to the line leading to the seacock and then pumping clear the line by reversing the flow. The plan worked, and Bob was a hero because for the past several days, the crew had been using a bucket for a head.

Nick, meanwhile, was finding ways to get under Marv's (admittedly thin) skin. While he insisted that potatoes, dirty though they may be, had

Figure 14.03. *Globe Star* leaving Whangaroa Harbor, New Zealand, in October 1983. (PHOTO COURTESY OF BOB ROUT.)

to be served with skins on, apple skins were not tolerated in applesauce. Back when Jesse was on board, Marv had bought Weet-Bix (a whole-grain wheat cereal high in fiber and apparently low in any other appealing qualities) for him because Jesse did not care for Nick's beloved oatmeal.[7] When Nick ran across some Weet-Bix, his comment was "What's this shit?!" Marv explained, and Nick told him that he was never to feed it to him. Then one morning when asked if he wanted oatmeal, his response was, "I don't want any more of that shit!" When Marv asked him what he should do with the many gallons of oatmeal they had on board, Nick's response was a cool, "Feed it to your next crew." Nick's standard breakfast after that was Weet-Bix. (Of course, Marv got back at him by incorporating some of the oatmeal supply into the bread he baked almost daily; Nick, who loved the bread, was eating oatmeal—he just didn't know it.)

Food was becoming a bone of contention, so to speak. Neither Nick nor Bob cared for the canned beef they had brought along. The two younger men were worried about "protein poisoning," which Marv dismissed as a trendy concern probably, or so he maintained, popularized in "commonly read, perhaps non-mainstream" magazines.[8] As it turns out, protein poisoning, also known as "rabbit starvation," appears to be very real—one cannot subsist on rabbit meat for very long, for example, because the body needs fats and other nutrients that rabbit meat lacks.[9] Protein poisoning is definitely an issue in certain rare circumstances, even if rabbit meat is not involved. It arises, says Registered Dietician Nutritionist Allison Jeter, "when one gets enough calories from food but one's body can still become malnourished due to lack of other nutrients—carbs, fats, minerals, vitamins, etc." This sort of "poisoning" could lead to GI upset, headaches, or, in extreme cases, even death. "A balance of macronutrients (carbs-proteins-fats) is key for best health outcomes," says Jeter.[10]

Nick, as it happens, thinks that the whole "protein poisoning" issue was overblown.[11] He contends that he—and to some extent Bob—simply did not care to have meat with every meal. Marv was a meat-and-potatoes sort of guy; meat at every meal, or at least with every dinner, was the norm for him. Nick says now, though, that when he sailed with Marv, he was pretty much a vegetarian, growing sprouts on board, taking supplements, etc., and was loath to eat meat in any case, except when he had to.[12] The reality is that the crew was actually getting multiple forms of carbohydrates and vitamins in the form of cereals, bread, potatoes, and so on, so "protein poisoning" was unlikely.

One source of protein that is *also* rich in other nutrients is fish, of which they had plenty. There was, for instance, an ongoing and apparently never-ending surfeit of tuna. The crew ate it steamed (a bit chewy), dried (even chewier), fried (quite tasty), and baked (a bit dry). They had tuna salad, slumgullion (tuna stew, more or less), and tuna chowder. For days, it was tuna for lunch, for dinner, and occasionally for breakfast. Oddly enough, while Marv got tired of it (and didn't care at all for either the dried tuna strips or the slumgullion), Nick and Bob loved it all—except for the baked version, which everyone agreed was just too dry to be palatable.

Figure 14.04. Bob Rout and one of the many tunas that were caught on this leg of the voyage. (PHOTO BY NICK GILL. IMAGE USED WITH THE PERMISSION OF THE CREAMER FAMILY.)

Figure 14.05. The baker at sea. Marv prepared dozens of loaves of bread and countless pies during the *Globe Star* voyage. (PHOTO BY NICK GILL. USED WITH THE PERMISSION OF THE CREAMER FAMILY.)

There was also plenty of fruit aboard, at least for the time being. Marv made applesauce (no skins, of course, at Nick's insistence) and apple pie; there were so many apple pies that the Pacific leg of the trip became known as "the apple pie leg." There were oranges and grapefruit brought on board as gifts from friends in New Zealand. With some help from Bob (who made scones), and using some freeze-dried strawberries, they even managed to have something approximating strawberry shortcake with lunch one day.

And there were more pies to come, but of a different sort. November 13, 1983, was a red-letter day for Marv: On that day, he baked his first-ever pizza pie, using white bread dough as a base for the crust, with toppings of stewed tomatoes, canned mackerel, onions, and garlic. It was a huge hit—although one wonders just how hungry one has to be to enjoy canned mackerel on a pizza. This was followed a couple of days later with a tuna pizza (naturally), and then a pizza made with oregano and chili powder.

Marv's dedication to serving decent food aboard *Globe Star* was impressive and unswerving, even if the occasionally baffling combinations reflected the somewhat limited contents of their larder.

In early November, Marv noted in his journal that they were making good time, even taking into account the extra week they'd had to wait for Bob to finish up some last-minute items and get a leave from his job so that he could join them. (One reason that Marv had figured the lost time could be made up was that, with a third hand aboard, they could make more frequent and more efficient sail changes than if they were double handing.)

Heading for their date with the Horn, they had covered some 890 miles since leaving Whangaroa. Their estimated latitude, it turned out, was in error by twenty-two miles, while their longitude was off by 120 miles. Overall, their estimated position was 122 miles west-northwest of their actual position, according to the ARGOS data they examined later.

They were now feeling the effects of the Southern Ocean's southwesterly swells, which resulted in "bed sheeting" the sails fairly regularly, and the air was becoming noticeably cooler. Soon, winds became stronger and more consistent. They were gradually working their way south, but also trying to move eastward. From Marv's journal of November 14:

> We are aiming for c.47° south where we plan to sail east until we get to c.100° west where we will begin to work our way south to c.57° south to clear Cape Horn. . . . We are really pounding out the miles! And in the right direction. Log says we are about 45° south and we have decided with good air to head east for a while. If air lightens we will angle off to the south. Right now c.1600 we are doing about 5k east with the yankee and triple-reefed main.[13]

Unfortunately, the ARGOS transmitter was once again giving them trouble. The indicator light was growing weaker by the day and, while they had a workable backup transmitter wired to the boat's batteries ready to go, that transmitter appeared to garble weather information in transmission. As a stopgap, Bob and Creamer replaced the batteries in the "good" transmitter; Nick punched in some weather and position information, and it emitted a strong green light, signaling a successful transmission. For now, they decided that the tracking equipment was doing its job.

As they slid into the Roaring Forties, the winds had shifted from northerly to southerly, which brought in crisp, cold air—and occasionally some blue sky—from the Antarctic.

On the boat, though, things were getting hot once again, and, as usual, friction between Marv and Nick was to blame. Marv, who was suffering from a bit of a head cold, wanted at least one of the hatch boards inserted, in order to stop some of the cold air circulating below. When he asked Bob to put the lower hatch board in, Bob couldn't find the board. The two men were worried that it had somehow gone overboard, but when Nick woke up, he told them that he had put it in a cockpit locker.

Marv was infuriated. He angrily asked Nick what would have happened if they had been rolled over, with water pouring in the hatch and no way to access the misplaced hatch board?! They could have drowned, Marv felt, all because Nick was trying to be neat. Marv had, he said, made it very clear that he wanted at least the bottom board in when in cold weather or rough seas, so to his mind, Nick was countermanding his instructions. Marv would have felt that this was, at best, sloppy seamanship, or at worst, a dereliction of duty—perhaps something akin to mutinous behavior.

The reality is that Marv, obsessed as he was with achieving his goal, and Nick, mercurial and not always the most diplomatic, were bound to have issues with one another. As Marv's daughter, Lynn, has noted about her own relationship with her father, he sometimes had "a rigidity about his opinion being the right way to do something—it was right or wrong, not just a different perspective or different way of looking at a problem or idea. This judgment could limit creative interactions or discussion."[14] We can assume that, while Marv dearly loved Lynn and the rest of his children, Nick was simply crew: a colleague at best, a hired hand (albeit an unpaid one) at worst. He could—and often did—treat his children with sensitivity and tenderness, but he was not likely to treat the obstreperous Nick the same way.

Later, Marv felt some regret about coming down so hard on Nick, but he felt strongly that the younger man had compromised their safety. The two men cooled off, but communications were strained afterward.

CHAPTER 15

ON TO THE HORN

Life is either a daring adventure, or nothing at all.

—HELEN KELLER

By mid-November, the winds were more or less directly behind *Globe Star*, and the three men were being propelled rapidly toward their goal. On the 19th, they made 150 miles of easting; the Roaring Forties were living up to their reputation. If this kept up, within a week they should be halfway from New Zealand to the Horn.

The next day, the winds abated a bit and Bob replaced the staysail with the working jib. Nick gave him a hand, and Marv noted in his journal that, whatever issues he himself might be having with Nick, the two younger men worked well together. They even teamed up to give Marv the night off from galley duty. Bob made supper, which consisted of veal in sauce over mashed potatoes with carrots and onions, with apple pie for dessert. Nick did the dishes, and Marv appreciated the opportunity to relax.

That Nick and Bob got along well makes sense. They were young men with similar interests and experiences. Nick, to be sure, seemed more brittle and combative than Bob, who was very laid-back and seemed to get along with everyone. Years later, Nick would say, "Bob and I had a good relationship on *Globe Star*; you couldn't ask for a better ocean buddy than Bob. When we got off in Port Stanley [after rounding the cape] we island hopped in the Falklands for a few weeks before joining the BAS [British Antarctic Survey] ship *John Biscoe*, which took us south to the South Shetlands and South Georgia and dropped us in Rio."[1] The two

Figure 15.01. The BAS (British Antarctic Survey), on whose ship (the *John Briscoe*) Nick and Bob traveled to Antarctica, maintains several research stations there. This is a photo of the *RRS James Clark Ross Rothera*, which replaced the *John Briscoe* in 1991. (IMAGE USED UNDER THE TERMS OF THE GNU FREE DOCUMENTATION LICENSE, COURTESY OF USER: *TOM L-C.*)

became good friends on the trip, and Nick even sailed again with Bob a couple of years later in New Zealand. But Bob was able to get along with Marv. He knew that Marv had what Bob called "strong views" about things. But, said Bob, "In those areas that I don't agree with, I don't debate. There's no point. And particularly when you live in close quarters with people, you've got to have some boundaries. My attitude was, I was there for a very positive reason, and I wanted to be part of it; the boat needs good harmony to work. There's no point having fights with people, because you're going to wake up and be in the cockpit with them tomorrow morning."[2]

Nick, on the other hand, was not always able—or perhaps willing—to avoid debate and, with Nick, the debates occasionally became rancorous.

It was a matter of temperament; Nick was constitutionally unable to agree with Marv solely because Marv was older and arguably more experienced. (And because it was, after all, Marv's boat and Marv's money paying for the voyage.) Nick needed to have his say, and he was not shy about contradicting Marv or complaining about the way he was treated. Of course, Nick was an adult and an experienced sailor; he *deserved* to have his say— but he was not always diplomatic about it, and Marv was not always willing to listen to contrary views in any case.

Later, Nick would comment, "Our differences came about mainly because we had our own way of doing things. Both of us were pretty headstrong, and also I tend to speak out rather than suppress."[3]

So far, all three men had been able to bury any serious divisions and continue working as a team. But would that continue?

As they neared the Horn, various strategies were discussed. In view of the strong southerlies of the past week that would have mitigated against much in the way of southward movement, they decided to take advantage of any southwesterlies to easterlies and move southward and eastward whenever they could. The *Pilot Charts* and the British *Routeing Charts* both showed fewer gales at the latitude of the Horn than further north, so they opted to head south when possible, keeping in mind that this would also mean cooler temperatures.

Things picked up on the 22nd and 23rd when the seas began to build. On the 23rd, *Globe Star* was moving smartly along on a broad reach in what looked like the beginnings of a gale. Still, they were making good time and were heading southeast, which was the direction they wanted.

The gale, when it came, was a knockout. They estimated steady wind speeds of thirty-five and forty knots, with sustained gusts of forty-five and fifty knots. They had been broad reaching—nearly running—on the starboard tack since before dawn of the 23rd, and seas were lumpy until they had accommodated to the new wind direction. The rough seas scrubbed any thought of making a pumpkin pie for the Thanksgiving holiday— which probably wouldn't have meant much to Bob and Nick, in any case, hailing as they did from New Zealand and Australia, respectively—so they made do with Scotch broth (a thick, filling soup containing beef or lamb and barley and other vegetables), boiled potatoes, and more of what seemed to be an endless but welcome supply of apple pie. Given the weather, this was a "three-step meal."

On Thanksgiving Day, *Globe Star* was 2,695 miles from Whangaroa, and her estimated position was about 251 miles southwest of her actual position. Their estimated latitude was off by 127 miles, and their longitude by 221 miles.

The storm ended before midnight, and good sailing—and cooking—conditions returned. Bob made a soufflé that he served with baked potatoes, so not only were culinary conditions improving, but Marv got another break from cooking. They were making a good seven or eight knots, but because they were surfing down a following sea in a stiff northwester, they would soon be forced to reduce sail.

Water temperatures continued to drop (it was now 50 degrees Fahrenheit, the lowest so far on this leg), and gales were coming again. On the 26th, Marv noted in his log,

> *Sailed downwind with poled out head sails during the period. Began with yankee and working jib, then working jib and staysail, then working jib, and finally staysail and storm jib. Gale conditions after c.1700 and up to noon (and beyond). Heavy seas with cross waves and breaking crests. Waves to 25' and winds 35k+. Speed 7–8 knots. Heading between 120° and 135°. EP at noon 49° 21'S. 127° 58'W.*[4]

As the wind eased, *Globe Star* yawed more and more, rolling downwind at about seven knots. Sleeping was tough while rolling downwind, but Marv noted that at least it provided some respite from being repeatedly banged and thrown about the cabin.

When the seas settled, though, another issue became apparent. Marv was an experienced seaman, a man who had sailed more than thirty thousand nautical miles even before he set off on *Globe Star*. He was used to rough water—he could sail in it, cook in it, eat in it, even sleep in it. What he found aggravating, though, was the deceptiveness of a sea that appeared smooth as glass but that was, as always, heaving. You could be thrown off balance, perhaps even end up overboard, in the middle of what appeared to be a "calm" sea.

Of course, the ocean is never *really* calm. The ocean "breathes," and in its breath we see and feel the sea surge and flow, sometimes gentle and hypnotic, sometimes fierce and brutal. This is undoubtedly a poetically anthropomorphic view, but it's not *just* poetic. Grant Deane, director of the Hydraulics Laboratory at UC San Diego, speaks of the sound of breaking waves—which is really, he says, the sound of air breaking into bubbles, "each one of which rings with its own tone, large low and small high." He notes that "their chorus forms a hissing roar, and provides an audible clue to the number and size" of those bubbles.[5] The breaking bubbles—and the breaking waves of which they are a part—form an air-sea interface in which gasses are transferred from one to the other, changing the color of the water, making underwater noise, and scavenging organic surfactants that, rising to the surface, create surfactant-enriched aerosols. All of which is to say that the ocean is never *really* calm; it's alive, constantly inhaling and exhaling, sometimes gently but sometimes not, giving life to the planet as it once gave life to us. There's an awful lot going on at and beneath the surface of the sea. Why would we expect it to be placid and docile?

Experienced sailors talk about getting their "sea legs," the ability to walk steadily on the deck of a vessel, even though that deck is constantly moving. Marv usually used the term "rubber knees," and he likened it to a type of tentativeness born of knowing that the deck may change position between the time you lift your foot and the time it next falls. Of course, "one hand for the boat" is the time-honored and sensible maxim used to remind us that an abrupt shift could send you sprawling. As Marv put it, "Swaying with the motion and letting it flow through the body is another way of coping with what at times resembles living in a giant tumble-action washing machine."[6]

On *Globe Star*, sleeping was made more comfortable—or at least possible—with the use of lee cloths, heavy fifteen-inch-wide pieces of sailcloth that kept captain and crew from being unceremoniously dumped to the cabin sole. With practice, a sailor can brace himself, lying with his knees wedged against the canvas. As the boat pitches and rolls, one can observe a sleeping crewman's arms and legs retract as needed to maintain balance and position, all while the sleeper is completely unaware of this activity. It's a tribute to the adaptability of men and women who sail the seas that they are able to sleep under such conditions.

The period of gales was followed, not surprisingly, by a frustrating lack of wind, and on November 27, *Globe Star* was slatting in an almost dead calm, while fifteen-foot swells banged the sails against shrouds and stays. At least it was peaceful, a respite after the past few days of wild sailing.

The captain and crew of *Globe Star* decided to have a holiday. Today, as near as they could figure, would be the day that they reached the half-way mark in longitude between Whangaroa and the Horn, so a party of some sort was called for. They opted for a noon picnic: potato salad, hot corn, deviled eggs, and fresh white cake with chocolate frosting. (Bob and Marv mixed the cake with an electric drill rigged up with a beater.) This was followed by a dinner of baked beans, scones, and applesauce.

Light air bedeviled them again the next day, and while they appreciated the chance to do some cleanup, they were frustrated that they were barely making steerageway. On the 28th, the wind picked up toward evening and they flew downwind, first with the chute and then with a double head rig in which, as necessary, a larger sail was replaced by a smaller one as wind speed rose. When they raised the working jib after dark, the leech was torn when it got caught on the hanks of the staysail, so Nick repaired it the next morning.

In addition to the damaged sail, the next day brought with it two problems. The first was that, while the *Globe Star*'s log showed their latitude to be 51°08'S, Creamer and crew did not believe that they were that far south.

> We've been plagued with weeks of cloudy weather so our estimates of direction have been inaccurate and nighttime latitude sights have been impossible. We should be getting closer to the latitude of Canopus, c.52° S.[7]

The other problem was food—again. The crew were turning up their collective noses at the Chunky Vegetable Beef and Beef Vegetable soups that Creamer had stowed. The secret, Marv discovered, was to disguise them, combining the two soups and perking them up with canned, mashed tomatoes, a can of mushrooms, some fresh cooked onions, and a bit of garlic. This was a hit, but Marv had to be wondering how many more times he'd have to put up with food-related near mutinies, especially given that he had tried so hard to provide a variety of nutritious, tasty foods. (One also has to wonder what, exactly, is the difference between a soup named Beef Vegetable and one labeled Vegetable Beef.)

By November 30th, they were in the Furious Fifties, and they were taking a beating. Marv noted that they averaged on that day about six knots downwind, and gales behind them created building seas that sent them surfing into troughs. The banging noises from inside the cabin were horrendous; the three men could only imagine what sort of damage was being done.

The overcast skies and driving rain precluded getting a decent view of the stars. It cleared up just before daybreak, but not in time for the meridian transit of Canopus and tau Puppis—the stars they wanted to use for latitude.

Just after midnight they encountered their latest calamity—which, looking back at it, could have been much worse. A monstrous breaking wave from astern crashed down on the cockpit, engulfed Bob, slammed open the sliding hatch, and cascaded torrentially into the cabin. Marv was on his bunk at the time and later said that it sounded like a mountain river as it roared past his bunk and came to a halt in the V-notch of the fo'c'sle. Fortunately, both hatch boards were in place (as Marv no doubt made sure to point out to Nick), but even so, the bilge was filled. Worse yet, the self-steerer was once again out of commission. One positive result of the dangerous mishap was that Bob, when he got off watch, was so keyed up that he made everyone a breakfast of pancakes and then baked an apple pie. (If there were skeins of wool aboard, one assumes that he would then have knitted sweaters for everyone, given his nervous energy after the near disaster.)

The weather was getting colder as they approached Cape Horn, and they were pelted with sleet around noon that day. It was cold enough for Nick to ask for a bowl of hot vegetable beef after he got off watch. Marv archly observed in his notes that Nick had apparently upgraded the soup from "shit" to "good soup."

Gales continued, and *Globe Star* barreled downwind with the storm jib and staysail both poled out.[8] It was rough and uncomfortable but, to Marv's eye, "sailable." Creamer had thought about the crashing seas of the past several days and came to believe that they were a product of the underwater configuration of the mid-Pacific Ridge, an underwater mountain system formed by plate tectonics. If so, then their estimate of longitude was pretty close to perfect, and shallower water should soon become apparent.

After getting a good look at Canopus and tau Puppis on the night of December 1, they realized that—as they suspected—they had overestimated their latitude, and so corrected their log. If their current pace continued, they should make Drake Passage in about two weeks. Their intent was to stay south of the Horn and Diego Ramirez because of deeper, and therefore less dangerous, water. At the same time, they needed to stay alert and recognize any signs that they were passing from the Pacific into the Atlantic. Most sailors, even forty years ago, would have had a fairly accurate notion of when they crossed that point, but Creamer and crew—lacking navigational instruments—would have to look for often subtle indications: water color change, bird life, bioluminescence, or the presence of icebergs or even pack ice.[9]

Before that, though, came another disaster and another test of the crew's resourcefulness. Just before midnight on December 2, Nick poked his head in the cabin and said, "Marv, the tiller just broke off."

Creamer couldn't believe that was possible, but Nick was right. The boat's stainless steel tiller was, in Marv's words, "hanging by a thin strip of metal that looked like the foil from a chewing gum wrapper," and it fell into his hands as he took hold of it.[10]

Bob Patterson had built that tiller into a supposedly indestructible monster. It was, he said, guaranteed never to break—bend, maybe, but not break. But here it was, in the middle of the Pacific Ocean, lying in Marv's hand with less than a three-inch tube left attached to the rudder post.

There was an inside steering station where they could insert a temporary tiller, but that would only work in relatively calm seas. In rough water, the inside tiller had neither the throw nor the leverage to keep *Globe Star* from yawing off and broaching in a gale.

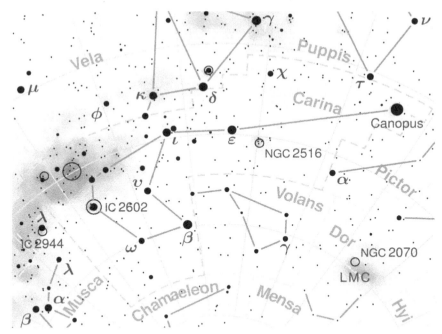

Figure 15.02. *Canopus* (at right, near the upper third of the image) is the brightest star in the constellation Carina, in the southern night sky. Creamer used it and its companion star, Puppis, to determine latitude. (IMAGE USED UNDER THE CREATIVE COMMONS ATTRIBUTION-SHARE ALIKE 3.0 UNPORTED LICENSE, COURTESY OF USER: *KXX*.)

At the moment, things were fairly tranquil, so there was some time to effect a repair of some sort, if they could come up with one. It had to be soon though; they had just entered the Furious Fifties and were approaching the Horn, which was notoriously stormy. Some kind of jury rig was called for, but it had to be robust and reliable.

Creamer's original plans had called for including a photographer/cinematographer to document the expedition, but the photographers they had interviewed had all eventually dropped out. (Not really being sailors, we might assume that the various photographers were understandably uncomfortable with the idea of sailing the globe without using navigation equipment.) However, there was as a result some unused photographic equipment on board, including a camera mounting bracket made up of several pieces of stainless steel tubing that could be used for an internal

Figure 15.03. Rough seas in the Pacific. (PHOTO COURTESY OF THE CREAMER FAMILY.)

splice. There was also a solid cube of stainless steel that would make a handy sledgehammer.

While Nick manned the inside tiller, Bob and Marv went to work with hacksaws. It took about an hour and a half to fit one piece of tubing inside another and then hammer both pieces into the stub still welded to the rudder post. The two men then drove the remaining section of the original tiller onto the double-walled internal splice they had just created. The joint worked a bit when steered, but when daylight came, they drilled holes in each side of the splice, threaded the holes, and then secured the splice with cap screws. The new tiller was solid, for now.

The tiller incident is indicative of a couple of things. First is the necessity of having tools and spare parts on board, even if parts meant for one thing end up being used for something else. Second, it reinforces the need for a certain amount of resourcefulness when it comes to dealing with problems that arise. And, as any sailor knows, they will arise. As has often been pointed out, fortune favors the prepared. Creamer was prepared in terms of equipment, personnel, resourcefulness, adaptability, and determination. Experienced sailors know that disaster could strike even one who is well prepared, but it almost certainly *will* strike one who is unprepared.

Creamer, not surprisingly, was prepared for almost any eventuality. His entire upbringing—and his previous voyages—had prepared him for this circumnavigation. Mostly self-taught, he had learned to build, weld, cook, and use metal and wood lathes. He could repair almost anything, even lacking the appropriate tools and materials. As Lynn Creamer Borstelmann says, "I have never met anyone else who had such a wealth of life experience, and no one else who could so effectively draw on that experience [using] his excellent memory . . . to learn from it."[11]

The list of the team's improvisations at sea is impressive. On this portion of this leg alone, in addition to coming up with a jury rig for the tiller, they

- repaired the vane steerer, removing some of the slop in the bevel gears by moving the horizontal gear closer to the vertical one, moving the thrust washer aft and backing it up with a one-eighth-inch long piece cut by Bob from a one-inch stainless steel tube;
- made a rolling pin out of two-inch plastic pipe and a dough board out of a plexiglass sliding door from a galley cabinet;
- modified the whisker pole cars, shaving some off of the pins so that they would, for the first time, seat properly;
- replaced a broken turnbuckle on the aft headstay;
- made a penlight battery charger by tapping off four cells of one of the engine batteries to give them 8V to use on the 4 AA cells (They got hot but took some charge. Marv made a note to try using three cells—6V—next time.); and
- got Marv's shaver working again. It had been doused repeatedly in saltwater, but they were able to resuscitate it using some wire and soldering it back together with the 12V soldering iron they had on board.

This commitment to overcoming obstacles was just the way Creamer was wired. Indeed, it's probably the way *most* sailors are wired. They have

Figure 15.04. Marv working on the boom. (PHOTO COURTESY OF THE CREAMER FAMILY.)

to be, if they wish to keep their vessels running smoothly. Of course, it also holds true for farmers, machinists, mechanics, and countless others, but it seems that the desire—and ability—to overcome such obstacles is on the wane. These days, most of us just toss things out when they break; few are able to repair or rebuild. But in the middle of a passage, no matter how much money you're prepared to throw at a problem when ashore, replacement may not be an option. Self-sufficiency is a requirement for blue-water sailors. Early in Marv's career, he and Blanche could not find a place to live that satisfied Blanche—and neither of them cared for apartment living. Marv bought a small lot in southern New Jersey, enlisted the help of a few relatives, and hand-built what they called "the little house." With a lumber shortage threatening the project, they cut trees, hauled them to a sawmill, and used the lumber to build the house in two months in the dead of winter, while Marv and Blanche lived in a small travel trailer. (A side note: They expected to live in the house for a year, but found it so comfortable that they stayed for eight.)

One gets the idea that Marv was imperfect—sometimes demanding, not always easy to get along with, and with his own ideas about the right way to do things. He had little patience for fools, and he was the one who decided if you were a fool. There's no doubt that this got on some people's nerves, but whatever one thinks of Marv personally (and many people loved him dearly), he was undoubtedly one of the most capable, confident, skilled, persistent, and resourceful men ever to sail a boat.

CHAPTER 16

ROUNDING THE HORN

Travel is never a matter of money, but of courage.

—Paolo Coelho

Two of Creamer's earlier "fixit" projects were rapidly becoming "unfixed." First, the tiller repair was already loosening a bit. There was nothing to do about that now except to keep an eye on it; they hoped that it would hold until they got around the Cape.

The other issue was the stove. It had been tormenting them almost from the start. They had been attempting to purge the stove's fuel lines for weeks, ever since they somehow got saltwater in the kerosene reserve tank back in the Indian Ocean. Marv took the stove almost completely apart in an attempt to clean up the fuel lines. His ministrations seemed to have the desired effect and, for now, the stove was working perfectly. This, of course, would not last.

Their long slant to the southeast ended early on the morning of December 9. About 1:00 a.m. they got a look at Canopus that seemed to confirm their latitude, but because clouds obscured stars needed to establish a north-south line, they couldn't be sure that the observation was made at meridian transit. The clouds also prevented their seeing alpha Dorado, which they would have preferred because its ground position is nearly 150 miles closer to Cape Horn and therefore nearer by about two and half degrees to the imaginary overhead point they were seeking.

In fact, their estimated latitude at noon on December 9 differed from satellite-determined latitude by less than two miles, this after a sail of nearly four thousand miles from Whangaroa, during which they'd had only four opportunities to see stars for latitude correction. That was pretty impressive.

Less impressive was their estimation of longitude, which had to be accomplished by estimating the distance run each day and the average angle of the track. Still, their estimated longitude was only 216 miles off.

Their estimated latitude of 56°13'S was just fourteen miles south of the Horn, so they changed their heading for an easterly run to the Cape, which they believed to be 925 miles distant. They had gotten to the latitude of Drake Passage well ahead of arrival there. If they could hold that latitude, they should be able to find their way into and through its waters and between the rocks of southern South America to the north and the floe ice that rims the Antarctic continent to the south.

Creamer had predetermined a "window of opportunity" during which passage around the Cape would be safest and during which they would be able to use the "twilight" method mentioned in chapter 14 to help determine latitude. On December 9, that window would open in six days and close in twenty, so they were feeling optimistic.

Globe Star was moving eastward fairly rapidly, even though winds were light. They had the chute up in the morning, but jibed exactly when Bob was getting ready to put a pumpkin pie in the oven. As a result, the cabin was a mess of sticky yellow goop; there was raw pumpkin pie everywhere. On the plus side, the temperatures were, so far, not nearly as cold as expected. In the cabin with the hatch open, it was a balmy 53 degrees Fahrenheit, a little cooler than it had been, but certainly bearable. It was an enjoyable day of sailing.

The next two days, however, were not.

On December 10, the wind backed from northwest to northeast and *Globe Star* changed from a broad reach to a close reach on a port tack. Gales from the northeast and rain and poor visibility made for tough going. The crew used various combinations of sails as winds varied from ten knots to thirty knots. As far as they could tell, they were on a heading of 95 degrees, but they had only occasional glimpses of the sun. The water temperature was a frigid 44.6 degrees Fahrenheit; things were cooling off even more.

The next day, clouds thinned enough for them to get glimpses of the sun, which was enough for them to verify their heading.

With no compass or other instruments, Marv spent much of his time looking for clues about their location and direction and extrapolating from those signs. (And, a teacher to the end, he also spent a great deal of time explaining to his crew how to do the same.) To him, the gale and the sea over which it blew were in themselves clues: Even though the wind had blown steadily for two days, the seas had not built up. This suggested to Marv a short fetch, and *that* suggested either a very small system or land to windward. As further evidence of the nearness of land, Marv noted the appearance of great numbers of birds: prions, albatross, sooty petrels, and more.[1] In addition, the water did not seem quite as blue and the low water temps continued. All of this combined to give the three men a serious case of Horn fever. They were sure they were getting close.

As they sailed, Marv made a simple discovery that greatly increased his comfort while steering from the cockpit. *Globe Star*'s configuration (similar to most small sailboats) meant that the helmsman sitting on a cockpit bench had to stand every so often to see over the cabin in order to make a 360-degree check. While he'd been seated, the cushion on which he sat kept him relatively warm and comfortable, but every time he'd stand, the cushion would become cold and wet, meaning that Marv—or at least the posterior portion of Marv—also became cold and wet. After a while, he came up with a solution:

Instead of placing the cushion between my waterproof pants and the cockpit seat, why not put it inside the foul weather pants where it would stay reasonably warm and dry when you stood up? I stripped the back out of a Stearns life vest, placed it between my outer pants and rain pants upside down so that the vee of the neck straddled the crotch of the rain pants, and then tied the attached laces around my waist to hold it in place. The difference in warmth was unbelievable.[2]

Though they had gotten latitude from Phact on each of the first three nights of November and then waited until the first night of December for observations of both tau Puppis and Canopus, it wasn't until around midnight on December 11 that Marv got a good look at Canopus during its meridian transit and decided that their dead-reckoned latitude was accurate. This was only the fifth time since leaving Whangaroa on October 30 that they had been able to make a meridian transit observation of a star for latitude finding. It was the last latitude check before reaching the Horn, now 425 miles away. (In fact, it would turn out to be the last meridian observation of the Pacific voyage. In total, the crew of *Globe Star* saw stars for latitude finding only five nights in the entire 5,500-mile leg.)

Early on the afternoon of December 13, *Globe Star* was engulfed by abnormally cold air coming from the north. For the first time, the crew could see their breath condense in the cabin. This made things uncomfortable, but it was in fact a very good sign: cold air from the north could not have originated over the ocean; its source had to be land, and given that the sun was quite high at that time of year, it must have originated over very *high* land—that is, mountains, probably snow-covered mountains.

They were now sure that they were in the vicinity of the Horn, although they'd not sighted any land. In fact, they thought that they might even have passed it and never seen it due to the poor visibility. By now, although they would have liked to have actually seen the Horn, they were perfectly satisfied not to have had any unforeseen land pop up in front of them in the gloom.

On that day (December 13), Marv and the crew decided that they must have reached Cape Horn, probably around noon.

It was time to celebrate, but in the midst of their celebration, naturally the stove quit working again; they had lukewarm minestrone soup for lunch. Later, they figured out that the problem was a faulty connector at the air pump. Kerosene had backed up into it and rotted some of the rubber; the result was that air pressure built up in the pump but was blocked from going into the galley tank. In the evening, Bob cooked up some rice to serve with ravioli, and the stove worked fine, so the problem was frustratingly intermittent. (That was unfortunate. As any auto mechanic or computer programmer will tell you, it's always easier to diagnose and correct a problem when it appears consistently.)

Another party was in order, the crew having decided that they had definitely passed the Horn and given that the stove was working again. Nick served fruitcake in the cockpit and they broke out a bottle of Tasmanian wine someone had given them. The wine was terrible, and the fruitcake was . . . well, it was fruitcake, but all three enjoyed it. After days of tension, there was a lot of wisecracking and laughter.[3]

Early in the morning of December 15, as Marv steered, Nick came on deck to make a sail change and saw land off to port—and a group of small islands dead ahead. As Nick recalls it, they did not simply sight and avoid the rocks, the voyage *almost ended on them.* At one point, the "rocks" were near enough that they could see sea spray at the base of the outcrops on the closest ones as they frantically maneuvered to avoid them; it was a close call, and they survived only because of the quick reactions of the skipper and the crew.

"Marvin intended to sight icebergs or ice as a navigational aid to get him through Drake Passage," says Nick. "He would then know he was far enough south and clearing the Horn. This never happened. The voyage very nearly ended on that group of islands/rocks that I sighted upon coming on watch at daybreak on 15 December, 1983. As we quickly changed tack and ran to the south, we were all a bit perplexed about what the land was."[4] (The islands would turn out to be the Islas Ildefonso, many miles *west* of the Cape.)

Marv cranked up the engine to ensure that they'd be able to clear the islands in front of them and veered to starboard in order to get outside the southernmost rocks. This was the moment that Marv had been anticipating when he had asked builder Bob Patterson to install the more powerful three-cylinder Volvo engine and a large three-bladed prop: in spite of currents pushing them forward, the engine was powerful enough to push them clear before disaster struck. (The people at Volvo had supplied the engine, with its thundering thirty-six horsepower, at no charge, one of only a few free items supplied by sponsors. Marv had actually picked up the engine in Virginia and hauled it to Canada on a utility trailer for installation in *Globe Star.*)

But disaster almost struck regardless. Although Marv was confident in the engine, out of habit he glanced at the engine's temperature gauge and was floored to see the indicator glide inexorably through the green and into the red. They shut down the engine. Marv steered, while Nick and Bob changed sails to a pointing rig; in the end, they cleared the rocks by about a mile.

It was time to see what had happened to the engine. Marv dug out the manual, located the water pump section, and—using a mirror while lying on top of the engine itself—managed to remove the end cap of the pump so that they could inspect the device. The problem was immediately obvious: all six of the blades of the rubber impeller had broken off and jammed in the outflow port. Antici-pating issues of this sort, the folks at Volvo had included a replacement impeller. Marv removed the old one, slipped the new one in, and replaced the cap. They started the engine, held their collective breaths, and watched the temperature gauge stay in the green. Marv and the engine both cooled off in a few minutes.

It's useful to note that Creamer was lucky here. Captain David Jackson, USN (Ret.), notes, "[Creamer was] extremely fortunate that all of the broken bits were caught in the outflow port. Oftentimes they pass on throughout the system and the engine will be plagued with over-heating issues until all the bits are found by breaking apart downstream connections and components."[5]

Blanche had brought the crew Helly-Hansen survival suits while they were in Tasmania, and a plum-meting barometer indicated to Marv that it was time to try them out. Sure enough, what turned out to be the Islas Ildefonso were barely out of sight when the wind cranked up to a steady forty knots with sustained

Figure 16.01. Hansen's latest Model 307 survival suit, the Mark III, is similar to the one that Creamer, thanks to his wife, Blanche, brought along on his circumnavigation. (PHOTO COURTESY OF HANSEN PROTECTION AS.)

bursts of fifty and sixty knots. These were the worst winds *Globe Star* had experienced since they were rolled in the Tasman Sea three months earlier.

As luck would have it, the winds were blowing in their direction. But any veer of more than 15 degrees from straight downwind brought rough riding, accompanied by crashing and shuddering that made it seem to Marv as if the boat were bring rammed by loaded barges.[6]

Seas continued to build and began flooding the cockpit. A breaker caught the rudder and, before Nick could get his thigh away from the tiller, the force bent the splice in the repaired section at about a 30 percent angle; when they tried it later, it became obvious that the bend was enough to make the self-steering inoperable. The same comber hit Marv in the face with enough force to drive water deep into his survival suit in spite of the suit's neck gasket.

That night they went to a two-man watch system in order to keep a better lookout in the twilight on which they were counting to judge their latitude. Peeling off layers of clothes and putting them back on consumed too much time, so they resorted to sleeping in their survival suits.

Luckily, the gales relented the next day, so, while Nick steered, Marv and Bob worked on repairing the damaged tiller. Marv made a note in his journal to make sure that the crew did not block the tiller with their bodies in rough weather. The gales had left their mark though: everyone was sleeping in wet clothes, and Marv's second shaver was ruined when it got knocked to the floor.

The crew's joy at having passed Cape Horn turned out to have been misplaced. The rocky islands they had encountered were not associated with the Cape's Staten Island, about eighteen miles off the eastern portion of Tierra del Fuego, but were in fact the Islas Ildefonso, about seventy-two miles west of the Cape. The ARGOS track showed that they had sailed southeastward from them to pass within eight miles of the Islas Diego Ramírez, a small group of subantarctic islands in the extreme south of Chile.

Though their original celebration had been premature, they actually did cross the Meridian of Cape Horn, thirty miles to the south, about 4:00 a.m. on December 16. That delayed crossing was still well within

Figure 16.02. Port Cook, on the north coast of Staten Island, eighteen miles off the eastern extremity of Tierra del Fuego. (IMAGE COURTESY OF USER: LENGNICK, USED UNDER THE GNU FREE DOCUMENTATION LICENSE.)

the window prescribed earlier by Marv, when he sought to establish a latitude-establishing "twilight" passage window. Said Marv,

> Globe Star *had proved to be a survivor. She had sailed through the world's stormiest oceans, had recovered undamaged from three knockdowns, and had survived forty-foot seas, crashing waves, and hurricane-force winds. We had not reached the home stretch but prospects at the back stretch were looking good.*[7]

The Ted-Brewer designed, Huromic-built vessel had certainly proved her mettle, surviving a near capsize, multiple knockdowns, and seas rough enough to chill the ardor of most sailors. *Globe Star* was quite a boat. But much credit for the voyage so far went also to the crew: they proved both resilient and resourceful, and they had learned to work together in spite of the occasional spat. It was an exceptional boat manned by a talented crew.

Figure 16.03. Nick Gill and Marv Creamer in their survival suits the day after they rounded Cape Horn. (PHOTO COURTESY OF BOB ROUT.)

On the day they rounded Cape Horn, their estimated position was 54°57'S, 61°58'W. Their true position at the time, as noted by the ARGOS transmitter, was 56°6.8'S, 64°46.7'W, 118 miles to the southwest.

Globe Star began to try to work her way northward in order to clear Shag Rocks, Islas Aurora, a group of six rocky islands that lay between them and Africa.[8] When Marv asked Nick and Bob what the two men thought about spending Christmas in the Falklands, they loved the idea, so they turned hard to port to see if they could find the wind-swept islands.

This is the point at which Marv, had he possessed a radio, should have radioed ahead to the authorities for permission to enter the harbor at Stanley. Of course, he had no radio—or, rather, it was packed below with the other emergency gear he had determined not to use—but securing permission ahead of time to approach what was essentially a war zone would surely have saved Creamer and crew a great deal of trouble.

But that was still ahead of them. For now, having passed the Horn, they were well clear of any danger from the rocks and small islands that dotted that area. But if they were going to fetch the Falklands, they would have to sail around two hundred miles north before gales from the west drove them irretrievably downwind.

Marv's logs from December 18 and 19 tell the story of their approach:

December 18: Weather is not cooperating with our idea of spending Xmas in the Falklands. First [winds] strengthened and came on the nose, now they are a little better in direction but have turned light. As a consequence we are beating into heavy dead seas with little wind, and with overcast sky and periods of rain. We believe we are southeast of Port Stanley and that it would take a "miracle" to permit us to sail northwest to fetch it. We might be inclined to burn some diesel fuel if we had some indication of direction other than swells, i.e., sun or stars.

December 19: We have been becalmed most of the daylight hours under cloudy skies. Burned 3 hrs. of diesel after being buzzed by an RAF, 4-engine plane. We tried to follow him but a completely overcast sky forced us to give up. Oil slicks tell us we are near the Falklands.[9]

By December 20, they were feeling gloomy. They had been certain that by now they would have found land. Even when a southwester blew in and the air was clear, there was still no land to be seen, although they were seeing penguins and white ducks in the water, which implied that land was indeed near.

Having earlier sighted thousands of diving petrels crossing their bow from starboard to port as they sailed northwestward, Marv then spotted some promising-looking cumulous clouds in the direction from which the petrels had come.[10] Bob put up a yankee and working jib, and within two or three hours they had the southern coast of West Falkland in view. That was the end of the gloom.

They sailed southeast across the Falkland Sound, and then eastward toward the harbor entrance, a distance of about ninety miles. They kept a safe distance from the coast as they went but were not inclined to start across the Sound, knowing that they would probably run out of daylight before finishing the crossing.

To ensure sea room, they sailed south, away from the mouth of Falkland Sound, and hove to for the night, getting underway at daybreak. By about 8:00 a.m., the charts identified Barren Island at the southwestern tip of East Falkland. They continued northeastward, trying to reach Stanley before dark, but ended up sailing west of Lively Island, crossing the Choiseul Sound, and spent the night in Mare Harbour, which looked calm and well protected. However, they could not get the anchor to bite, and got the anchor line and rode tangled up in kelp. Sunset was approaching, so they sailed to what appeared to be some mooring buoys under military control (the Falklands War was only a year past). A helicopter buzzed them, and when they neared the buoys, two men on the deck of the *Merchant Providence* gave them permission to use one of the mooring buoys.[11]

They were in an iffy spot. The Falklands War, which pitted the United Kingdom against a woefully overmatched Argentina, began in early April 1982 and ended only seventy-four days later. When *Globe Star* arrived (slipping uninvited into what was basically a military installation), the area was still bristling with British warships and shore installations, and soldiers and marines patrolled the area. Creamer had blundered into what was still essentially a war zone.

Heading for some much-needed showers, they soon noticed that they were never alone. Security officers oversaw their arrival and one of them called the pilot of the chopper that had buzzed them. It turned out that the chopper had been sent out to investigate the strange boat entering military waters, but the pilot was confused because he had been told to look for a black and white boat; *Globe Star* was blue and white, so he ignored her. Marv and company were ordered to report to Chief of Police Bill Richards as soon as they got to Stanley—and they were told that they should make for Stanley with all possible speed.[12] The ship's baker brought them a dozen fresh breakfast rolls, which they took as a cue to leave.

.THE FALKLANDS

A life lived every day doing only what needs to be done may seem con-
venient but your heart and soul don't live for convenience they live for
exploration, imagination, and the pursuit of dreams.

—Avina Celeste

THE FALKLANDS WAS STILL A HOTSPOT WHEN *GLOBE STAR* ENTERED THE
harbor on December 21, 1983, but efforts were underway to stabilize relations between the two warring countries. Britain was exchanging mes-
sages with Argentina's new civilian government as a first step toward that
normalization; then Foreign Secretary Sir Geoffrey Howe characterized
communications from Prime Minister Thatcher as "a friendly signal."[1]
On the diplomatic front, things were cooling down.

At ground zero in the Falklands, however, things were still dicey. It
turned out that military rules required radio contact and permission before
entering within a two-hundred-mile circumference of the Falklands.
Globe Star, which possessed no radio, had never been granted permission
to enter. The three men had more or less been under "house arrest" since
their arrival, which explained why they were never alone; an officer even
stood guard outside the bathhouse when they showered.

Globe Star left her mooring buoy in Mare Harbour and headed for
Stanley under power. Upon arrival, Creamer and crew could see Harrier
jets taking off and landing off the port bow as they threaded their way
among dozens of warships and civilian vessels lying at anchor. As they
pulled up at government dock number one, a customs officer directed
them to lie alongside the government research vessel *Forrest*.

They were quickly escorted to the office of Police Chief Bill Richards. He took care of the entry formalities and then explained how Nick and Bob might gain transport out of the country and how crew from the United States might reach Stanley.

The most sobering moment of the encounter occurred when a police clerk handed the three men local terrain maps for use when tramping about the country. The maps did not show tourist sites, local restaurants, shops, and the like; they were descriptions of known and suspected mine-fields. While out and about in Stanley, Marv and the crew were advised to avoid areas thought to be mined, a directive they were probably quite careful to obey.

Once the formalities were taken care of, the three men were permitted to move around Stanley without any restrictions, other than avoiding mined areas, so Marv went looking for provisions and discovered that there was a decent supply of staples and canned fruits and vegetables. (The three men tramped about the town in their yellow foul-weather gear, soon earning the sobriquet "yellow penguins.") Nowhere, however, could the men buy eggs, poultry, or bread. (The locals, it turned out, baked their own bread.) Cuts of mutton were available if you bought in quantity, delivered by the town butcher on his rounds. Marv really wanted beef but was told that farmers were too busy at the time to sell beef cattle; they were advised, if they wanted beef, to go out and shoot a cow. Instead they opted for mutton.

Supermarket owner Norman Clark had recognized Marv's accent and wondered aloud how an American had come to be in the Falk-lands. Given the answer, he responded by inviting Creamer and crew to a Christmas party he was giving on December 23.

Marv met several people while in Stanley, many of whom offered drinks, free meals, and even an airplane ride around the islands (courtesy of Mike Goodwin, who ran a commercial charter service). One interest-ing—and, ultimately, quite valuable—encounter occurred when he met then Lieutenant (spelled as we have it here, but pronounced "leftenant") Mark Stanhope of the Royal Navy. At the time, Stanhope commanded the submarine *Orpheus*, and he was intrigued (Marv's term was "freaked out") by Creamer's navigation methods. Stanhope, who would eventually become a Rear Admiral and First Sea Lord and be awarded an OBE, was at first doubtful about Creamer's claims. He was, after all, a career naval officer, though young at the time, and had trouble believing Marv's story when they met at a pre-Christmas luncheon:

> *He looked at me and said crisply, "They told me in there that you just sailed around the Horn without a compass. Is that true?" Disbelief was written all over his face. I replied, "Yes. Moreover, we sailed without sextant, clock, or electronics." His immediate response was, "How in the hell did you do it?" Answers led to more questions—questions about finding directions, latitude, how we managed at night and in overcast. And then the surge was over. He relaxed and said, "I know it's Christmas Eve tomorrow, but you've got to come out to my submarine and tell your story to my officers."[2]*

Marv was never one to miss an opportunity to talk about *Globe Star* or about his own accomplishments. They took an eighty-five-foot personnel carrier out to Prince William Sound, where *Orpheus* was moored, and Marv spoke to the crew of the sub. They were, in Marv's words, "flabbergasted."

But Marv got more than just praise from the officers. One of them asked if they had sustained any damage, and Marv told him about problems with the tiller, the steering oar, and the dodger frame. The officer noted that they were currently tied up to *Bar Protector*, which he called "the best repair ship in the world," and had a runner carry a note over to the repair officer, Barry Collins.[3]

The response from Collins was gratifying: "Tell him to bring in whatever needs fixing and we'll take care of it."[4]

The offer was a godsend. Creamer had been asking around, desperately trying to find someone who could repair his equipment, and had struck out: no civilian facilities could handle this sort of repair, but the Royal Navy could and did.

In the meantime, it appeared that—even in the harbor—*Globe Star* was in danger, threatened by the rising winds and by her precarious mooring. She was tied up to the *Forrest*, the Falkland Islands government research boat, fended off with two tires, two reed fenders, and one Taylor fender. It was not an optimal arrangement, and Creamer feared what might happen when *Forrest* departed on January 9; the option of tying off to the pier itself in such weather was not at all appealing. For the time being, though, there was little he could do about it: Stanley was serious about observing the Christmas holiday, and all the shops and government offices were closed up tight for four days.

While he waited, Creamer had no choice but to accept multiple invitations to dine with acquaintances. At one of those gatherings, he noted that Nick and Bob, busily helping themselves to platters of beef and mutton, had seemingly overcome their earlier fear of "protein poisoning." Creamer apparently managed not to make any snide comments to the two men, but it had probably been difficult for him to forbear the pleasure.

At a carnival, Creamer had again run into Commander Stanhope, who introduced him to Barry Collins of the *Bar Protector*, and also its captain, Pat Middleton. Collins told him that the requested stainless steel welding jobs on the tiller, vane, and dodger would be no problem and that Creamer should bring the items over to the ship on the 27th. Even better, when he heard about Marv's mooring troubles, Captain Middleton said that he'd see about getting Marv permission to moor in "the Camber," a rivetted rectangular enclosure measuring about three hundred feet by four hundred feet. It would be perfect: safe and out of "the slop." Marv was hoping that Middleton would save the day.

On the 28th, Creamer picked up the restored tiller from *Bar Protector*'s chief shipwright, Jim Berry. The repair was a thing of beauty. Berry had shaped the internal sleeve, brought the two pieces of the tiller together so the two met parallel, welded the break, put stainless-steel pins through both sides, and welded the ends of the pins to hold them in place. Marv couldn't imagine a better-crafted restoration.

Oddly, once the issues with Marv's ignorance of military protocol were taken care of, the crew of *Globe Star* was afforded the friendliest of welcomes. It was much different than the prevailing attitude at Cape Town or Sydney. Everyone was friendly—even the military officers who at first had been suspicious of *Globe Star*'s more or less surreptitious entry—and went out of their way to make them feel welcome. Two young men who were interested in crewing (Marv was still trying to round up crew) stopped by to chat; they were contracted to work for the City of Stanley, however, and had to bow out of accompanying Creamer on the next leg. (On the plus side, they dropped by later with apples and oranges for *Globe Star*'s mess.) Captain Middleton came by to let Marv know that he was still trying to find *Globe Star* a safe berth at the enclosure at Navy Point, and the assistant harbormaster, Lieutenant Commander David Atterbury, stopped by to invite Marv over to take a look at soundings, with a view of moving *Globe Star* over. From Marv's perspective, Navy Point would be even better than a mooring because he wouldn't have to use a small boat to get back and forth to Stanley. (That would have been a problem because it was far too windy in the sound to use the inflatable; with the weather as changeable as it was there, an adverse wind could push the little rubber boat miles away while he was trying to get to shore.)

Atterbury and Middleton came through. *Globe Star* was allowed to make her way over to a very small enclosure at Navy Point and tie up to a solid timber floating dock. An added benefit was that this new location meant that Marv could circulate around the harbor more easily and could even accept dinner and overnight invitations.

Another piece of good news: Blanche called and told Marv that Bob Watson had committed to fly to Stanley to crew for the last leg of the trip. Now all Marv had to do was find at least one more, and preferably two more, crewmembers for his final leg.

On the morning of the 29th, Marv took off to check out charts of the enclosure that would be *Globe Star*'s home for the next several days or weeks. They looked good, so he told Lieutenant Commander Atterbury that he would bring his boat over in the afternoon. He then headed over to the telephone station to receive a call from Blanche, receiving assurances from Bob and Nick that they would be present and ready to help move *Globe Star* when he returned.

Thus, the stage was set for the final blow-up between Marv and Nick—and Bob, in this case.

When he returned, neither crewman was in sight, and *Globe Star* was being slammed against the *Forrest* by gale-force winds and cross-sound waves. This was a potential disaster. There was no way Marv could move the boat by himself in this sort of weather, so he scrambled around, finding and deploying more fenders between the two vessels.

Adding insult to injury, the two crewmen had left a mess: there was flour all over the counters, stove, and galley floor; a stack of dirty dishes in the galley; a dough hook and other utensils in the sink; crap in the head; and the trash basket was simply missing.

Theoretically, this being Bob and Nick's final stop, they were free to move on. But they had promised Marv that they would be available to help move *Globe Star*. In the meantime, they were expected to be good crew because they were still living aboard.

Things got ugly. Bob told Marv that the older man could have at least cleaned up because Bob had made bread that day. Marv agreed that there was some merit to that argument, but then the two set Marv off—not all that difficult a task, it seems—by staying up late and talking after Marv went to bed. Nick smoldered but kept his temper.

The real eruption occurred the next morning. Marv gave the two a blast detailing their various offenses, and then Nick went a step too far: He told Creamer that Marv "used" people and that they never would have gotten around the Horn if it weren't for him. He continued his tirade, calling Marv "mercenary" and noting angrily that Marv should have paid them to crew.[5]

The conflicts between Marv and Nick were completely predictable once one realizes that in some ways these two men were in fact quite similar. Both were "alpha males" who were used to bossing others around and who were definitely *not* used to having their orders questioned or their wishes denied. Both were highly intelligent, headstrong, demanding, quick to anger, and sometimes unable (or unwilling) to suppress that anger. As Nick says now, looking back at the voyage, "We were both opinionated and wanted to be dominant."[6]

But there were also ways in which the two were different. Nick, young and hotheaded, was quick to take offense and was often unable to curb his temper. Marv, often equally headstrong and quite sure that his point of view was the correct one, was nonetheless usually capable of holding his temper in check and was not completely averse to being overruled in certain cases. (Keep in mind, though, that this was his vessel and his journey—he *was* the captain in this situation and he was used to his orders being followed.)

Creamer's eldest daughter, Andra, points out that Creamer did not *always* need to be the one in charge. He knew how to take a back seat when necessary, and he was unfailingly polite to his superiors and to the people with whom he worked, whether on a boat or at the college at which he taught:

> *On land and at sea, if Dad was not the designated leader, he played his part. As a young man, he worked as a carpenter on the equivalent of a construction crew where he had no difficulty taking orders. He worked for years for Dr. Harold Wilson, the Social Studies Department chair, and Dr. Thomas Robinson, the college president of Glassboro State, and was consistently respectful and never insubordinate. Several of my friends' fathers were also professors, so I heard via the grapevine how Dad was perceived among his peers. His peers appreciated that he could express an opinion and challenge authority, but he did so with humor and tact. He participated in a number of community organizations and initiatives. Sometimes he was the chair and sometimes he was not, but he would never have been regarded as domineering. While people crewed for him at sea, he also crewed for others. He was invited back. Dad might have questioned what his captain was doing, but would never have attacked his authority, as Nick Gill seems to have. And while Dad may have been quick to anger in a stressful situation, [he] was perfectly capable of mature diplomacy.*[7]

Nick, for his part, had been having marriage troubles before shipping out, and so was engaged in a certain amount of self-reflection aimed at helping him to understand his own personality and deal with his own foibles. "I was much like Marv in character," he said later, "and if I didn't want to end up like him—which I didn't—I'd better resolve to change myself. It was a great revelation to me when I realized that Marv was treating me (and others) in the same way I treated [my wife] all those years. I was hypercritical, I was a perfectionist, I wanted [my wife] to do things my way because I thought it was the best way."[8]

That sounds a bit like Marv. The older man could be hypercritical and demanding, and he surely thought that, on board his boat, his way was the best—essentially the *only*—way. The fact that he was often right, that his way *was* often the best way, did not reduce the friction that sometimes ensued when Marv insisted on his way or ignored others' suggestions or desires. Marv was a good man, and he could be—and often was—affable, caring, and kind. But he was not a saint, and he had his failings.

Still, by all accounts, the reality was that Marv was not abrasive by nature, while Nick—at least at the time of the *Globe Star* circumnavigation—tended to be. Marv was capable of controlling his temper most of the time, while Nick was rarely able—or willing—to do so. The resulting clashes were inevitable.

In the end, the two men helped Marv move *Globe Star* to her new berth and then took a boat back to Stanley. It was the last Marv would see either of them. Marv noted later, "As usual it is not the sea or boat that makes the biggest problems—it is the crew."[9]

From Nick's perspective, the trip was worthwhile, even though he and Marv often clashed and he felt that Marv didn't always give his crew the credit they deserved. "I don't hold any grudge against Marvin at all," he says. "He gave me an adventure of a lifetime, and gave me direct experience that people who are on a mission, who are obsessed with being record holders or the 'first' to achieve a goal, are so full of their own ego that they often cannot see or recognize the efforts of others to get them there."[10]

In fact, years after the voyage, Nick and Marv exchanged "olive branch" emails, patching things up as best they could.

The holiday parties continued, but Marv did not attend them. On New Year's Eve, he came down with the worst cold he'd had in thirty years. This isn't that surprising, really. Sickness at sea is fairly rare; it's when long-distance sailors come into contact with people that they come down with contagious diseases. He spent the next few days in bed, but he took comfort in the fact that his boat was safely sheltered; if he had not changed berths, he would have had a terrible time, sick as he was, trying to hold *Globe Star* off in the gales that had been blowing.

He took the time to pamper himself a bit, listening to music (the soundtrack to *The Music Man* gave him a lift), working crossword puzzles, and playing solitaire. He enjoyed the time alone, relishing the peace and quiet.

When he finally felt well enough to leave *Globe Star*, he bundled up and ran a few errands. After speaking to Blanche via a ham radio telephone patch, he boarded the ferry back across the harbor. On the way, he spoke to a ferry crewman, Brad Bailey, who wanted to know if he could take him to New Jersey to see a girl he had met in the Bahamas. When Marv asked him where in New Jersey he wanted to go, he was astonished to hear him say, "Glassboro." He told Bailey that Glassboro was where he was headed, but it turned out that the timing was wrong for Brad, so he couldn't make the trip. That was too bad because the young woman he wanted to visit lived less than a mile from Creamer's home.

Marv was having trouble rounding up more crewmembers. Partly, this was due to military rules governing travel. One could fly from Ascension Island to Stanley only on a "compassionate basis," meaning the death or sickness of a close relative. The alternative was an eight- to eleven-day boat trip, which Marv felt would cause potential crew to shy away.

Bob Watson was definitely on his way though. Blanche told him (via ham radio again) that Watson had called the Colonial Office in London and had secured air passage all the way to Stanley. Marv was delighted to get this bit of information but decided to keep it under his hat lest a local bureaucrat find a way to recover lost control.

More good news soon arrived from the repair wizards on *Bar Protector*. Jim Berry had finished straightening the bent steering oar from the self-steering vane and had welded the dodger frame. Berry arrived that afternoon with the repaired equipment and two associates to help install it. Marv was grateful to have help with the self-steerer because its weight and awkward shape made remounting it a two-man operation. Marv noted that, while military rules prevented monetary payment, he was able later on to provide them with what he coyly termed a "spiritual" reward.

The RN folks were really going all out to be helpful. In addition to arranging a safe berth and gratis repairs to *Globe Star*'s equipment, Royal Navy personnel checked in on Marv when he was ill and, once he was

Figure 17.01. The supply and repair vessel *Bar Protector*, as it looked in 2011. (IMAGE USED UNDER THE CREATIVE COMMONS CC0 1.0 UNIVERSAL PUBLIC DOMAIN DEDICATION, COURTESY OF USER: *ALFVANBEEM.*)

feeling better, often stopped in for a morning cup of tea. When he needed to work on repairs, there were offers of tools, the use of shop equipment, materials, and expertise. He was invited to use the ship's laundry facilities and told to help himself to fresh-baked bread whenever he needed it. Further, he was often invited to lunch with the officers and provided information on navigational aids that he might encounter on the upcoming (and final) leg. If gales made using ladders to descend to the floating docks unsafe, he was assigned a bunk so that he could sleep over. If he spent the evening at the Officers' Club, one of the members would accompany him to make sure he got back to the boat safely.

It's safe to say that the Royal Navy had adopted Creamer as one of their own.

On January 12, word came from Blanche that Dr. Ed Gibson—an old friend of Marv's who had crewed on one of Creamer's previous voyages to

Africa—and Dave Lansdale, Ed's brother-in-law, had signed on to crew for the Stanley–Cape May leg and would join Bob Watson for the flights to London, Ascension Island, and Stanley.

The new crew was made up of Marv's friends—and relatives of friends. Ed Gibson was a surgeon about the same age as Creamer (he passed away in 2017 at the age of 102), who spent much of his early career in Army MASH units in and near Berlin during and just after World War II. An experienced sailor, he was at one time commodore of the Boothbay (Maine) Harbor Yacht Club and he had crewed with Marv on noninstrument transatlantic trips before. Gibson was interested in scientific pursuits such as the data gathering performed by Marv on this trip and was an honorary trustee of the Bigelow Laboratory for Ocean Science, in East Boothbay. An old and trusted friend of Marv's, Ed was a steady and experienced hand on a boat.

Dave Lansdale, Ed's brother-in-law, was a retired Scott Paper Company executive and a licensed pilot with adventure in his blood. After his wife passed away in 1983, he resolved to complete as many of his "bucket list" items as possible; one of those items was sailing across an ocean, so he was keen to join Creamer on the last leg of his circumnavigation. (Lansdale passed away in 2010.)

Bob Watson was a younger man, thirty-three years old at the time of Creamer's circumnavigation. A recent graduate of architectural college, Watson specialized in restoration architecture—repairing and redesigning buildings in such a way as to preserve their heritage. He had met Creamer a couple of years prior at a meeting of the local historical society, when Creamer gave a speech there. Enthralled by Marv's descriptions of his instrument-less journeys, Bob had half-jokingly asked Marv to give him a call if he needed crew on his upcoming circumnavigation. Somewhat unexpectedly, the older man *did* call and ask him if he'd like to join in on the final leg of the journey. Bob accepted with alacrity and says that he never regretted that decision.[11]

Shortly after his arrival in Stanley, Marv had encountered American Giles Mercer. Mercer had been born in Maryland but had yearned for a more rugged environment. He had lived with his wife Crystal in Scotland for some time, but Scotland wasn't demanding enough for the two of

Figure 17.02. The crew for the final leg of *Globe Star*'s journey. From left to right, Marv, Ed Gibson, Bob Watson, and Dave Lansdale.
(PHOTO COURTESY OF THE CREAMER FAMILY.)

them; they both wanted a life with fewer amenities. Stanley, a place where you couldn't buy bread or have garments dry cleaned (and where you had to shoot your own cow for beef), was more to their liking.

Marv knew all about seeking a more rugged life. In the 1960s, when he had driven his family to Alaska while towing a small travel trailer, he had encountered many such folks: hardy types who had found themselves attracted to rugged environments and who therefore left the stresses of modern urban life behind to live simpler lives in the forty-ninth state. The Mercers and their two daughters lived such a life, and Marv was treated to a meal cooked over a peat fire in an old-fashioned kitchen range. When he left, he took with him a gift of a big bunch of red radishes and a batch of fresh eggs laid by hens kept in a coop in the Mercers' backyard.

Marv must have felt a certain kinship with the Mercers, although as far as we know he never saw them again. Marv too sought a more rugged life and was himself one of those "hardy types." He found *his* "rugged life" on the sea, but he was certainly kindred spirits with the Mercers and people like them who longed for a simpler existence, however harsh and demanding that existence might be.

Then again, Marv's early life had been somewhat rugged, even on land, and he raised his children to be as self-sufficient as possible. The two Creamer daughters learned early to sew their own clothes and the family had an extensive vegetable garden and canned and froze their own vegetables and fruit. Marv had a machine shop in the basement of the family home, and he repaired any household items that needed fixing. (Son Kurt was essentially an unpaid apprentice, working alongside Marv and learning the tricks of the trade.) Lynn Creamer Borstelmann recalls, "Our life was different and required more work than [that of our] friends and neighbors. In this regard, it was simpler, but also work! Not that we didn't watch TV, listen to music, go to concerts, etc. Our parents ensured we had lessons and activities as well."[12]

Waiting for his crew, Creamer tackled some catch-up jobs aboard *Globe Star*. His journal notes:

January 18: Got after the fo'c'sle door. Planed off the hinge side and reset the hinges. It has been a royal pain! Also got after the fridge. The fan motor shaft is tight and the fan motor fuse was blown. Royal Navy man has taken over the fan motor repair.

January 19: Reattached the dodger frame this morning. The frame makes an excellent hand hold but this in time works the screws out of the teak trim alongside the hatch where it is secured. Found some . . . [bolts] so drilled out the frame and tapped the steel sides of the hatch . . . and bolted the frame with 3 bolts on each side. That should hold it for a while. Also reassembled the ignition switch and ran the engine for a half hour or so to oil the cylinder walls and charge the batteries. Will try to take the [refrigerator] motor housing apart and free up the shaft.[13]

Creamer didn't spend all of his time working on the boat. There was time for relaxation and even a bit of nostalgic philosophizing. In a letter to his daughter, Lynn, he wrote that he hoped to make it home in early May (which would allow him to attend her graduation from nursing school) and wondering about her future plans. Alone in a foreign port, Creamer felt keenly the absence of his family, writing that he missed them terribly and would be glad to get back home. Indulging in a bit of sentimentality, he noted that he was enjoying having this opportunity to reminisce, recalling "what a joy it was to watch all of [the kids] grow up." Poking a bit of fun at his own peripatetic obsessions, he wrote, "when this bit of idiocy is completed, I'll be ready to settle down to the serious business of fathering and grandfathering."[14]

On January 27, Creamer stepped from the galley to the cockpit to investigate what sounded like an outboard motor. It *was* an outboard motor, and it was attached to an RAF inflatable. The boat's two crewmen asked if he were in need of anything. They lent Marv a "torch" (flashlight) and said that they would find him some jerry cans of fuel. After Marv explained that he planned to return to a fort built to protect Philadelphia from British invasion during the American Revolution, they brought over an RAF Union Jack and asked him if he would fly it as he sailed up the Delaware. Marv assured them that he would.

On January 28, Creamer's crew arrived. Ed Gibson, Dave Lansdale, and Bob Watson landed at the airport with a phenomenal amount of gear, mostly their own but also a lot of things that Blanche had gotten together at Marv's request. The four men piled into a taxi, gear and all, and rode to the Public Jetty, where they transferred to a passenger ferry that dropped them off at the Camber.[15]

The four men spent the next morning getting caught up and laying out their departure plans, but there was—as always—a slight hitch. The new lithium batteries for the ARGOS transmitter had been improperly packed, or so said the authorities, so they were held over for approved packing and subsequent shipment. It was anticipated that the delay wouldn't cause a problem because they expected the return to Cape May to take about three months and had targeted the middle of May as a good time to arrive in order to avoid spring storms near the New Jersey coast. As far as the timeline went, things were looking good.

Then came the oregano crisis. Marv had made spaghetti using mutton instead of hamburger and, against all odds, they all decided that spaghetti

Figure 17.03. Ed Gibson shaving while underway.
(PHOTO COURTESY OF THE CREAMER FAMILY.)

with muttonburger tasted great. However, this exercise highlighted a shortage of one of Marv's favorite spices, oregano. Marv was aghast; he couldn't see how the four men could possibly survive for three months without oregano. An emergency oregano-hunting expedition was quickly launched. When they couldn't find oregano at any of the local stores, they were downhearted. A clerk at one of the stores suggested checking with the British research ship the *John Briscoe*. (This was the same ship that would eventually take Bob Rout and Nick Gill to the arctic.) On their shopping rounds, they encountered an ornithologist who actually worked aboard the *John Briscoe* and who recommended they speak with Steve, the ship's head steward, about obtaining some of the precious herb. After finishing their shopping (more mutton), they headed over to the ship and met with Steve, who gave them a generous amount of oregano and wished them well. Crisis averted.

On to the next calamity, which, not surprisingly, involved *Globe Star*'s cantankerous galley stove. Theoretically, a kerosene stove is a simple enough machine: The burner of a pressure kerosene stove ejects preheated kerosene through a small orifice that vaporizes the liquid. The "atomized" fuel then exits a sieve-like cap where, in theory, it burns with a blue and very hot flame. However, the high temperature of the flame tends to carbonize some of the kerosene, which eventually clogs the orifice. The burners of Creamer's stove featured internally mounted "prickers" that could be rotated by a control knob to clean the openings. When Ed and Marv took the burners apart, they found that their spare orifices were too large for the burners and the spare prickers were too large for the old orifices. They wound up repairing the old ones and hoping for the best. (As it turns out, this hope was misplaced, but for now, the stove worked superbly. Dave, who had taken over the cooking, roasted a leg of mutton for four hours and served it with frozen peas and baked potatoes. There were no problems with the stove and the meal was delicious.)

A couple of days later, Keith Mursell and Bob Griffith brought their new ARGOS batteries; when the package was opened, the batteries immediately shot out of the slippery bag and into about eight feet of murky water. Not surprisingly, panic ensued. The lithium batteries had made a long, torturous, *expensive* journey and were essentially irreplaceable. The nontransmission of position information was not a major concern to Marv, but he was committed to sending out weather data as part of an associated research project and was unwilling to sail without an operational transmitter. The crew agreed that *someone* should search the bottom, and no one objected when Dave volunteered.

Dave endured three fruitless dives before Bob and Keith returned with an identical package of batteries—which turned out to be flashlight batteries. The ones on the bottom were not their precious transmitter batteries but a dozen expendable "D" cells for flashlights and the like.

On February 5, fifty-knot winds swept the islands. This was bad weather, even for the Falklands. Two ships dragged anchor and moved slowly across the harbor, as if captained and crewed by slightly impaired, ghostly seamen. A Greek ship anchored in Port William was driven onto a rocky lee shore. Marv was afraid that the floating dock holding *Globe Star* would give way, so he borrowed a sledgehammer, some heavy steel

Figure 17.04. *Globe Star* secure in "the Camber" at the British Navy compound at Port Stanley, the Falklands.

pins, and some hawser-weight rope, and went out onto the wall to help secure the dock. The jury rig helped relieve the strain on the lines, as well as the strain on the *Globe Star* crew.

As part of their departure preparations, Creamer turned on the transmitter, plugged in the weather data, and sent a transmission. Almost immediately, he received word that the transmitter's voltage had dropped from 227V to 191V, so he and the crew installed the new batteries. Then word came that the weather data had been garbled, just as it had been between Hobart and Sydney. When they pulled the set apart, they discovered that a twenty-prong plug had been reversed. Curious, they opened the spare set that had been modified to run off the 12V onboard batteries and found that *its* twenty-prong plug was also reversed. They restored the plug to its intended position and packed the set away to use in the event of battery failure, which they figured was almost certain.

Marv had planned to depart on February 8 but waited another day because of the continued bad weather. At about 3:00 p.m. on the 9th, they cast off their lines, cranked up the engine, and motored out of the Camber's narrow entrance into Port Stanley. Marv had been in Stanley for forty-nine days, had made a number of very good friends, and had enjoyed an even larger number of very good meals. Now he and his crew were headed for home.

CHAPTER 18

HEADING FOR HOME

The world is a book and those who do not travel read only one page.
—St. Augustine

It was a *long* way home. In the end, the *Globe Star* crew would spend ninety-eight days at sea on this leg, and they would sail some 7,400 nautical miles. The final leg, then, would end up being almost as long as the first in terms of both miles sailed and days at sea. It was a long time for four people to spend cooped up on a small boat.

Because of the very light air, *Globe Star* continued under power northward into Port William and then east to Point Pembroke. At that point, they entered the South Atlantic and set a course a little east of north. Their plan was to move toward the equator while paralleling the South American coast at a distance that would keep them clear of the southwestward flowing Brazil Current, a weak mirror image of the mighty Gulf Stream of the North Atlantic. (The former current actually splits, with one component flowing eastward and the other hugging the coast and flowing southwest.) The plan was that their heading would shift from east of north to west of north after they had reached the bulge of Brazil. From there, it would be a matter of heading to about one hundred miles from where they began their journey and then bending abruptly westward toward Cape May.

Creamer and crew continued under power for the first night, anxious to get clear of land as quickly as possible, just in case the weather turned. The next morning, they raised a double-reefed main, yankee, and staysail and galloped off under a stiff breeze.

They were headed home, on course, under sail—as a sailboat is meant to be, of course—and each day put them incrementally closer to home. Creamer was cautiously optimistic. Prospects seemed good: They had survived the stormy Southern Ocean, they had cleared the fabled Horn, and they carried a fresh and capable crew. On top of that, their planned route was through open ocean, which was always a plus for a small boat, as far as safety was concerned, and as they moved toward and then away from the equator, their chances of meeting violent weather became less and less likely. Moreover, the only remaining landfall was on a familiar coast and at a time when lengthy storms were unlikely.

Although they had expected to meet bad weather at the outset, instead the wind was frequently light or nonexistent. The crew had to work to find sails that would give them some headway in a suitable direction. Creamer's log repeatedly mentions being becalmed those first several days,

On the plus side, Dave and Bob, who had been suffering the ravages of seasickness, were now feeling better. Soon, Dave was able to take over the galley, a domain he had claimed for himself at the outset of this leg. Ed, Bob, and Marv took turns doing dishes, and on the 25th, Dave undertook his first apple pie, which, by all accounts, was a rousing success.

As always, there were plenty of repair and maintenance tasks to keep everyone busy. Marv's journal notes:

> *Ed and I had a look for diesel fuel line leak but came up dry. Ed tightened the packing nut on the shaft stuffing box. Worked on stove. Got forward burner working. Sewed patch on genoa. Lubricated winches.*[1]

Naturally, the stove was giving them trouble. Marv and Ed replaced a burner. They then got the rear burner working again, but not to full heat. The stove would continue to torment them all the way back to Cape May.

On the 24th, Bob spotted something bobbing in the water: A mystery—a real-life, honest-to-God message in a bottle. Ostensibly, the note was written by twelve-year-old Carolina Susana Cortes, who said that for two years she had been throwing bottles in the ocean and receiving answers from all over the world. Ms. Cortes said that she had been studying the Malvinas Current and sent a message of peace and friendship from the children of Argentina. However, Marv's suspicions were aroused when he noted the return address: Liga Naval Argentina, Revista "Billiken," Lineas Maritimas Argentinas (ELMA), Prefectura, Naval Argentina. This was not the address of a schoolgirl but—indirectly—an arm of the Argentine Navy, specifically an Argentine shipping line formed after Peron national-ized the shipping industry in the late 1950s and early 1960s.

In any case, the mystery was never resolved: after he returned to Cape May, Creamer sent off a letter to the address noted, but received no reply.

On February 25, the new crew received their first taste of heavy weather. Just after midnight, forty-five-knot gales struck, and the wind then made a 170-degree shift under completely cloudy skies; this made direction finding exceedingly difficult. On the bright side, the storm brought warmer temperatures: the air temperature was now 72 degrees Fahrenheit and the water was a relatively balmy 68 degrees Fahrenheit. This improved night watch conditions immensely; getting a slap of warm-ish seawater in the face is always more pleasurable than getting doused with cold. A few days later, the air and water temperatures had risen to 79 degrees and 75 degrees, respectively. The weather was definitely turning.

Globe Star's EP on February 28, nineteen days out of Stanley, was 33°15'S, 40°42'W, which was 276 miles west northwest of the position established by ARGOS. According to the tracker, Creamer's latitude was off by 112 miles and his longitude by 250 miles.

More repairs awaited. *Globe Star* was headed for the tropics, so a func-tioning refrigerator would have been useful. Theirs had failed weeks ago. Puttering with it, they got the compressor to run, but only for a moment. They decided that the problem was in the controls, so they tried—and failed—to bypass them. It wasn't a matter of life and death, but chilled water and juice would have made the steamy tropical days easier to bear.

The fridge wasn't the only piece of failed equipment. (Experienced sailors know that all equipment eventually fails. *Really* experienced sail-ors know that this failure is bound to occur at the worst possible time.) While puttering with the compressor, they noticed that the alternator on the engine was not working. This was more serious, as it could eventually mean a lack of battery power to start the engine in an emergency situa-tion. The boat's solar panels might power the running lights for a short period of time, but they would not reliably provide enough juice to fully charge the engine's starting batteries. Today's panels might have done the job, of course, but Marv's 1980s-era solar panels operated at about 10 percent efficiency at most. (A few years after Creamer's circumnavigation, efficiency rose to about 20 percent. And in 2019, the National Renewable Energy Laboratory in Colorado achieved an efficiency rating of over 47 percent.)[2]

There was a theoretical backup plan, which was to begin a hand-cranking operation with the included crank and then call for whatever help the starter could provide at the same time that compression was restored to one cylinder. Marv figured that, with a bit of luck, the engine would start on that cylinder and then with the restoration of compression to the other two, one at a time, the engine could be coaxed to full power.

It was a nice plan, but a lot depended on hoping that the timing was right and that luck was with them; in sailing, as in many things, *hope* is not a good strategy, and Marv knew it.

Luckily, they came up with another approach. Checking out the alternator, Marv discovered that it worked fine when a live lead wire was touched momentarily to the exciter terminal (the 12V wire that transmits DC power directly to the alternator) on the balky device. The source of the problem was in the control panel, which had succumbed after more than a year's drenching of seawater. They realized that they'd have to "hand-tease" the alternator for the rest of the voyage. To make this easier, Marv jury rigged the device, adding one wire from a 12V source on the engine and one from the exciter into the galley; he then used a makeshift switch to provide a brief shot of "juice" to the alternator when needed. Creamer had just hot-wired his own boat.

Globe Star was becalmed much of March 4, but that afternoon the winds picked up and they jolted along with genoa and a single-reefed main. Heavy rains the previous day had allowed them to collect about twenty gallons of water, so each of the crew managed a full bath on the fantail and a freshwater rinse. The next day, they were treated to a hard blow from the port side that almost knocked them down: at Marv's direction, Bob tried to run it off to starboard, but the boat heeled severely on the starboard side and water poured in the open port over the starboard settee berth. The tape recorder, Marv's clothes, and several cans of food stored under the berth were soaked. Afterward, they lay in lumpy seas with sails slatting—not the most pleasant of days.

The lumpy seas continued for a while and then, on March 8, they motored in a dead calm for over four hours. At 6:00 a.m., they were underway, but had wind on the nose; they were having a tough time making headway toward the equator. The next day, they found themselves motoring in calms. Marv felt that this might have been due—or at least the issue exacerbated by—the relatively short sail rig on *Globe Star*, which made the going slow in light air.

On March 12, the cockpit was enlivened by shouts of "Fish on the line!" as Bob hauled in a twenty-five-pound dorado. They tried to pickle the fish in a glass jar, an attempt that might have gone much better had they been sailing away from the equator rather than toward it. A few days afterward, the pickled fish was delicious, but after that it was a mess: By the end of the week, the container frothed, said Marv, "like fermenting toddy made by an African palm tree tapper."[3] (Which Creamer may have had occasion to taste, having sailed to Africa before and having traveled—by plane—around the world in 1969, after spending that summer in multiple African countries.)

The dorado pickling may have failed, but landing the fish may have provided a clue to their whereabouts. The stomach of the dorado had been filled with small fish that looked, to Marv's eye, like bottom fish, leading them to suspect that they were sailing over a shallow area shown on the chart. He surmised that they were therefore crossing the Continental Shelf.

This seems like quite an inferential leap to make on Marv's part. How would he know that the fish in the dorado's gut were bottom feeders? What bottom feeders would be present there? How shallow *is* the Continental Shelf? Is his assumption a reasonable one to make based on such "evidence"?

Dr. Richard Searles is the former head of the Botany Department at Duke University. He notes that the dorado (also known as the mahi-mahi or dolphin fish) is a *pelagic* fish, meaning that it lives up in the water column, in contrast to *benthic* fish, which live on or near the bottom.

*There are plenty of fish which are benthic and distinguished ecologi-
cally as such. A dorado which was over the continental shelf might
have some benthic fish in its gut, but I think it feeds mostly on other,
smaller pelagic fish. A dorado in the open ocean beyond the continental
shelf would certainly not have benthic fish in its gut.*[4]

The logic of Creamer's supposition is at least partly supported by the
facts. If the fish in the dorado's gut *were* benthic, then he is probably—
though not definitively—correct because, as Dr. Searles points out, a fish
caught beyond the shelf would most likely *not* have been feeding on such
fish. (But see next for another viewpoint.)

Dr. Searles says that the shelf is by definition a shallow area, generally with a depth of less than one hundred meters, so if Creamer's *premise*
is correct, then yes, he had reached and was very likely sailing over the
Continental Shelf.[5]

This sort of extrapolation may be a bit of a stretch, but then, to a great
extent, extrapolation and guesswork were all that Marv had to go on. His
entire journey was in fact speculative, relying on repeated instances of
conjecture, supposition, and educated speculation, all complemented by a
lifetime of experience. But even if he were occasionally wrong, which he
was, he was correct enough—often enough—to find his way around the
world using nothing but those "speculations."

At least one leading ichthyologist believes that Marv could have
been mistaken here. Dr. Steve Ross, of the University of North Carolina–
Wilmington, has some doubts about Marv's deduction. First, he disputes
Marv's characterization of the sea being in any way "shallow" in that area.
"Even sea mounts in that area," he notes, "are quite deep." As far as the
mahi-mahi,

*Not only does it matter what species of fish they were eating but it
matters what life stage or size they were. For example, mahi (dolphin
[the fish, not the aquatic mammal]) often feed on juvenile fishes, like
triggerfish and filefish, which are pelagic in the upper water column
when young but are benthic as adults. I very much doubt the mahi
were feeding on the bottom as that is quite rare, and in the supposed*

position of the vessel, I suspect the water was quite deep. In short, I think Marv was incorrect about the water depth and the mahi diet.[6]

In sum, we just don't know, possibly because we simply don't have enough information about the fish he caught and exactly what was in its gut. But if his deduction based on the mahi was incorrect, he was apparently right enough about a number of other things—enough so that he did in fact find his way to the Atlantic Coast.

On March 12 and 13, they were finally able to get latitude from Mars, beta, and delta Scorpii. It was the first time they had been able to use celestial bodies for latitude finding since leaving the Falklands. (In that time, they had sailed about 2,250 miles through the horse latitudes and into the tropics.)

The weather was, as expected, changing as they got deeper into the tropics. They still had the occasional cool evening, but the days were hot, the skies full of clouds, and the boat drenched by daily showers in the late afternoons.

On March 16, they raised the drifter in northeasterly air—the first easterly air they had encountered in these latitudes. Their direction had been poor, but was improving. The next day, Creamer noted:

Still moving well with easterly air. We are able to sail straight north (as near as we can judge), and at fairly good speed, c.4 knots. We all look forward to clearing the Brazilian hump c.7° south latitude. At that point we will be able to sail directly toward home.[7]

The easterlies continued to propel *Globe Star* toward the equator, and on the 23rd, they turned northwestward. They were finally heading more or less directly toward home.

Creamer did surprisingly well at navigating by the stars and by educated guesswork. When he could get a decent sighting of the stars, his latitude was close to right on. Longitude, though, was another story. As sailors know, and as noted earlier, it is very difficult to ascertain longitude accurately without an accurate chronometer and tables; Marv had neither. Instead he had to go by whatever clues he could gather from the clouds in the sky, the wind, the color and temperature of the water, the birds he might spot, and by whatever dead reckoning positions he'd managed to plot earlier. (Which themselves may have been off.) It's no surprise, then, that checking the ARGOS data later, Creamer discovered that his March 23 EP was way off. The latitude, naturally, was not so bad: he was off by 116 miles. His longitude, though, was off by a whopping 692 miles.

As they neared the equator, they sailed under a greater number of stars useful for latitude finding, and from March 20 to March 26, they were able to confirm their latitude based on observations of Spica, Alphard, and gamma Virginis. This meant—among other things—that they were able to determine fairly accurately the day on which they crossed the equator. That would occur, they judged, around midday on March 27; naturally, hijinks ensued, as is the custom when crossing the equator. (The origins of such "line-crossing" celebrations are shrouded in mystery, but they go back to well before the eighteenth century, and seem to have taken place in the navies and maritime academies of most countries. They have on occasion devolved into brutal hazing that has been the subject of investigations and resulted in punitive actions, but these days they are mostly good-natured exercises in—occasionally ribald—fun.)

In *Globe Star*'s case, Ed poked fun at Marv by planting a blowup woman (that is, a doll) in Marv's bunk. The doll was clad in a not particularly erotic-looking Bigelow Labs jersey. Ed, of course, denied any knowledge of how "Mary" might have gotten aboard, in spite of the fact that he'd been taking water temperature readings for Bigelow Labs while on this voyage. Then Ed shaved his moustache as a sacrifice to the sea gods. (Which seemed to have worked because shortly afterward, the wind picked up.)

It's unfortunate that Ed didn't have a *second* moustache to sacrifice because two days later they were in the doldrums, motoring along as best they could with an engine that kept leaking fuel. That leak, caused by some corroded banjo washers, was eventually repaired, but they found another leak when they pulled up the cabin sole hatch cover to look at the water level in the bilge: Clear water was pouring into the bilge from a hose end. Thinking it was siphoning from the fresh water tank, they tasted it—it was salt water, and the only possible source was an overflowing hopper bowl; someone had failed to close the inlet valve after flushing the toilet.

Progress was being made, and Marv was feeling optimistic that he might make it back to Cape May in time for his daughter Lynn's Chapel Hill, North Carolina, nursing school graduation on May 13.

His optimism was misplaced; they would not make landfall until May 17 and, says Lynn, this was not the first graduation he'd failed to attend: He had missed her high school graduation when he was out sailing, and had been on a sailing trip to Africa in 1980 when she graduated from Duke University. (Then again, Lynn herself had also decided not to attend the latter.) Marv's missing her nursing school graduation hurt a bit, but it wasn't the emotional calamity it might have been:

> *Although it was important to me, I did have other close friends at the time who acted in the role of family for me, so I did not feel a loss. I was older and nearly my entire nursing school experience happened while dad was heavily involved in planning or executing the circumnavigation, so he wasn't really part of it. I was also very independent from the time I left home in 1975. I had not gone back to NJ except to visit, even in the summers. And it was part of a larger pattern of my dad missing my graduations. From 1970 when he got his first sailboat,* Scotia, *summers were for sailing.*[8]

That doesn't mean that summers were always spent *without* the kids, because the children sometimes sailed *with* Creamer. However, the other children actually spent more time at sea with him than Lynn, perhaps because she was prone to seasickness. After high school she planned a trip to Bermuda with Marv and Blanche but had to turn back because she was so ill. Younger brother Kurt Creamer did accompany Marv and Blanche on that trip, and Marv took Andra and her new husband on a sailing trip to Bermuda for their honeymoon.

Lynn's experience growing up with (and sometimes without) Marv mirrors to some extent many others' experiences with their parents. Especially during her teens and twenties, their relationship was sometimes troubled and distant, but that's often the case with children of that age as they seek to find themselves, establish their own identities, and free themselves of the parental yoke. In the Creamers' case, this might have been aggravated by Marv's tendency to overlook his family's needs in his desire to sail more and sail farther. There's much to admire about Marv Creamer, but there's no getting around the fact that Marv was gone many summers and that during those absences, he missed taking part in his kids' emotional and personal lives. (Still, Lynn loved her father, she says, and their relationship did in fact improve in later years.)[9]

Early the next morning, the wind shifted to east of northeast and a few hours later a line of large cumulus clouds crossed their bow from starboard to port. A few hours later, they replaced the ARGOS transmitter, whose batteries had given out, with the one that John O'Brien and Ian Milne had rigged to run on their 12V boat batteries. (This was the set that had garbled weather data when sailing from Hobart to Sydney, but Creamer figured that the problem had been solved by reversing the multipronged plug in the Falklands.)

Winds continued out of the northeast on March 31. The sky turned a powdery gray, filled with dust, and the sun was a very pale yellow when it neared the horizon. Creamer suspected that the source of the dust was the Sahara: the same they had seen more than a year ago when traveling in the opposite direction.

For several days in a row, they moved steadily northwestward with the yankee, staysail, and main occasionally changed between single and double reef. On April 2, Creamer was able to obtain latitude from Procyon (actually one of the stars nearest to Earth, at only 11.46 light-years' distance), but on the 6th came a big moment: the *Globe Star* crew was able to get a good look at Polaris, low in the sky on the starboard bow:

> *Even though it stands directly above the ice-covered Arctic Ocean, it gave us a very warm feeling knowing that we were back in its realm where it provided instantaneous orientation at the merest glance.*[10]

By April 8, the winds were turning light and the seas heavy. They landed a twelve-pound dorado, which made for fine eating for the next two nights, but progress was slow. They had the drifter up for the first time in a long while.

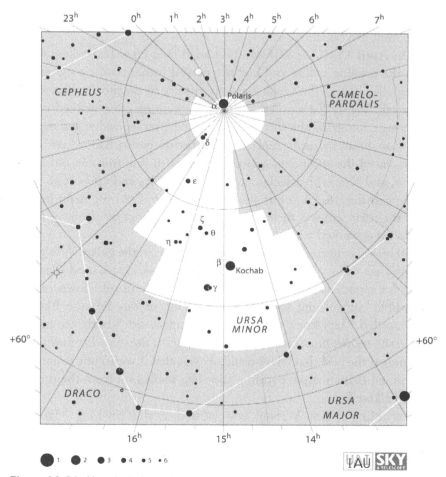

Figure 18.01. Here is Polaris, in the constellation Ursa Minor. (IMAGE USED UNDER THE CREATIVE COMMONS ATTRIBUTION 3.0 UNPORTED LICENSE, COURTESY OF USER: *BOIVIE*.)

On Friday the 13th, the wind had dropped off and was exceptionally light. When it veered to east, they put up the chute, which worked well until that evening.

About 4:45 p.m., they had a visitor: A ship bore down on them from the east, veered to port seemingly to pass astern, then veered to starboard, passed on their port side, then circled them clockwise and gave a three-blast salute. Passengers and crew came to the rail to wave. It was a Soviet ship, the *Krasnodon*, with a deck load of machinery headed east, presumably bound for Cuba.[11]

On April 15, *Globe Star* was becalmed. The crew had taken all sail down the evening before and had not moved (other than via current) in twenty-four hours. They took the opportunity to do more maintenance and repair. While Ed worked aloft, the remaining crew worked on the mast plug connecting the solar panels to the batteries, exchanged topping lift and mainsail halyards, replaced the primary genoa halyard with new line, replaced the secondary genoa halyard with line from an old genoa halyard, and scraped barnacles, etc., from the sides and aft bottom. They also tapped the mast and put another cleat on to hold the main halyard when the main sail was furled to the boom. The boat didn't move much, but the crew worked a lot.

Dave was continuing his culinary adventures in the galley. While they tried to coax *Globe Star* through the horse latitudes, Dave used Blanche's recipe for sponge cake to try to make a pineapple upside down cake. It was edible but nothing to write home about, mainly because Blanche, knowing that Marv knew how many eggs to use, didn't bother to include eggs in the recipe; thus, Dave included no eggs in the cake. Damning with faint praise, the best that Marv could say was that it wasn't any worse than the canned British apple pudding they had picked up from the military in the Falklands.

According to Bob Watson, who crewed on that final leg, Marv was somewhat dissatisfied with Dave's cooking—or at least used his cooking as an opportunity to needle him. Although they'd known each other for quite a while, and in fact had sailed together previously, Marv criticized Dave quite a bit during that final leg. Recalling a conversation with Dave during that trip, Bob notes, "Dave said to me, one day when Marvin was out of earshot, 'I don't understand why he's so critical of me and very negative about everything I do. I sailed with him before and it was like my best friend and he's a totally different person now than he was on that previous trip.'"[12] Of course, Marv was several years older now and racing the clock to get back to New Jersey; perhaps he really *was* a totally different person, at least temporarily.

Figure 18.02. Ed Gibson, Bob Watson, and Dave Lansdale arrive in the Falklands.
(PHOTO COURTESY OF THE CREAMER FAMILY.)

Figure 18.03. *Globe Star* docked in the Falklands.
(PHOTO COURTESY OF THE CREAMER FAMILY.)

The food was a minor issue, really, compared to the fact that they spent so much time becalmed. It was hot and dry. As had many other vessels before it, *Globe Star* bobbed ineffectually in breezes that were so light as to be unusable, or absent altogether. This close to their goal, it was a frustrating experience—but then many generations of sailors had been equally frustrated trying to sail through the horse latitudes. Sailors of old may or may not have jettisoned their equine cargoes to lighten their load and to conserve precious water (origin stories about the term differ), but there's no doubt that many a captain sought desperately for some way to urge his vessel out of the deadly calms and into the wind.

CHAPTER 19

HOME IS THE SAILOR

One's destination is never a place, but a new way of seeing things.
—HENRY MILLER

FINALLY, THE CALMS ENDED. ON THE AFTERNOON OF APRIL 21, WINDS picked up and then kept picking up. Eventually, they howled through the rigging, blowing in excess of thirty knots; over two days' time, the seas had built to thirty feet.

Globe Star was now moving smartly along, and they began crossing major shipping lanes, which of course resulted in more ship sightings. On April 23, they sighted four ships, all of them bobbing like corks in the foaming breakers. It didn't seem possible to Marv that simple air and water could exert the kind of pressure needed to fling these multi-million-pound leviathans around. He wondered how many more storms lay ahead and what kind of weather they would face when they made landfall.

Bad luck turned into good on the 24th—depending on how one wishes to interpret "good." In midmorning Dave spotted a sloop-rigged sailing yacht flying a spinnaker and a French flag headed northeast. Thinking they might enjoy some conversation with fellow sailors after seventy-six days of talking to each other, they lowered their genoa and cranked up the engine to give chase. A dirty fuel filter stalled the engine and scuttled that plan. They replaced the fuel filter, bled the lines, and tried again. Again, the engine failed. They eventually got the engine running well, but it took several more bleedings, and by that time, the French yacht was long out of sight. They had missed their opportunity to speak with other humans for the first time in months, but they had also found and repaired an engine problem that might have caused them great difficulty—and possibly placed them in grave danger—later on when they tried making port.

They had had hopes of finding Bermuda, thinking that they were about 230 miles east of it, but because of the direction of the wind, a little south of west, they could not maintain a due-west course in order to run it down. Even so, early on the morning of April 26, Marv thought that he caught a momentary smell of the island, and late in the day he saw streak lightning off to port as they proceeded on what they guessed was a course of 300 degrees.

Their approach to the population centers of the northeastern United States brought more and more ship sightings and an occasional glimpse of a jet. On April 29 toward the end of a day of numerous clouds, including towering cumulus, they watched a waterspout dance against the background of the setting sun.

They were getting close to home now, and they were joined by a tired barn swallow:

He tried perching on furled sails, Ed's knee, and the tiller lines. The strong west winds that had blown him to sea and overcast skies were now making it difficult for us to reach that land. In the early morning hours we got a look at Cor Caroli and Vega and at noon estimated our latitude to be that of Cape May, i.e., 39°. All we needed now was to sail directly west to intercept it by the parallel sailing method.[1]

It should have been simple. They had managed to find their way to the correct latitude. All they needed to do now was sail west until they were home, but what should have been an easy few days of sailing turned into over two weeks of frustration. They were beset by gales, overcast skies, dead calms, adverse currents, and strong headwinds. By noon on May 3, they were ten miles *farther* from Cape May than they had been the day before.

The next day was worse: southwesterly gales, wind-driven surface water, and the underlying Gulf Stream wiped out a hundred miles of

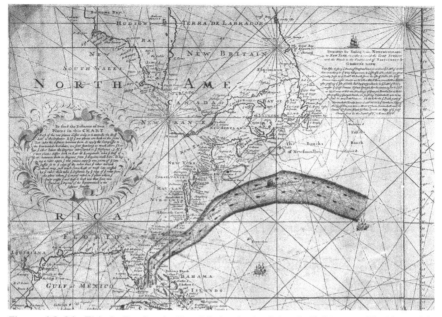

Figure 19.01. This is Benjamin Franklin's chart of the Gulf Stream. Working with Timothy Folger, a Nantucket whaling captain, the two men named and mapped out the current in a chart that was published in London in 1769—and subsequently ignored by most British sea captains. (IMAGE IN THE PUBLIC DOMAIN.)

movement through the water to give them a net loss of eight miles for the twenty-four-hour period. They were going backward, losing ground instead of gaining it.

On May 4, heavy cloud cover made direction finding difficult, but during the night, a wind shift occurred. When Marv came on watch, he noted that the cabin was warmer and the hatch didn't squeak (meaning, or so he surmised, that the humidity was higher), so he changed over to the port tack and set a course that was mostly guesswork. When the sun came out a few hours later, they found that they were within 10 degrees of their desired course.

The wind cranked up on the 5th, and churning seas made sleep almost impossible. Trying to maintain some westing in southwest gales, they gradually reduced sail to the storm jib and storm trysail and still averaged about four knots, but they took a lot of heavy thumps during the course of the night.

The next day, gales from the west forced them to reduce sail, first to jib and trysail, then down to storm jib only. It was another rough night.

The water kept getting warmer, which, while more comfortable in the cockpit, was not a good sign; *Globe Star* was fighting to get free of the warm Gulf Stream and find her way into the cold green coastal waters. The reappearance of blue water was demoralizing because it indicated that they were not near the coast. Instead they were stuck on the Gulf Stream, an endless, warm-water conveyor belt that carried them, unwillingly, toward Europe at the rate of 36 miles per day. According to the ARGOS data, in the past seventy-two hours they had gotten only sixty-eight miles closer to Cape May, and the winds were still from the west, the direction they had to sail to make their landfall.

Despite a brief respite during which southerly gales propelled them along their way, a few days later they noted that the water color was back to blue and that the water temperature was up to over 67 degrees Fahrenheit. Their run on May 10 was only twenty-six miles, and the next day's was hardly better, at thirty-eight miles. They were still stuck on the Gulf Stream and their easy few days of sailing had turned into a frustrating multiweek slog.

On May 11, they saw Vega at meridian transit and were able to figure their latitude, noting with shock that storms and currents had pushed them much farther north than their EP showed. They came over on the starboard tack and began sailing southward, hoping to clear Cape Cod before turning southwest for Cape May.

May 11 was a red-letter day for a few reasons. First, Marv got a good look at Vega and was able to correct his latitude. Later, the crew spotted two large flocks of land birds—smaller birds flying north and larger ones flying south. But the biggest shot in the arm came that afternoon when they spotted the largest bird of all:

What a surprise we got about 1230 LAT [Local Apparent Time]. A P3 Orion from the Navy base at Brunswick, Maine, dropped five large boxes of mail, newspapers, fruits, vegetables, cokes, etc. [meat, shrimp, cookies, asparagus, oranges, grapefruit, lettuce, tomatoes, and two kinds of salad dressing] via triple parachutes and marked by flares. The "care" packages had been picked up in Norfolk, Va., arranged by Lee Houchins. Phillip S. Hughes, Acting Sec'y, of Smithsonian, requested the drop in a letter to the Sec'y of the Navy, John F. Lehman, Jr., dated May 9. We made three passes to pick up the first package but got each of the other four on the first try.[2]

As it turned out, Lee Houchins, their Smithsonian project leader and the man in charge of the ARGOS transmitter they carried, was actually in the Orion, supervising the food drop. And as it also turned out, Blanche Creamer was the original impetus behind the operation: she had gotten concerned about the crew's food and water supply, wondering whether they might have used up their reserves in the three months they had been at sea, and called Lee Houchins to see if he could arrange an airdrop.

Aside from having to take care not to get the parachute shrouds entangled in their prop, they were able to pick up the dropped items with no real problem. Ironically, they had been sitting in the cockpit eating a lunch of baked beans when the air drop began. They weren't really low on food, but they were definitely running out of *good* food, especially fresh fruits and vegetables. They gleefully abandoned the baked beans and feasted on shrimp, tomatoes, and lettuce salad. There would be fresh asparagus with dinner that night.

Interestingly, during the air drop they noticed a tanker off to their port side and heading in the same direction. At first, they thought that the ship was waiting for the currents in the Delaware to change, but Marv later decided that the vessel's captain thought a rescue might be underway and hove to until it was clear that he was not needed.[3]

The next day, more excitement. They spotted a spouting whale, pilot whales, porpoises, a ship, and a housefly. Of them all, the fly caused the most excitement because usually the only flies found on a boat are the ones that board when the passengers board. In all his years of sailing, Creamer had rarely seen a fly more than fifteen miles offshore unless it had boarded with the crew or guests. So having first gotten longitude hints from Saharan dust, rocky islands, and a barn swallow, they were

Figure 19.02. Marv, Ed, and Dave unpack goodies after the P3 Orion's airdrop.
(PHOTO COURTESY OF THE CREAMER FAMILY.)

now proposing to extract east-west information from a housefly. The crew assured themselves that land could not be far away.

On the afternoon of May 13, they spotted four fishing boats that they guessed were fishing on or close to Georges Bank, a large, elevated area of the sea floor between Cape Cod and Cape Sable Island, Nova Scotia. They were now fairly sure that they had cleared the Gulf Stream, but the price they paid was a greatly diminished range of vision.

They were reduced to about a half mile of visibility. Ordinarily, this was good enough, but then the fog set in. Marv was on watch and, as he sat in the cockpit with his feet resting on the fiberglass box that held their life raft, he began worrying: If they were to get run down in the fog by a freighter or other large vessel—a maritime misfortune that occurs all too regularly, especially in busy shipping lanes—could they get the raft released, inflated, and launched in time to save themselves? As he sat there musing about their possible deaths, Marv saw the big black bow of a ship less than a hundred yards away. Panic stricken, he yelled, "We're being rammed!" and called for the key to the engine, but before he could get the engine started, the ship passed by, very close—so Marv thought—to

Globe Star's stern. The ship was a Hapag-Lloyd container ship out of Hamburg, Germany, its deck deserted and its fog horn strangely (and illegally) silent.[4]

They had escaped disaster, but they were still in the fog and still in some of the busiest shipping lanes in the world. There was no relaxing until the fog lifted a few hours later.

By then they were a bit *too* relaxed, because they were once again becalmed. A band of dark clouds passing tantalizingly overhead promised usable air but did not deliver. They needed a fix but could not get a glimpse of the setting sun. For a moment, they thought they had spotted two long rows of lights affixed to land, but they turned out to be the lights of fishing boats hove-to for net tending.

However, among the fishing boat lights was a white light that appeared to blink every five seconds. They searched the *Light List* for a light with a five-second interval but found nothing. Stuck in shipping lanes with no wind, they felt compelled to motor close enough for identification. The hour-and-a-half ride used up a great deal of fuel, but they believed that they had no other recourse. The blinking light turned out to be attached to "N" buoy, a replacement for the old Nantucket Light Ship. The switch had been made while they were at sea, and the light characteristic had been changed from a double flash every ten seconds to a single flash every five seconds.

By the time they had cleared the buoy and the main body of the fishing fleet, a previously stalled front advanced and provided enough air for them to move under sail, although quite slowly.

By Creamer's reckoning, they were now free of the Gulf Stream and had entered the cold coastal waters; he believed that Cape May lay 255 miles west of southwest. The cold extension of the Labrador current, he figured, would now be adding rather than subtracting miles.

Their initial speed was poor, and the best heading they could make was about 30 degrees off target, but over the next few days, the wind veered and strengthened. Their speed, their heading, and their visibility were now quite good. On May 17, when he came on watch, Marv got a good look at Vega and determined that they were on the latitude of Cape May, that is, about 39 degrees.

Globe Star was now streaking for home. The triple-reefed main was set on the starboard tack and the genoa was close-hauled. Creamer knew that the genny was straining but was reluctant to strike it. That was a mistake. The sun was edging above the horizon when it popped like a rifle shot. The clew grommet had pulled out of the heavy canvas, and the sail flogged wildly in the early morning wind. (The genny was their hard-luck sail—it was both the first and the last to be damaged.)

The next morning, Marv was awakened by Bob Watson in the cockpit shouting for him. A Coast Guard chopper from Cape May was circling above. On his way up the companionway ladder, Marv had spotted a red marker line on the starboard bow, so when Bob asked which way to steer, Marv pointed and said, "Toward that buoy." It was the "F" marker, just fifteen miles south of Cape May harbor. They pointed *Globe Star*'s bow northward and supplemented sail with diesel power to keep from losing way to lee.

In spite of the fact that they were now so close to Cape May that they could almost *see* it, their troubles were not over, and their circumnavigation almost ended only a few miles short of their goal. Heading into Delaware Bay, Creamer let his boat wander too far toward the left bank, where *Globe Star*'s propellor struck a fixed object of some sort that almost stalled the engine. The engine recovered but then sped up as they glided to a halt in a dead calm. Creamer knew without even looking that the inch-thick stainless steel propeller shaft had twisted off. The crew put down an anchor to hold the boat against the outgoing tide and then considered their options. One of those options was obvious: Simply hail a boat with a radio and ask for a tow. This did not appeal to Creamer; how would it look to have circumnavigated the globe and then have to be *towed* to the site of their homecoming festivities?

There had to be a better alternative. They opened the sidewall of the engine compartment, only to discover that the engine compartment was flooding; when the propeller shaft had twisted off, it had pulled through the stuffing box, allowing water to gush in. Creamer describes their next steps:

Figure 19.03. Marv and crew on their return to Cape May.
(PHOTO COURTESY OF ROWAN UNIVERSITY ARCHIVES.)

> *Luckily the rudder had prevented the shaft and attached propeller from dropping into Delaware Bay. By unclamping the stuffing box we managed to get hold of the barely visible end of the shaft and haul it back into the boat. With the shaft inboard we replaced the stuffing box and stemmed the flow of water.[5]*

The shaft, having sheared where it exited the transmission flange, had left about three-quarters of an inch of keyway on the shaft. The crew needed to remove the flange, but the four cap screws securing it were rusted tight; if they used open-end wrenches (there was no room for any other type of wrench) to attempt to loosen the bolts, they could strip the heads. That would leave them almost literally "up the creek."

Eventually, though, by hammering and "wrenching" at the same time, they were able to loosen the bolts and then remove the two set screws—an operation that required heating the flange on the galley stove (which worked, for once) and then boring the other screw out with a 12V lug

Figure 19.04. A wan and pensive Marv Creamer rests after dealing with a broken propeller shaft as *Globe Star* nears Cape May.

nut wrench that had been converted into an electric drill. Creamer then used a tiny grinder that he had made from the motor of an automobile window crank to grind a piece of key stock, which he used to worry the sheared end of the propellor shaft into the flange. It was not a good fit and wobbled badly when they tried moving forward; they didn't dare try reverse. But it held, and Creamer decided that it *might* work if they stayed at reduced RPMs.

The propellor shaft kludge worried Marv, because a typical docking maneuver would require reversing—a task he was not sure his boat could manage with a jury-rigged prop shaft. That meant a change in plans: Although they had originally intended to dock in Essington for the night, giving the people assembling to welcome him home some time to gather at Cape May, Creamer now felt that this was too risky. Instead, they would anchor for the night on the Delaware.

This was a good plan—except for the water-befouled engine that greeted him at 4:00 a.m. when Creamer went to check the engine oil: water, lots of it, had gotten into the crankcase. Would it hold together for

Figure 19.05. Marv and Blanche meet the press after making port in Cape May.
(PHOTO COURTESY OF THE CREAMER FAMILY.)

the last ten or so miles? He opted to try for it, well aware that he could ruin the engine.

It worked, just barely. They entered Cape May Harbor about 1:00 p.m. on Thursday, May 17. Alerted by the ARGOS monitor, a small plane (in which rode Marv's son Kurt) flew welcoming passes above them. Blanche's brother, Charlie Layton, who had followed them around the world via the ARGOS system, was racing up from Baltimore, but he arrived at the dock about forty-five minutes too late, deceived by the boat's final burst of speed.

When *Globe Star*'s bow touched the fuel dock at Cape Island West Marina, it brought an end to a dream that originated a half century earlier in the mind of a teenager reading about an oceangoing sailboat, a dream that was then nudged along by the failure of a compass light some forty years later.

After 351 days at sea, and a voyage of some 29,000 nautical miles, *Globe Star* was home. Marvin Creamer, a slender, balding geography professor from a small-time college, had accomplished his dream. He had shown the world that men and women could indeed sail the globe with nothing but a good boat, their brains, their senses, and equal measures of grit and determination. And a good deal of luck, of course.

EPILOGUE

We travel not to escape life, but for life not to escape us.

—Unknown

At sixty-eight years of age, Marv's life was far from over when *Globe Star* docked at Cape May after her eighteen months at sea. He would carry on sailing, though never again would he take such a long voyage. He continued enjoying life, working in his garden, puttering around the house, and sailing his much smaller boat, a Flicka 20 christened *Jubilee*. At one point he had intended to sail *Jubilee* across the Atlantic, but advancing age and problematic arthritis convinced him to shelve that plan. This was just as well, really. The Flicka 20 is a beautiful boat, a pocket cruiser that is sturdy enough to go anywhere—but not necessarily in comfort.

The current owner of *Jubilee*, Rob Cheshire, bought the boat from Marv shortly before Creamer's death, and he notes that the boat is "built like a tank. [But] in a boat that small, it's a matter of discomfort. You know the boat's made sturdy enough to take you anywhere, but it's not going to be a pleasant ride if it gets rough."

Creamer continued driving well into his nineties, and after giving up driving, continued to ride a bicycle, then a scooter. (Companionable and irrepressible to the last, he remarried in 2010, five years after Blanche's death.) Marv died on August 12, 2020, having achieved something dreamt of by many but accomplished by very few and having led a life of exuberant exploration and adventure that most of us could only imagine or read about in the pages of a book such as this one.

During his lifetime, Marv received dozens of accolades and awards. In 1980, even before the *Globe Star* voyage, he had received the Medal of Achievement for Performance Cruising from *Yacht Racing/ Cruising Magazine*. After his instrument-less circumnavigation, in 1984, he was made an honorary member of both the Slocum Society and the

E.01. Rob Cheshire became friends with Marv late in Marv's life, helping him spruce up *Jubilee*, which Cheshire eventually bought. This is *Jubilee* at the dock in the early 2000s. (IMAGE COURTESY OF ROB CHESHIRE.)

E.02. Marv Creamer's Blue Water Medal. (IMAGE COURTESY OF ROWAN UNIVERSITY/CRAIG TERRY.)

Circumnavigators Club. In 1989, Creamer was inducted into *Cruising World*'s Hall of Fame. In 1985 came perhaps the greatest honor of all: he was awarded the coveted Blue Water Medal, sailing's highest honor, by the Cruising Club of America.

And yet few have heard of Marvin Creamer. Certainly, some dedicated sailors have read about his circumnavigation, but many—even in the sailing community—are unfamiliar with his accomplishments. And certainly, few *outside* of the sailing community know about Marv and his many voyages, with and without instruments. That's a situation this book aims to correct.

Interestingly, Marv—who would eagerly speak about his voyages and accomplishments at the drop of a hat—was not terribly interested in showing off his awards. They were not displayed in a case or on a "trophy wall." In fact, by and large, they were not displayed at all. Several people (Rob Cheshire among them) have said that the awards—including the prestigious Blue Water Medal—simply sat in a cardboard box on the floor in his office. He would happily drag them out to show visitors, but he never got around to building a display of them. It's odd for a man who was very proud of his maritime endeavors to have been so reticent about displaying his many honors, but it appears to be the case: Cheshire notes that the only reason he knew about them at all was that they happened to be sitting in a box on Marv's floor when he went over one day to help Marv get his Internet connection working.

Bold sea ventures earn Pitman sailor yachting award

By TONY MULDOON
Of the Courier-Post

A series of increasingly bold sea ventures has earned Marvin Creamer, Pitman's globe-girdling sailor, the Cruising Club of America's (CCA) Blue Water Medal, long-distance yachting's equivalent of the Pulitzer Prize.

Creamer, a 69-year-old retired Glassboro State College professor who circumnavigated the globe without the use of modern navigational instruments, received the award Thursday night at the New York Yacht Club.

The Blue Water Medal award ceremonies are held in conjunction with the National Boat Show, which ends tomorrow at the New York Coliseum.

In a voyage lasting from Dec. 21, 1982 to May, 1984, Creamer sailed Globe Star, his 35-foot, cutter-rigged sloop, around the world from Cape May.

The CCA Blue Water Medal confirmed Creamer's place in the pantheon of small boat voyagers beside such legendary figures as New Englander Joshua Slocum who, in a voyage lasting from 1895 to 1898, became the first person to sail alone around the world.

But it was not so much that Creamer sailed around the world (such voyages are increasingly common) but that he did it with fewer navigational instruments than 10th Century Vikings.

A compass, sextant and radio were carried in a sealed bag in case of emergency, but Creamer relied solely on his system of naked eye celestial observations and his highly developed sea-sense.

MARVIN CREAMER
. . . out-navigated ancient Vikings

E.03. When Marv was awarded the Blue Water Medal, it was big news in New Jersey. (PHOTO/SCAN COURTESY OF THE CREAMER FAMILY.)

Marv was different than most of us. In an age in which many of us are simply passive wanderers, he was an active *doer*. He was not simply *of* the world; he was actively *in* the world. He sought to know—and succeeded in knowing—a good deal more about how the world worked than many in his generation and certainly a great deal more than those of later generations, wedded as we are to technology and wandering through life with our faces stuck in our smartphones. While so many of us are blind to our environment, Marv was alive to his: He took note of the wind, the texture

E.04. Author/sailor Patricia Wood in her natural element. (IMAGE COURTESY OF PATRICIA WOOD.)

and smell of the earth, the size and direction of the waves, the passing of seasons; he knew where he was at all times and could pinpoint his place in the world, while all the time wondering about and planning to travel to other places. He could successfully travel the world partly *because* he paid attention to where he was in the world in the first place.

Patricia Wood, mentioned in chapter 7, is an author and a veteran of several transpacific crossings. Based in Hawaii and living aboard her sailboat, *Orion*, Patricia understands what it's like to be alone in the midst of seemingly endless water and infinite horizon. She was quick to point out that Marv understood more than just how to sail; he brought to the challenge his scientific background, his questing intelligence, and his broad understanding of the real world.

> *He understood not just scientific treatises or doctrines or theorems or hypotheses—not just scientific data, but how it applied to his immediate world. The cabin door's swelling? It's probably humid. Oh, the door shuts easily? It's probably really dry out. He was able to understand clouds in order to understand what he saw on the water.*[1]

Wood also pointed out that, in this day and age, Marv would likely be *unable* to sail without technology simply because it wouldn't be allowed.

> *Back then, one could just show up and clear customs, as it were. Now I can't just show up, even at a port in [relatively nearby] Mexico.*

You have to have charged cell phones, because you have to notify [the authorities] ahead of time. You have to have your paperwork filed ahead of time. Now you're completely dependent on technology because countries require it.[2]

In fact, as Marv's daughter, Lynn Creamer Borstelmann, notes, part of the reason her father ran into a bit of a problem in the Falklands—having arrived in conflicted territory—was the fact that the *Globe Star* crew *had* no technology. If the crew had had a radio, for instance, someone on board could have radioed ahead and either been warned off or gained permission to enter the area.

Two seemingly contradictory themes have emerged in this story of Marv Creamer's incredible journey. First, Marv and his crew were admirable examples of a sort of Thoreauvian self-reliance, overcoming all obstacles, sometimes by clever engineering, sometimes simply by dogged perseverance, often by a combination of the two. One cannot sail the world without a strong (some might say stubborn) streak of self-sufficiency. On a boat—as on a farm or in a machine shop—things break and there is simply no one else around to fix those things. Obstacles arise and must be overcome, not handed off, ignored, or complained about; they must be surmounted, then and there. As Michael Stadler points out in *Psychology of Sailing*, seamen must "develop the special personality traits which are useful in this environment . . . such as reserve caution, level-headedness, and . . . deliberation."[3] Which is to say, decisions on a boat must be made promptly, but not hurriedly; actions must be taken self-assuredly, but not recklessly. Self-reliant men and women are capable of such decisions and such actions, and at sea, they must make those decisions and take those actions if they, their vessel, and their shipmates are to survive.

On the other hand, being confined on a boat is not too dissimilar from being in a cloister, a prison, or, for that matter, being afield in wartime. (Paraphrasing Samuel Johnson, living on a boat is *very* much like being in a prison, but with the added possibility of drowning.) Yet, as with workers on a farm or soldiers at war, the crew of a sailboat—although they must remain calm, civil, self-reliant, and industrious—must grow to trust and depend on one another.[4] The "social density" on a yacht is quite high: several people are crammed together in a small space and under extreme pressure. This does not always go well. (In one bizarre instance, the result was the murder of two of the crew by two other members.[5] It's safe to assume that such an outcome is rare these days.) In Creamer's case the crew, with rare exceptions, learned to work together as a team, which is the only way a boat can sail safely and efficiently. On a small boat at sea, one's life is literally in the hands of the other crewmembers: one dozing sailor on watch at night; one woman who slacks off when inspecting toggles, shackles, and turnbuckles; one person's sloppy math at the chart table; one man too slow to reduce sail—any of these can spell the disastrous end of what should have been an enjoyable cruise.

Marv himself was undoubtedly a self-reliant, self-sufficient man. He could tune an engine, figure out his latitude from the stars and his longitude from debris in (or the color of) the water, repair a tiller or a cabin hatch, or make a small grinder out of a discarded auto window motor. He could grow and harvest vegetables and then cook them in a stew of his own making. He was a tinkerer, a fixer, a man not given to allowing obstacles to overwhelm him. And yet he got along with people. Not all people, and not all the time; his was a strong personality, after all. It had to be: on board a vessel at sea, someone must be in command, and that someone was clearly and inarguably Marvin Creamer. On top of that, he was driven to accomplish an extraordinary goal—circumnavigating the earth without the use of instruments. He was known to insist that his way was the right way, the *only* way to do something; unsurprisingly, this occasionally irritated people. Also unsurprisingly, he was often correct, which must have at times been even *more* irritating. But, on the whole, people liked him and wanted to work with him, this in spite of what must have occasionally seemed like an iron and unbending will.

Creamer sailed around the world without instruments simply because he felt he could and because he wanted to prove a point. No one had done that for a thousand years—or possibly ever, we can't really know—but Creamer did it. A voyage like that took a special kind of person, a person so complicated and so accomplished that it's difficult to sum up such a man in just a sentence or two.

E.05. Marv cutting the cake at the party honoring the twenty-fifth anniversary of the *Globe Star* voyage. The party was held in 2008; he would have been ninety years old when this photo was taken. (PHOTO COURTESY OF THE CREAMER FAMILY.)

And that's a third theme that emerges when one looks at the life of Marv Creamer: he was a *complex* man, as are most of us—especially those of us driven to achieve great things. He was a planner who strove to predict—and find ways to overcome—every potential obstacle, but also a man who set off on a journey around the world in an unproven boat. A man patient enough to while away months at home while he tried to figure out ways to navigate by the stars alone but impatient enough to set out in the middle of winter when, by all rights, he should have waited six months or more to fully assess and shake down his vessel. A man who loved his family dearly but who often prioritized his sailing expeditions above them, missing many graduations and family events because they were, to him, less important than his voyages. A man who was garrulous and sociable but who was capable of being remote and cool. A man who touted the democratic process but was not always capable of being democratic (or even thoughtful) in his dealings with family and crew. A man who loved to learn and to teach but who later in life commented that he didn't care to use new navigation technology, didn't know how to use it, and didn't intend to learn. (This was an odd statement for a lifelong teacher to make, but according to his obituary in the *New York Times*, it was apparently his attitude—at least at the time he was interviewed.)[6] And yet Marv loved *some* newer technologies: in his later years, he was a fan of Google voice assistant and was an early adopter of instant messaging and chat rooms. He posted on Facebook almost daily—usually politically oriented limericks he had written. Perhaps Creamer, steeped in the nautical traditions of sailors of the past, simply preferred to avoid some of the more modern technologies used by today's sailors? As we said, he was a complex—and not always consistent—man.

Lin Pardey—who, both on her own and with her late husband, Larry, has written several now-classic sailing books—understands something about what drove Marv. "Nowadays it's hard to find something that hasn't been done before," she says. "And [Marv] found something new and interesting to do, but it also fit into his whole psyche of enjoying trying to understand the physical world. It fit who he was very well."[7]

Lynn Creamer Borstelmann, surely one of those who knew him best, recalls her father this way:

E.06. Sailor/author Lin Pardey, who wrote or cowrote several now-classic sailing books. (PHOTO COURTESY OF LIN PARDEY. PHOTO CREDIT: MICHAEL MARRIS.)

I have never really met anyone else who was like my father. I do see him as something of a unique individual, highly intelligent and with a repertoire that covered so many different disciplines—a true renaissance man. He drew on a font of general knowledge while also drawing on specialized knowledge in particular areas that enabled him to excel at this effort—geography, mathematics, celestial navigation, public relations, teaching, machine shop, growing up in the depression, cooking and provisioning. He also had a phenomenal memory, and could commit to memory a lot of detail and recall it later; this made him an avid storyteller, but [it also meant that he could] entertain others and himself with songs, word games, and stories for long periods of time at sea.[8]

As his daughter points out, Creamer was a polymath, a man who was an expert or near expert in several fields. He had to be in order to accomplish what he did. An autodidact, he never took a navigation course (though he eventually taught one) or a sailing lesson, never studied under a shipwright, never worked in a loft. He never studied psychology and yet was able to get along with even fractious people (no one works in academia for thirty years without learning to get along and deal effectively with others) and, for the most part, to keep his vessels running smoothly in spite of any disagreements or clashes that may have occurred on board.

There are few left like him, and while our world is a little less interesting because of his absence, it may also be a bit richer—and we a little wiser—because he lived in it.

APPENDIX A

MAP OF *GLOBE STAR*'S ROUTE

BELOW IS A MAP OF *GLOBE STAR*'S VOYAGE, PLOTTED WITH MARV Creamer's *estimated* positions. Note that these will vary—sometimes greatly—from the actual positions plotted by ARGOS, most of the data from which is either no longer available or was incomplete to begin with. (Of *Globe Star*'s 351 days at sea, only seventy-eight days of ARGOS data are available.)

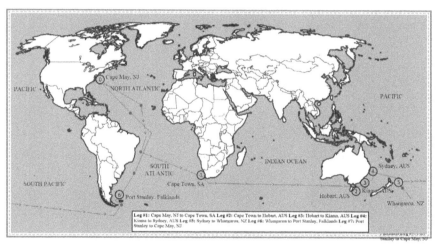

Appendix.01. (MAP BY THE AUTHOR, WITH THANKS TO LOUIS LILLEGARD OF LOU'S DESIGN GARAGE FOR THE BASE IMAGE.)

APPENDIX B

CREWS AND LEGS OF THE
GLOBE STAR VOYAGE

Dates: December 21, 1982—May 17, 1984								
Port	Crew Members	Date of Arrival	NM Sailed	SM Sailed	Days at Sea	Days in Port	Departure
Cape May, NJ	George Baldwin, Jeff Herdelin						12/21/82
Cape Town, SA	Jeff Herdelin, Rick Kuzyk	3/31/83	7,800	8,980	100	57	4/27/83
Hobart, AUS	Jesse Edwards, Nick Gill	8/12/83	6,800	7,830	77	41	9/22/83
Kiama, AUS	Jesse Edwards, Nick Gill	9/29/83	600	690	7	3	10/2/83
Sidney, AUS	Nick Gill	10/2/83	60	70	1	6	10/8/83
Whangaroa, NZ	Nick Gill, Bob Rout	10/23/83	1,300	1,500	15	7	10/30/83
Port Stanley, Falklands	Ed Gibson, Dave Lansdale, Bob Watson	12/22/83	5,500	6,300	53	49	2/9/84
Cape May, NJ		5/17/84	7,400	8,500	98		
		Totals	29,460	33,870	351	163	

APPENDIX C

MARV CREAMER ON NAVIGATING WITHOUT INSTRUMENTS

Excerpted from Marv's unpublished manuscript, *The Globe Star Voyage.*

Navigating Without Instruments

Clues taken directly from the sky and sea provide the navigator with the information he needs to guide a boat over long distances without the use of navigational instruments such as compass, sextant, chronometer, or electronics. He can check the nearness of specific stars to the boat's zenith (the point in the sky directly overhead) to find latitude, and use the sun, moon, planets, stars, clouds, waves, and the wind for finding and maintaining direction. Because finding longitude is dependent upon a knowledge of correct time, the navigator, when navigating without a timepiece, must keep a running record of longitudinal change by deducing the amount of change from distances and directions made good. Occasionally longitude can be checked against water color and temperature (as sensed by the hand), bird species, seaweed, and outcrops of rock, but in general dead-reckoned longitude cannot be trusted, so the navigator must rely on parallel sailing, a method widely used before the introduction of the chronometer. In parallel sailing, the boat early in the voyage is maneuvered in a north or south direction to the latitude of the desired landfall and then sailed directly east or west until the objective is run down.

Hour-to-Hour Steering Directions

Noninstrument steering is easiest on clear nights in the northern hemisphere. Polaris is always within about one degree of true north and provides excellent direction. For setting a course other than north, the hands placed palm-to-palm and opened to a right angle, then closed halfway, two-thirds of the way, etc., can be used as a pelorus to measure ninety-degrees, forty-five degrees, thirty degrees, etc., from a northerly or other known direction. A distinct advantage of using the pole star rather than a compass is that all headings are true. There is no need to correct for deviation or variation. Once a course is set, an appropriate star can be selected, fore or aft, for use as an interim steering guide. As the selected star changes direction with the earth's rotation, a new one can be chosen by checking the boat's heading against Polaris at the time of selection.

By using amplitude tables or formula ($\sin A = \sin d \, 7 \cos L$) in which A = amplitude, d = declination, and L = latitude, the direction of the sun and moon at the time of rising or setting can be determined and used to confirm or correct the boat's heading when these bodies are on the horizon. Sudden shifts in wind direction can be detected by keeping note of where the sun appears on the rail, but ordinarily a gradual wind shift will go unnoticed. To identify gradual wind shifts on clear days or any shift on cloudy days, it is desirable for the helmsman to keep in mind the angle between the boat's keel line and the crest lines of waves and swells. Long distance swells are reasonably constant in direction and waves of a larger size do not change direction immediately upon a wind shift. Sometimes it is possible to see the wave-top curls slanting to the left or right as they tumble down the face of a wave after a wind shift has occurred. These are clues to a changing wind direction. Accommodation to a new wind direction is easiest when it is accomplished immediately following a change. The helmsman should estimate the amount and direction of change and make a mental note of the new angle between the wind and the boat's center line.

Wind shifts on cloudy nights are the hardest to deal with. As the helmsman becomes sensitive to the total environment, he will probably notice a subtle change in the boat's rhythm, sound, or motion that will alert him to a changing wind direction. Experimentation with the boat's heading may yield the needed adjustment, or it may be possible when bioluminescence outlines wave crests, to read and use wave crest-keel line angles in the same way as suggested for cloudy days. Even if cloud cover persists, it is rare when the sun, moon, and usable planets and stars are hidden for as much as twenty-four hours at a time.

Because there is no pole star in the southern hemisphere, setting a course there on a clear night is more difficult than it is north of the equator. Both for steering and latitude finding, it is essential to be able to designate a polar point in the southern sky. An imaginary line drawn from Gacrux in the Southern Cross through Acrux and beyond passes very close to the polar point, and because nearby Hadar and Rigil Kentaurus are almost identical in declination (equivalent to latitude), an extended perpendicular that bisects the line between them also passes very close to the polar point. The spot where this perpendicular, a near meridian, and the extended Gacrux-Acrux line, a near meridian, cross in the Southern Void, is a satisfactory polar point. This imaginary point can be used for direction in the same way that Polaris is used in the opposite hemisphere.

Latitude from the Stars

To determine latitude, the navigator selects stars, preferably bright ones, and planets whose declinations match the latitudes of intermediate check points or final objectives. Each selected star or planet is observed at the time of meridian transit. At that time, if a star stands directly over the observer, i.e., at his zenith, his latitude is equal to the star's declination. If it is not directly overhead, but still on the meridian, it will stand either north or south of him. The angular distance north or south of the zenith can be estimated by comparing this zenith distance to the pre-calculated angular distance between stars in the area of the sky above the observer.

The navigator must be careful in determining the time of meridian transit. This can be facilitated by drawing an imaginary line from the polar point to the rising, preselected star. When the star is near the east horizon, the imaginary line extended in both directions will make an uneven distribution of the firmament, but when the extended line moved by the earth's rotation, reaches a place in the sky where it divides the sky equally into an eastern half and a western half, the revolving imaginary line coincides with the observer's meridian. At that time, the star, fixing one point of the line, is on the observer's meridian and, therefore, is making meridian transit. At this instant in time, if there is any departure of the star from the observer's zenith, the departure occurs in a north-south direction only. To make a judgment of the star's location with reference to his zenith, i.e., at his zenith, north of his zenith, or south of his zenith, and angular distance, if any, involved, the observer should fix his shoulders in a north-south direction, stare upward, fix an imaginary zenithal point and then make a zenith distance judgment. This should be followed by facing in the opposite direction, east or west as the case may be, and making a second zenith distance judgment. Normally, an observer has a bias to his left or his right, which will affect where he "sees" the star. By averaging the two "sights," one facing east and the other west, he can fix a point for the star and estimate his latitude based on the star's declination. Experience shows that the bias of a particular observer may be fairly constant or may vary from one time to another. As a rule, the greater the degree of concentration, the greater the accuracy will be. A caveat is in order, however. In theory, at least, meridian transit occurs for only the slightest instant in time so lengthy deliberations tend to decrease the accuracy of the observations because the star moves away from the meridian.

Vane Steering

Without vane steering it is necessary for the helmsman to be engaged in direction decision making during every minute of his watch interval. He must constantly determine the direction of the wind and the heading of the boat and make appropriate decisions to accommodate to both of these. Stars at night and the sun, moon, and distant clouds by day make the job a lot easier. Steering in cloudy weather, whether it is by night or day, can be very tiring.

When a vane steerer is used the helmsman's task is decidedly easier. He can check the various direction references, set the vane and relax until, in his judgment, changed conditions call for a resetting of the vane. The wind itself, when a reliable vane is used, becomes a direction reference and can be relied upon for guidance a greater proportion of the time than all other references combined.[1]

APPENDIX D

GLOBE STAR'S SPECS AND SAIL PLAN

Globe Star was a steel-hulled Goderich 35, designed by Ted Brewer and built by Huromic Metal Industries, based in Goderich, Ontario, Canada. The boat was first built in 1977. She displaced 17,000 pounds and carried 6,200 pounds of ballast. Her LOA was 35.67 feet, her LWL was 28.33 feet, and she was fairly beamy, at 11.50 feet. She had a maximum draft of 4.75 feet.

The Goderich 35 (also known as the Huromic 35) could be rigged as either a ketch or a cutter. Creamer's vessel was set up as a cutter, with a sail area of 649 feet.[2]

The vessel carried seventy-five gallons of water, and Creamer carried no extra water on his circumnavigation.

Ted Brewer had come up with a "motion comfort ratio" calculator meant to predict the speed of the upward and downward motion of a vessel as it encounters waves and swells. In theory, the faster the motion, the less comfortable the boat will be for passengers. Higher values denote a more comfortable ride. The Goderich 35 came in at a comfort ratio of 33.27, which was decent, but lower than some vessels of similar size, including the Irwin 37 MK V (36.93), the Mariner 35 (42.3), Southern Cross 31 (38.8), and the Tayana 37 (40.78). Many (but not all) larger boats, of course, tend to ride more comfortably, including the Vagabond 47 (48.71) and the early Allied Seawind (39.69). Many, including the Catalina 350 (21.12) and the Ericson 33 (20.26), are much less comfortable, at least as measured by Brewer's calculations. (Some sources say that Brewer dreamed up the comfort ratio tongue-in-cheek, but it has in fact been accepted as a reasonable measurement and as a useful way to compare vessels of similar types and size.)

APPENDIX D

Following are images of *Globe Star*'s sail plan and arrangement, generously provided by Ted Brewer.

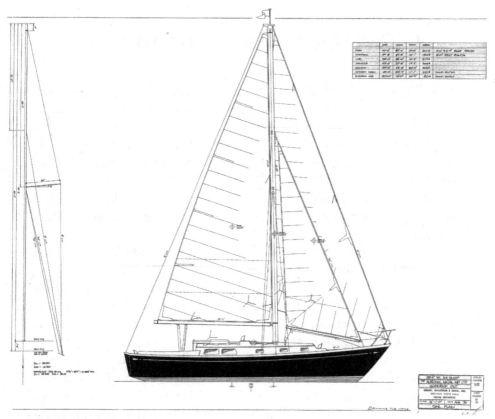

Appendix.02. Goderich 35 Sail Plan.
(IMAGE COURTESY OF TED BREWER.)

266

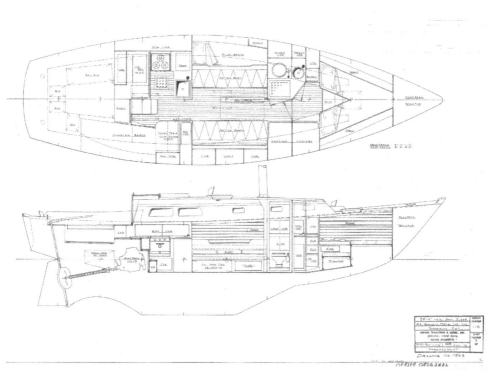

Appendix.03. Goderich 35 Arrangement.
(IMAGE COURTESY OF TED BREWER.)

NOTES

Prologue

1. Mike Tomlinson, "Wave Information," email to Rod Scher, March 21, 2021.
2. Ibid. Interestingly, Tomlinson also says that, in some circumstances, sailors may actually be better off in a small boat rather than a larger one: "Smaller boats may fare better than large ships in waters with waves with long wavelengths such as rogue waves. This is because a large ship may find its bow and stern supported on the peaks of two waves with no water midships to support the vessel, thereby causing the hull to break in two."
3. Marvin C. Creamer, *The* Globe Star *Voyage*, unpublished manuscript, 2017. Creamer's manuscript has never been widely distributed, though this author used it as an important source. The manuscript was rejected by publishers, possibly because they felt it lacked a dramatic arc. Creamer, for his part, felt that providing such an arc would be dishonest, tantamount to "heating up" the material just so that it would sell. This author hopes that the story, as he has told it, is dramatic enough on its own.
4. Ibid., 78.

Chapter 1: Groundwork

1. The name *Globe Star* was something of an accident. Creamer had intended to name his vessel *Globestar* (one word), but a mistake resulted in the wrong name being painted on the hull.
2. Ted Brewer, email to author, April 4, 2021.
3. Scientists today posit the existence of at least nine senses, in addition to the basic five. The basic senses are sight, smell, hearing, touch, and taste. More recently, however, neurologists and psychologists tend to add several more. These include a sense or perception of pain, heat, and cold; the sense of balance; and a sense of body awareness, among others.
4. Creamer, *The* Globe Star *Voyage*, 40. Bob Patterson ran Huromic Metal Industries (HMI) of Goderich, Ontario, Canada. He built the first Ted Brewer–designed Goderich 35 in 1976.
5. *Census Reports of the New Jersey Department of State*, Census of New Jersey, 1915 § (1916).
6. Andra (Creamer) James, interview with author, July 14, 2021.
7. *Census Reports of the New Jersey Department of State*, Census of New Jersey, 1915 § (1916), 4.
8. R. Schuman, "The Only Thing Worse Than Getting a Ph.D. in Today's Academic Job Market," *Slate*, August 1, 2014, accessed March 12, 2021, https://slate.com/human-interest/2014/08/abds-all-but-dissertation-ph-d-candidates-who-cant-quite-finish.html.

9. The Allied Seawind 30 ketch began production in 1962, and the first fiberglass boat to circumnavigate was a Seawind 30.

10. Creamer, *The* Globe Star *Voyage*, 5.

11. "Digest of Education Statistics, 2008," *National Center for Education Statistics (NCES) Home Page, a Part of the U.S. Department of Education*, https://nces.ed.gov/. Teachers' salaries were no better in 1978, the year the author took his first teaching job. He was paid the staggering sum of $9,280 per year to teach high school in rural Oregon.

12. Creamer, *The* Globe Star *Voyage*, 9.

13. Ibid., 11.

14. Kurt Creamer, interview with author, February 24, 2021.

15. Ibid.

16. Creamer, *The* Globe Star *Voyage*, 19.

Chapter 2: Departing Cape May on Board **Globe Star**

1. Note that, referring to the town in New Jersey, Greenwich here is pronounced "GREEN-witch," *not* "GREN-itch." Woe to the New Jersian (or visitor) who pronounces the name as if it referred to the Greenwich in either Connecticut or England.

2. Bob Rout, interview with author, March 8, 2021.

3. Ibid.

4. Jeff Herdelin, interview with author, March 14, 2021.

5. Ibid.

6. Creamer, *The* Globe Star *Voyage*, 43.

7. Jeff Herdelin, interview with author, March 14, 2021.

Chapter 3: *The Open Ocean, Galley Fires*

1. "Women in the Navy Chaplain Corps," The Chaplain Kit, June 11, 2016, https://thechaplainkit.com/history/women-chaplains/women-in-the-navy-chaplain-corps/.

2. "Causes of Boat Fires," BoatUS, accessed April 23, 2021, https://www.boatus.com/expert-advice/expert-advice-archive/2015/december/causes-of-boat-fires.

3. Creamer, *The* Globe Star *Voyage*, 89.

4. Jeff Herdelin, interview with author, March 14, 2021.

5. Ibid.

6. Most diesel engines, it turns out, will run fine on kerosene, though it is recommended that lubricants be added to kerosene when it's used as diesel fuel.

7. Creamer, *The* Globe Star *Voyage*, 50.

8. Rüdiger Trimpop, email to author, July 23, 2021.

9. Kathleen Saville, email to author, July 20, 2021. Saville is an incredible writer in her own right, which is not surprising, given that she is a senior instructor in the Department of Rhetoric and Composition at the American University in Cairo. She is also director of the AUC Writing Center and Faculty Coordinator of the AUC Literacy Program. In 1981, she and her husband rowed from Morocco to Antigua. Three years later, they rowed from Peru to Australia. Saville earned two Guinness Records as the first woman to make these crossings in a rowboat.

10. Julian Sancton, *Madhouse at the End of the Earth* (New York: Crown Publishing Group, Penguin/Random House, 2021), 129.

Chapter 4: Headed for Africa, If All Goes Well

1. Creamer, *The* Globe Star *Voyage*, 51. One of the rules—in this case laws—that Creamer certainly flouted has to do with the carrying of firearms into a foreign port. (Creamer had on board a .357 revolver and a semiautomatic rifle.) As a US-registered vessel, *Globe Star* could carry *in international waters* any firearm it would have been legal to possess in a US domicile. Bringing undeclared weapons into a foreign port, however, may have violated the laws of the country whose port the vessel entered.
2. Of course, ships are not the only floating danger one might encounter. Many boats have struck—and even been sunk by—floating logs, whales, half-submerged shipping containers, and other such items.
3. "The History of LED Lights," *LED Lighting Basics*, June 15, 2020, https://sitlersled-supplies.com/the-history-of-led-lights/.
4. Commander John E. Harrington, USCG (Ret.), email to author, August 2, 2021. Like many transoceanic sailors in 2019/2020, the Harringtons found themselves stuck in New Zealand, unable to begin a passage home due to the fact that COVID-19 lock-downs had cut off access to supplies and places to stop for repairs and reprovisioning.

Chapter 5: Heading for Cape Town

1. Creamer, *The* Globe Star *Voyage*, 53.
2. Ibid.
3. Ibid., 54.
4. US Department of Commerce, National Oceanic and Atmospheric Administration, "What Are the Horse Latitudes?" NOAA's National Ocean Service, May 5, 2014, https://oceanservice.noaa.gov/facts/horse-latitudes.html.
5. Commander John E. Harrington, USCG (Ret.), email to author, August 2, 2021.
6. Ibid.
7. Blanche Creamer, letter to Lynn Creamer, March 22, 1984.
8. Herb Benavent, interview with author, February 6, 2021.
9. "Lithium-Ion Batteries: Timeline," *Naval Technology*, June 15, 2020, https://www.naval-technology.com/comment/lithium-ion-lib-timeline/.

Chapter 6: Landfall in South Africa

1. Creamer, *The* Globe Star *Voyage*, 55.
2. Lynn Creamer and family, interview with author, February 2, 2021.
3. The original Cape Agulhas light, now almost two centuries old, was replaced by a newer structure in 1962 but still stands as a museum.
4. Creamer, *The* Globe Star *Voyage*, 56.

Chapter 7: Finding Your Way: Traditional Navigation

1. Peter Tyson, "Secrets of Ancient Navigators." PBS, October 6, 1998. https://www.pbs.org/wgbh/nova/article/secrets-of-ancient-navigators/.

2. To put that into some sort of perspective (at least for US readers), Greenland, at about 836,000 square miles, is larger than Alaska and Texas combined, but it has roughly one-tenth the population of Wyoming.

3. Although they are sometimes mistaken for one another, ravens are larger than crows and have a wedge-shaped tail, while crows have a flat tail and a smaller bill.

4. "Ravens & Crows," McGill University, accessed May 20, 2021, https://unis.mcgill.ca/en/uw/birds/ravens_crows.html. Crows are not the only highly intelligent, tool-making birds. Cockatoos have recently (2021) been shown to create and use multiple tools to (A) drill into a sea mango pit, (B) wedge open the pit, and then (C) scoop out the pulp. This is apparently a learned behavior, as only older cockatoos created and used the tools.

5. Loretto Matthias-Claudio, Richard Schuster, and Thomas Bugnyar, "GPS Tracking of Non-Breeding Ravens Reveals the Importance of Anthropogenic Food Sources during Their Dispersal in the Eastern Alps," *Current Zoology* 62, no. 4 (2016), https://www.researchgate.net/publication/282506668_GPS_tracking_of_Non-breeding_ravens_reveals_the_importance_of_anthropogenic_food_sources_during_their_dispersal_in_the_Eastern_Alps.

6. Albatrosses can fly incredibly long distances and may not touch land for years, though they may stop and float on the water while they sleep. They regularly cross entire oceans, and some species can circumnavigate the globe in only forty-six days.

7. Bob Rout, interview with author, March 8, 2021.

8. The ancient Chinese actually used several types of compasses, beginning with a "compass spoon" or *sinan* (475–221 BC), a spoon-shaped bit of magnetite. The spoon shape allows the device to rotate on a base.

9. Tyson, "Secrets of Ancient Navigators."

10. Daniel J. Boorstin, *The Discoverers* (London: Phoenix, 2001), 221.

11. Although the author tried many times, he was unable to contact anyone from the PVS. Thus, we have no commentary on Marv's journey from the group. At the time of this writing, they seem to be down to a skeleton staff and somewhat inactive. This is a shame because it would have been interesting to have had the organization's perspective on Marv's circumnavigation. An even larger shame would be if the PVS had to abandon their cultural and educational missions; one hopes that does not come to pass.

12. Patricia Wood, interview with author, March 21, 2021.

13. "Polynesian Navigation," Polynesian Voyaging Society, March 24, 2017, accessed May 23, 2021, http://www.hokulea.com/education-at-sea/polynesian-navigation/.

Chapter 8: A Cold Shoulder at Cape Town

1. Creamer, *The Globe Star Voyage*, 57.

2. Ibid., 58.

3. Douglas Livingstone, "The Other Job," *English in Africa* 40, no. 3 (2013): 105–12, accessed May 25, 2021, http://www.jstor.org/stable/24389673.

4. Boyce Rensberger, "Neutercane a Meteorological Rarity," *New York Times*, September 7, 1972. A neutercane is somewhat rare; it is, according to this *New York Times* article, "a cross between the tropical hurricane and the temperate zone's common frontal, or 'inter-type' storm."

5. Creamer, *The* Globe Star *Voyage*, 59.

6. "The Horn" in this case meaning Cape Horn, at the southernmost tip of South America, one of the most hazardous passages one can make by sea.

7. Stephen Murray-Smith, "Bass Strait: Lighthouses and Wrecks," *The Great Circle* 10, no. 2 (1988): 74–78, accessed May 26, 2021, http://www.jsturraor.org/stable/41562622.

8. Alexander Babitsky, "90 Facts about Sailing," iNsailing, January 25, 2021, accessed July 7, 2021, https://insailing.com/blog/90-facts-about-sailing. Babitsky is of course not the only one to have come up with this somewhat tongue-in-cheek pithy aphorism, often worded differently, but with much the same meaning.

9. Joshua Slocum, of course, was the revered mariner who sailed his thirty-seven-foot sloop, *Spray*, around the world solo in the mid-to-late 1890s. He wrote *Sailing Alone Around the World*, which has become required reading for serious sailors. Sadly, the Slocum Society was disbanded in 2011.

10. US Department of Commerce, National Oceanic and Atmospheric Administration, "What Are Barnacles?" NOAA's National Ocean Service. National Oceanic and Atmospheric Administration, March 30, 2016, https://oceanservice.noaa.gov/facts/barnacles.html. If barnacles and weeds cover much of the hull, they can increase the weight of the boat drastically and reduce its speed by as much as 60 percent.

11. Several experienced sailors interviewed for this book noted that Marv's heading out without a dodger was an example of poor planning. If nothing else, it probably did reflect the fact that he was impatient to be off.

12. Creamer, *The* Globe Star *Voyage*, 61.

13. Brendan Jones, "Metric Trend Leaves U.S. Kilometers Behind," *New York Times*, September 6, 1970, 9. South Africa went metric in 1967, and this 1970 article pointed out that most of the rest of the world was—or soon would be—using metric, leaving the United States as "the only country still using yards, quarts and pounds."

14. "South Africa Cuts Blacks' Tax," *New York Times*, March 31, 1983, A3.

15. Carolynne Lengfield Sr., ed., *Understanding Apartheid* (Southern Africa: Oxford University Press, 2006).

16. Creamer, *The* Globe Star *Voyage*, 66.

Chapter 9: Heading for Australia

1. There is an urban myth about a supposed disastrous attempt by the Royal Navy to disprove this superstition. According to the story, the Navy purposely laid the keel of a new vessel on a Friday, launched her on a Friday, and placed her under the command of a Captain Friday. She began her maiden voyage on a Friday and was allegedly never seen again. The story is often recounted as fact, in spite of the fact that it has been disproved many times.

2. Creamer, *The* Globe Star *Voyage*, 67.

3. Ibid.

4. "Provisioning for Offshore," *Sailing Magazine*, September 4, 2013, https://sailing-magazine.net/article-1378-provisioning-for-offshore.html.

5. Creamer, *The* Globe Star *Voyage*, 68.

6. Marvin C. Creamer, "My World Is a Circle," unpublished poem, date unknown.

7. Herb Benavent, email to author, October 4, 2021 .

8. Creamer, *The* Globe Star *Voyage*, 69.

9. Ibid., 70.

10. Ibid. Some stoves are equipped with a galley bar against which one leans while cooking. As with Marv's method, this might strike one as somewhat unsafe, but it's also true that if one is strapped to the front of the stove, it would be hard to escape when a hot pot is headed in one's direction. The majority of sailors interviewed by the author do not restrain themselves when working in the galley, regardless of the weather. (Of course, many simply do not *use* the stove in rough weather, though many may use the *oven* when the weather turns bad because its contents are not as likely to fly out and strike the cook.)

11. Creamer, *The* Globe Star *Voyage*, 72.

12. Several sources note a phenomenon known as *boater's fatigue*, a state of exhaustion caused mostly by a combination of wind, vibration, noise, and (sometimes sudden or jarring) movement. Especially when combined with a lack of sleep, boater's fatigue is something to beware of.

13. Creamer, *The* Globe Star *Voyage*, 72.

Chapter 10: *Can They Find* and *Avoid Tasmania?*

1. Ibid., 74.

2. Ibid., 75.

3. Ibid.

4. The "Bight" is a huge open bay off the central coast of Australia.

5. Creamer, *The* Globe Star *Voyage*, 76.

6. Ibid., 77.

7. Ibid.

8. Ibid., 78.

9. Chilblains are painful swellings due to damage to capillaries from repeated exposure to very cold, but not quite freezing, temperatures.

10. Creamer, *The* Globe Star *Voyage*, 8.

Chapter 11: *Six Weeks in Tasmania*

1. Andra Creamer James, email to author, October 27, 2021.

2. Nonboaters may not know that zincs are used to minimize corrosion when dissimilar metals are used together. Fittings that touch fittings made of certain other metals are subject to galvanic corrosion and will dissolve quickly, especially in salt water. The idea is that, instead of the metal fittings themselves corroding, the zincs—placed between the fittings—corrode instead and are replaced regularly. This is why they're known as "sacrificial" zincs.

3. Creamer, *The* Globe Star *Voyage*, 82.
4. Lynn Creamer Borstelmann, email to author, September 3, 2021.
5. Ibid.
6. A submarine, of course, is always a "boat," irrespective of its size; this one was more than 361 feet in length, with a crew and officer complement of over one hundred sailors. In 1983, she was a relatively new boat; she would be decommissioned in 2002.
7. Creamer, *The* Globe Star *Voyage*, 85.
8. Ibid., 87.

Chapter 12: Leaving Hobart

1. Captain David Jackson, USN (Ret.), email to author, August 29, 2021.
2. Creamer, *The* Globe Star *Voyage*, 90.
3. Daniel Schneider, interview with author, March 24, 2021.
4. Ibid.
5. Ibid.
6. Ibid.
7. Creamer, *The* Globe Star *Voyage*, 91.
8. Ibid.
9. Ibid., 92.

Chapter 13: Across the Tasman Sea

1. Bligh and all of his crew landed safely at Timor, at the eastern end of the Lesser Sunda Islands; years later, Bligh briefly became governor of New South Wales, Australia.
2. Lord would eventually rise to the rank of Rear Admiral in the Australian Navy and was, from 1999 to 2000, Maritime Commander of Australia.
3. Creamer, *The* Globe Star *Voyage*, 95.
4. Ibid.
5. Patricia Wood, email to author, July 29, 2021.
6. Nick Gill, email to author, August 13, 2021.
7. These are standard retail/home improvement store prices. We all know that anything purchased through a chandlery or with the words "boat" or "marine" on it will cost at least four times more than the exact same item purchased at your local hardware store.
8. Herb Benavent, interview with author, February 6, 2021.
9. Creamer, *The* Globe Star *Voyage*, 100.

Chapter 14: To the Horn with a New Crewman, More Conflicts

1. Ibid., 101. This was actually a not-uncommon reaction from crewmembers who joined up later in the voyage. Bob Watson, who crewed on the Falklands to Cape May leg, was asked if he had any doubts. He noted that he simply waited for Creamer to have made it three-quarters of the way and then joined up for the final leg, feeling that Creamer must know what he was doing to have made it that far. Bob Rout felt much the same, joining up in New Zealand after Marv had made it halfway around the world.
2. Ibid., 103.

3. Ibid.
4. Ibid., 106.
5. Ibid.
6. Ibid.
7. Weet-Bix is still made (in Australia, as it always has been) and is imported to many countries, including some specialty stores in the United States. No one knows why. The taste has been described as ranging from "bland" to "like oaty paper." The version sold in Britain is known as Weetabix.
8. Creamer, *The* Globe Star *Voyage*, 108.
9. This is not, by the way, the same as "protein toxicity," which is actually a malady linked to kidney issues.
10. Allison Jeter, email to author, June 16, 2021.
11. Nick Gill, email to author, August 13, 2021.
12. Nick Gill, email to author, August 19, 2021.
13. Creamer, *The* Globe Star *Voyage*, 111.
14. Lynn Creamer Borstelmann, email to author, June 30, 2021.

Chapter 15: On to the Horn

1. Nick Gill, email to author, June 7, 2021.
2. Bob Rout, interview with author, March 8, 2021.
3. Nick Gill to Blanche Creamer, March 24, 1984.
4. Creamer, *The* Globe Star *Voyage*, 113.
5. Grant Deane, "When the Ocean Breathes," CAICE, University of California at San Diego, January 10, 2020, https://caice.ucsd.edu/when-the-ocean-breathes/.
6. Creamer, *The* Globe Star *Voyage*, 114.
7. Ibid., 115.
8. Generally speaking, poles would be used as a way of keeping the sails open in light winds, but Bob Rout, who had some racing experience, convinced Marv to sail with poled out sails even in heavy seas. Captain David Jackson (USN, Ret.), who teaches sailing at the Naval Academy, tells the author that he feels having both jib and staysail out was actually too much sail for the weather conditions.
9. In fact, Marv had decided on a steel-hulled boat precisely because he thought that *Globe Star* might encounter icebergs or floating ice.
10. Creamer, *The* Globe Star *Voyage*, 116.
11. Lynn Creamer Borstelmann, email to author, August 20, 2021.

Chapter 16: Rounding the Horn

1. The sooty petrel is a brownish-black bird that lives in the South Pacific, but that migrates to the north Atlantic and north Pacific. It's also known as the sooty shearwater. The bird can be found in the open ocean but tends to concentrate around upwellings and the continental shelf. Thus, Marv's surmise about his location based on this sighting could have been correct.
2. Creamer, *The* Globe Star *Voyage*, 120.

3. People, and especially hungry sailors, really do eat fruitcake, a buttery, very sugary treat that was actually banned in Europe for a time because it was seen as too rich and decadent. Many hate it, but the ongoing Great Fruitcake Debate will surely not be settled here.

4. Nick Gill, email to author, August 5, 2021.

5. Commander John E. Harrington, USCG (Ret.), email to author, August 2, 2021.

6. Creamer, *The* Globe Star *Voyage*, 122.

7. Ibid., 123.

8. The islands are uninhabited and cover only about fifty acres. Thus, they were a small target and should have been easy to miss. However, because they are so small, and given that the tallest of them is only 246 feet above sea level, *Globe Star* could easily have run into one of the islands—especially in poor visibility—with little warning.

9. Creamer, *The* Globe Star *Voyage*, 122.

10. There are actually multiple families of petrels, and several species within each.

11. The *Merchant Providence* was originally a German ship, *Tabora*, built in 1965. In 1983, she had recently been sold to Cencargo Ltd. and chartered for service in the Falklands with the United Kingdom's Ministry of Defence.

12. Walter George (Bill) Richards, having joined London's Metropolitan Police in 1956, would retire in 1985, shortly after *Globe Star* passed through. He had been seconded to the Falklands in 1983.

Chapter 17: The Falklands

1. "Britain Seeks to Revive Ties with Argentina," *New York Times*, December 12, 1983. Note, however, that Britain made clear that it would *not* be interested in discussing the possibility of the Falkland Islands becoming a sovereign domain. The question of who owns the Falklands has been a political hot potato at least since the 1920s.

2. Creamer, *The* Globe Star *Voyage*, 129.

3. Robin Des Bois, "Shipbreaking #50," robindesbois.org, February 15, 2018, https://www.robindesbois.org/wp-content/uploads/shipbreaking50.pdf. The repair ship, with a LOA of 367 feet, was launched in 1981, so she was quite new at the time; in July of 2017, she would be sold for scrap in Turkey.

4. Creamer, *The* Globe Star *Voyage*, 129.

5. Ibid., 133.

6. Nick Gill, email to author, August 13, 2021.

7. Andra Creamer James, email to author, October 27, 2021.

8. Nick Gill, letter to Blanche Creamer, March 24, 1984.

9. Creamer, *The* Globe Star *Voyage*, 133.

10. Nick Gill, email to author, June 7, 2021.

11. Bob Watson, interview with author, September 12, 2021.

12. Lynn Creamer Borstelmann, email to author, August 20, 2021.

13. Creamer, *The* Globe Star *Voyage*, 137.

14. Marvin Creamer, letter to Lynn Creamer, January 22, 1984.

15. The Stanley Public Jetty is a bustling part of the waterfront where cruise ship passengers are dropped off by tenders.

Chapter 18: Heading for Home

1. Creamer, *The* Globe Star *Voyage*, 142
2. J. F. Geisz et al., "Building a Six-Junction Inverted Metamorphic Concentrator Solar Cell," *IEEE Journal of Photovoltaics* 8, no. 2 (March 2018): 626–32 .
3. Creamer, *The* Globe Star *Voyage*, 144.
4. Richard Searles, email to author, June 29, 2021.
5. Ibid.
6. Steve Ross, email to author, July 22, 2021. Dr. Ross is currently research faculty at UNC-W and has led offshore studies for the US Geological Survey. His area of specialization is ichthyology, particularly in areas of ecology and life history studies (age, growth, feeding, and reproduction).
7. Creamer, *The* Globe Star *Voyage*, 145.
8. Lynn Creamer Borstelmann, email to author, June 30, 2021.
9. Ibid.
10. Creamer, *The* Globe Star *Voyage*, 147.
11. Krasnodon is a city in eastern Ukraine. (As of 2016, efforts were underway to rename the city Sorokyne, but those efforts seem to have stalled.) There are several ships with the former name; the one that greeted Creamer was probably the 210-meter cargo vessel that now flies the Ukrainian flag.
12. Bob Watson, interview with author, September 12, 2021.

Chapter 19: Home is the Sailor

1. Creamer, *The* Globe Star *Voyage*, 150. Barn swallows usually do not travel far out to sea, although there have been reports of them building nests on anchored or moored fishing boats and then following the boat when it heads to sea, taking their nest—and possibly their nestlings—with it.
2. Ibid., 151.
3. As most sailors are aware, International Maritime Law (as well as long-standing seafaring tradition) notes that a shipmaster "has an obligation to render assistance to those in distress at sea without regard to their nationality, status or the circumstances in which they are found." Similarly, UNCLOS (The United Nations Convention on the Law of the Sea) and SOLAS (The International Convention for the Safety of Life at Sea) mandate that any shipmaster render assistance to any person found at sea in danger of being lost and must "proceed with all possible speed to the rescue of persons in distress." The captain of the freighter off to *Globe Star*'s port side, if he was doing as Creamer surmised, was simply doing his duty, as required by both the law and by the humanitarian principles embraced by those who sail the seas. Every sailor knows that the next time, it could be him or her. Very few sailors—perhaps *no* sailors—would fail to offer aid to a stricken vessel. Sailors competing in races have even lost ground because they stopped or went out of their way to rescue a competitor in distress. It's simply what one does when in charge of a vessel on the water.
4. *International Regulations for Preventing Collisions at Sea*, 1972. International Maritime Organization. 1990 Edition. London. According to '72 COLREGS 35(a), in

restricted visibility, "A power-driven vessel making way through the water shall sound at intervals of not more than 2 minutes one prolonged blast."
5. Creamer, *The* Globe Star *Voyage*, 155.

Epilogue
1. Patricia Wood, interview with author, March 21, 2021.
2. Ibid.
3. Michael Stadler, *Psychology of Sailing: The Sea's Effects on Mind and Body*. (Camden, ME: International Marine, 1988), 92.
4. Ibid., 93.
5. Ibid., 95–96.
6. Margalit Fox, "Marvin Creamer, a Mariner Who Sailed Like the Ancients, Dies at 104," *New York Times*, August 17, 2020. Creamer had recently purchased a sailboat that had GPS and other such technology already installed. He removed it from the boat.
7. Lin Pardey, interview with author, February 14, 2021.
8. Lynn Creamer Borstelmann, email to author, June 30, 2021.

Appendix D: Globe Star's Specs and Sail Plan
1. Creamer, *The* Globe Star *Voyage*, 165–67.

BIBLIOGRAPHY

PRINT AND EBOOKS

Blewitt, Mary. *Celestial Navigation for Yachtsmen*. Camden, ME: International Marine, 1994.

Boorstin, Daniel J. *The Discoverers*. London: Phoenix, 2001.

Bowditch, Nathaniel. *The New American Practical Navigator*. New York: E and G Blunt, 1854.

Creamer, Marvin C. *The* Globe Star *Voyage*. Unpublished manuscript, 2017.

Dutton, B., and E. S. Maloney. *Dutton's Navigation & Piloting*. Annapolis, MD: Naval Institute Press, 1981.

Harari, Y. N. *21 Lessons for the 21st Century*. Ireland: Random House Publishing Group, 2019.

Henderson, Richard. *Sea Sense*. Camden, ME: International Marine Publishing Company, 2009.

International Regulations for Preventing Collisions at Sea. 1972. London: International Maritime Organization, 1990.

Lengfield, Carolynne, Sr., ed. *Understanding Apartheid*. Southern Africa: Oxford University Press, 2006.

Lovette, Irby, ed. *Handbook of Bird Biology*. Cornell University Laboratory of Ornithology. West Sussex, UK: John Wiley and Sons, 2004.

Maloney, Ebert S. *Chapman's Piloting, Seamanship, and Small Boat Handling*. Sixty-sixth edition. New York: Hearst Marine Books, 1989.

Murray, John. *Rescue at Sea: A Challenge for the Shipping Industry*. PowerPoint presentation, June 29, 2021. London. International Chamber of Shipping.

Rodgers, Paul. *Sailing by the Stars*. Dobbs Ferry, NY: Sheridan House, 1988.

Sancton, Julian. *Madhouse at the End of the Earth*. New York: Crown Publishing Group, Penguin/Random House, 2021.

Sartre, Jean-Paul. *Being and Nothingness*. Translated by Hazel E. Barnes. New York: Washington Square Press, 1992.

Saville, Kathleen. *Rowing for My Life*. New York: Arcade Publishing, 2017.

Sobel, Dava. *Longitude*. London: Fourth Estate, 2014.

Stadler, Michael. *Psychology of Sailing: The Sea's Effects on Mind and Body*. Camden, ME: International Marine, 1988.

Trimpop, Rüdiger M. "The Psychology of Risk Taking Behavior." PhD diss., Department of Industrial/Organizational Psychology, Ruhr-Universität Bochum, Germany, 1994.

Tyson, Peter. "NOVA Online: The Search for Longitude: Secrets of Ancient Navigation." University of Arizona. Accessed May 22, 2021. http://ircamera.as.arizona.edu/NatSci102/NatSci/images/extnavigationsecrets.htm.

Vigor, John. *The Practical Mariner's Book of Knowledge*. Camden, ME: McGraw Hill Education, 2013.

JOURNALS, INTERVIEWS, AND WEBSITES

Babitsky, Alexander. "90 Facts about Sailing." *iNsailing*, January 25, 2021. https://insailing .com/blog/90-facts-about-sailing.

Benavent, Herb. Interview with author. February 6, 2021.

Brewer, Ted. Email to author. April 4, 2021.

"Britain Seeks to Revive Ties With Argentina." *New York Times*, December 12, 1983.

Burke, Cathy. "Why Johnny Can't Read: Teacher Can't Teach, Professor Says." *United Press International*, April 28, 1982.

"Causes of Boat Fires." BoatUS, accessed April 23, 2021, https://www.boatus.com/ expert-advice/expert-advice-archive/2015/december/causes-of-boat-fires.

Census Reports of the New Jersey Department of State. Census of New Jersey, 1915 § (1916).

Creamer, Blanche. Letter to Lynn Creamer, March 22, 1984.

Creamer, Kurt. Interview with author. February 24, 2021.

Creamer, Lynn, and Family. Interview with author. February 2, 2021.

Creamer, Marvin C. "My World Is a Circle." Unpublished poem. Date unknown.

Creamer Borstelmann, Lynn. Email to author. June 30, August 20, and September 3, 2021.

Deane, Grant. "When the Ocean Breathes." CAICE. University of California at San Diego, January 10, 2020. https://caice.ucsd.edu/when-the-ocean-breathes/.

Des Bois, Robin. "Shipbreaking #50." robindesbois.org, February 15, 2018. https://www .robindesbois.org/wp-content/uploads/shipbreaking50.pdf.

"Digest of Education Statistics, 2008." *National Center for Education Statistics (NCES) Home Page, a Part of the U.S. Department of Education*. https://nces.ed.gov/.

Fox, Margalit. "Marvin Creamer, a Mariner Who Sailed Like the Ancients, Dies at 104." *New York Times*, August 17, 2020.

Gill, Nick. Email to author. June 7, August 5, 13, and 19, 2021.

Gill, Nick. Letter to Blanche Creamer. March 24, 1984.

Geisz, J. F., et al. "Building a Six-Junction Inverted Metamorphic Concentrator Solar Cell." *IEEE Journal of Photovoltaics* 8, no. 2 (March 2018): 626–32.

Goodwin, Ian D., Stuart A. Browning, et al. "Climate Windows for Polynesian Voyaging to New Zealand and Easter Island." *PNAS* 111, no. 41 (October 14, 2014): 14716–21. https://doi.org/10.1073/pnas.1408918111.

Harrington, CDR John E., USCG (Ret.). Email to author. August 2, 2021.

Herdelin, Jeff. Interview with author. March 14, 2021.

Jackson, Captain David, USN (Ret.). Email to author. August 29, 2021.

James, Andra (Creamer). Email to author. October 27, 2021.

James, Andra (Creamer). Interview with author. July 14, 2021.

James, Naomi. *Alone Around the World*. New York: Penguin Publishing Group, 1979.

Jeter, Allison. Email to author. June 16, 2021.

Jones, Brendan. "Metric Trend Leaves U.S. Kilometers Behind." *New York Times*, September 6, 1970.

"Lithium-Ion Batteries: Timeline." *Naval Technology*, June 15, 2020. https://www.naval-technology.com/comment/lithium-ion-lib-timeline/.

Livingstone, Douglas. "The Other Job." *English in Africa* 40, no. 3 (2013): 105–12. Accessed May 25, 2021. http://www.jstor.org/stable/24389673.

Loretto, Matthias-Claudio, Richard Schuster, and Thomas Bugnyar. "GPS Tracking of Non-Breeding Ravens Reveals the Importance of Anthropogenic Food Sources during Their Dispersal in the Eastern Alps." *Current Zoology* 62, no. 4 (August 2016): 337–44.

Montenegro, Alvaro, Richard T. Callaghan, et al. "Using Seafaring Simulations and Shortest-Hop Trajectories to Model the Prehistoric Colonization of Remote Oceania." *PNAS* 113, no. 45 (November 8, 2016): 12685–90. https://doi.org/10.1073/pnas.1612426113.

Murray-Smith, Stephen. "Bass Strait: Lighthouses and Wrecks." *The Great Circle* 10, no. 2 (1988): 74–78. Accessed May 26, 2021. http://www.jstor.org/stable/41562622.

"NSW Cruising Ports." *Sail World*, May 14, 2006. https://www.sail-world.com/Australia/NSW-Cruising-Ports/-23924.

Pardey, Lin. Interview with author. February 14, 2021.

"Polynesian Navigation." Polynesian Voyaging Society, March 24, 2017. Accessed May 23, 2021. http://www.hokulea.com/education-at-sea/polynesian-navigation/.

"Provisioning for Offshore." *Sailing Magazine*, September 4, 2013. https://sailing magazine.net/article-1378-provisioning-for-offshore.html.

"Ravens & Crows." McGill University. Accessed May 20, 2021. https://unis.mcgill.ca/en/uw/birds/ravens_crows.html.

Rensberger, Boyce. "Neutercane a Meteorological Rarity." *New York Times*, September 7, 1972.

Riley, C. "Understanding and Utilizing the Secrets of Waves." *Boatsafe*, April 18, 2020. Accessed March 9, 2021. https://www.boatsafe.com/understanding-utilizing-secrets-waves.

Ross, Steve. Email to author. July 22, 2021.

Rout, Bob. Interview with author. March 8, 2021.

Saville, Kathleen. Email to author. July 20, 2021.

Schneider, Daniel. Interview with author. May 27, 2021.

Schuman, R. "The Only Thing Worse than Getting a Ph.D. in Today's Academic Job Market." *Slate*, August 1, 2014. Accessed March 12, 2021. https://slate.com/human-interest/2014/08/abds-all-but-dissertation-ph-d-candidates-who-cant-quite-finish.html.

Searles, Richard. Email to author. June 29, 2021.

"South Africa Cuts Blacks' Tax." *New York Times*, March 31, 1983.

"The History of LED Lights." *LED Lighting Basics*, June 15, 2020. https://sitlersled supplies.com/the-history-of-led-lights/.

"The Weight of a Wave." *Surfer Today*. Accessed March 9, 2021. https://www.surfertoday .com/surfing/the-weight-of-a-wave.

Tomlinson, Mike. "Wave Information." Email to Rod Scher. March 21, 2021.

Trimble, Ben. Interview with author. March 31, 2021.

Trimpop, Rüdiger. Email to author. July 23, 2021.

Tyson, Peter. "Secrets of Ancient Navigators." PBS, October 6, 1998. https://www.pbs
.org/wgbh/nova/article/secrets-of-ancient-navigators/.

US Department of Commerce, National Oceanic and Atmospheric Administration.
"What Are Barnacles?" NOAA's National Ocean Service. National Oceanic and
Atmospheric Administration, March 30, 2016. https://oceanservice.noaa.gov/facts/
barnacles.html.

US Department of Commerce, National Oceanic and Atmospheric Administration.
"What Are the Horse Latitudes?" NOAA's National Ocean Service, May 5, 2014.
https://oceanservice.noaa.gov/facts/horse-latitudes.html.

Watson, Bob. Interview with author. September 12, 2021.

"Wave Energy." Ocean Energy Council. Accessed March 9, 2021. https://www.ocean
energycouncil.com/ocean-energy/wave-energy/.

"Women in the Navy Chaplain Corps." The Chaplain Kit, June 11, 2016. https://
thechaplainkit.com/history/women-chaplains/women-in-the-navy-chaplain-corps/.

Wood, Patricia. Interview with author. March 21, 2021.

INDEX

shark encounter and, 53
vane steerer and, 64–65
bananas, as unlucky, 34
Bar Protector, 205, 206, 211, *212*
bare poles, sailing under, 107
Barren Island, 201
Bass Point, 147
Bass Strait, 90–91, 112
Benavent, Herb, 56, *57*, 109, 159
Benavent, Maddie, *57*
Berry, Jim, 206, 211
beta, 227
Big Dipper, 135
Bigelow Laboratory for Ocean
    Science, 213, 228
bilge pump, 115
binnacle, 78
birds, navigation using, 74–76,
    75, 193
Bjarni Herjolfsson, 74
Bligh, William, 151–152
blowup doll, 228
Blue Water Medal, *248*, *249*
BoatUS (Boat Owners
    Association of the United
    States), 35
BOC race, 151
Bom Jesus, 67
boom, shortening of, 131
Boothbay (Maine) Harbor Yacht
    Club, 213
Borstelmann, Lynn Creamer
    (daughter)
    Blanche and, 55, 67, 133
    Creamer's letter to, 133, *134*

current work/location of, 8
on father, 174, 187, 215–216,
    229–230, 251, 254–256
Boston (submarine), 134, *135*
Botha, P. W., 95–96
Bounty, 151
Boy Scout troop, 134–137
braai, *95*
braaivleis, 94, *95*
Brash Island, 146
Brazil Current, 221
Brewer, Ted, 1, 3, 93, 146, 198
British Antarctic Survey (BAS),
    177, *178*
Brown, Rick, 13

C. E. Ryder Corp., 19
Canaries Current, 49
Canary Islands, 49
Canopus, 183, 184, 191, 193–194
Cape Agulhas Lighthouse, 68–69
Cape Brett, 161
Cape Horn, 131, 197–198, *199*
Cape Island West Marina, 246
Cape Runaway, 165
Cape Verde Islands, 40, 43, *48*,
    49–50
Cataraqui, 90–91
cats, as lucky, 34
Centre National d'Études
    Spatiales, 59
charts, 23, 82–83
Cheshire, Rob, 247, *248*, 249
Chinese, 77, 78
Choiseul Sound, 201

East Cape, 165
Eduard Bohlen, *68*
Edwards, Jesse, 132, 139,
141–142, 145, 146, 148,
155–156, 169
Endeavour, HMS, 24
engine
damage to, 125
problems with, 28–29, 156,
195–196, 228, 235–236,
242–243, 245–246
provision of, 22
repairs to, 215
testing of, 119
equator, crossing of, 228
Erik the Red, 73–74, 80

"F" marker, 242
Falkland Sound, 200
Falklands, 165, 177, 199–201,
203–220, *219*, *233*
Falklands War, 201
farm equipment, repairing, 5
fetch, xi
fire, 34–36
Flicka 20, 247
Floki, 75
fog, as sign of land, 49
Folger, Timothy, *237*
food
air drop of, 238–239, *240*
Boston (submarine) and,
133–134
Creamer's skills with, 110–112,
113, 117, 166, 172–173, *172*

dissatisfaction with, 105–106,
182–183, 232
Gill and, 162, 168–170
oregano for, 216–217
Thanksgiving and, 179–180
Forrest, 203, 205–206, 207–208
Franklin, Benjamin, 80, *237*
fully developed sea, xi
Furious Fifties, 165, 183, 185

Gacrux, 53, 135–136, *137*
gamma Virginis, 228
genoa, *58*
Georges Bank, 240
Gibson, Ed, 212–213, *214*, 216,
217, 218, 222, 228, 232,
233, *240*
Gill, Nick
on approach to Cape Horn,
194–195, 197
ARGOS transmitter and,
173–174
background of, 142
conflicts with, 154–156,
162–163, 168–170, 174–175,
178–179
Creamer's shoulder injury
and, 143
Falklands and, 199, 204
final blow-up with, 207–210
food and, 166, 168,
169–170, 206
illness and, 156–157
John Biscoe and, 217
joining crew, 132

INDEX

toilet problem, 168
Tomlinson, Mike, xi, xii
trade winds, 78, *79*
Trimble, Ben, *9*
Trimpop, Rüdiger, *41*
Trinidade, 51
Tupaia, 24, *25*
turnbuckles, 58
Twardowski, Ed, 11
twilight, as navigation aid,
    165–166, 192, 197, 198
Tyson, Peter, 73

Understanding Boat Design
    (Brewer), 3
Ursa Minor, *231*

vane steerer, 93, 131
Vega, 238, 241
VHF antenna, 138
Vikings, 73–76
Viljoen, Marais, 95–96
Viña del Mar, Chile, 139, 141
Volvo, engine provided by, 22. *See
    also* engine

Ware, Ron, 151–152, 154, 168
water makers, 66–67, *66*
water supply, 65–66
Watson, Bob, 207, 211, 213, *214*,
    216, 222, 232, *233*, 242
Watson's Bay Royal Naval Base,
    152, 156

waves
    formation of, xi
    navigation using, 10–11
    power of, xi–xii, *xii*
weather
    on approach to Cape Horn,
        183–184
    on approach to Tasmania,
        122–123
    in Indian Ocean, 112, 117
    in ITCZ, 54
    red sky and, 33
    in Tasman Sea, 141, 157–158
Weet-Bix, 169
Whangaroa, 160, 161–163, *169*
whistling, bad luck and, 34
Wignall, Bill, 126, 129
Wilson, Harold, 209
windlass, 47
winds, navigation using, 78, *79*,
    80, 193
Wisdom, *57*
women, as unlucky, 34
Wood, Patricia, 81–82, 155,
    250–251, *250*

yacht clubs, 86
*Yacht Racing/Cruising
    Magazine*, 247
yellow flags, 98

296